CHORA: Intervals in the Philosophy of Architecture
Managing Editor: Alberto Pérez-Gómez
Edited by Alberto Pérez-Gómez and Stephen Parcell

Volume 1 (1994)
Volume 2 (1996)
Volume 3 (1999)
Volume 4 (2004)
Volume 5 (2007)
Volume 6 (2011)

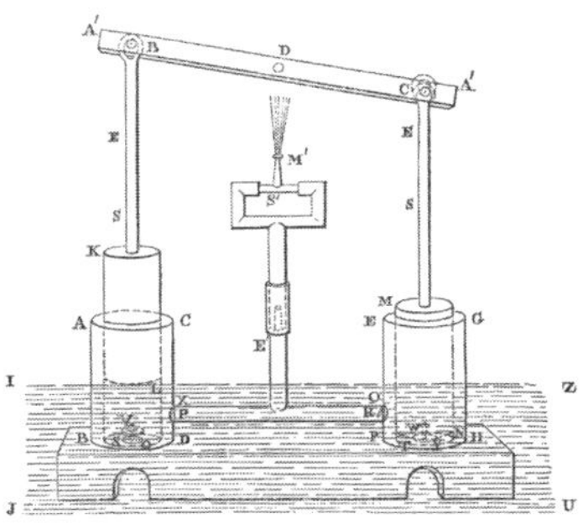

Chora 6: Intervals in the Philosophy of Architecture

Intervals in the Philosophy of Architecture

CHORA

VOLUME SIX

Edited by Alberto Pérez-Gómez and Stephen Parcell

McGill-Queen's University Press
Montreal & Kingston • London • Ithaca

CHORA is a publication of the History and Theory of Architecture graduate program at McGill University, Montreal, Canada.

For author information and submission of articles please contact
www.mcgill.ca/architecture-theory/chora/

Legal deposit third quarter 2011
Bibliothèque nationale du Québec

Printed in Canada on acid-free paper

ISBN 978-0-7735-3858-0 (cloth)
ISBN 978-0-7735-3859-7 (paper)

Library and Archives Canada has catalogued this publication as follows:

Chora: intervals in the philosophy of architecture

Each issue also has distinct title.
Irregular.
Vol. 1 (1994)–
ISSN 1198-449X
ISBN 978-0-7735-3858-0 (volume 6) (bnd)
ISBN 978-0-7735-3859-7 (volume 6) (pbk)

1. Architecture—Philosophy—Periodicals. I. McGill University. History and Theory of Architecture Graduate Program. II. Title.

NA1.C46 720'.1 C94-900762-5

This book was designed and typeset by studio oneonone in Sabon 10/13

Contents

Preface

Continuing its dedication to innovative and open scholarship that challenges the conventional view of architecture's history, this sixth volume of CHORA also revitalizes efforts to establish an effective, interdisciplinary dialogue on architecture. Characterized by a cross-cultural and temporal scope, and supported by diverse approaches to the problem of architecture's history, the individual topics examined here are united by their desire to investigate alternative models of architectural meaning. Beyond the orthodox reading of architecture defined by the drive of aesthetics or technology, CHORA's academic forum presents research that recognizes the potential of architecture to ethically and poetically connect with humanity. It also addresses a need for an architectural discourse that embraces histories of architecture as evidence of cultural difference and as precedents for responsible action. The authors of the thirteen chapters included here recognize the imperative of such scholarship.

One recurring concern in this volume of CHORA is the ritual and cosmological origins of architecture and their connection to the public realm of political and social interaction. For example, in "On Fire and the Origins of Architecture," Lian Chang probes the metaphorical significance of fire in architectural origin myths, beginning with the Vitruvian story of fire as the linguistic origins of architecture. Chang's study looks at the Greek associations of fire with the civilized, the social, and the technological and at how this strengthens architecture's connection with both language and society. With similar emphasis on the cultural value of architectural origins, Santiago de Orduña relates Aztec mythology and ritual sacrifice to architecture's potential to engage humans with the phenomenal world. By illustrating the cultural specificity of Aztec symbolism, Orduña illustrates that the Christian appropriation of Aztec symbolism was at odds with the Aztecs' embodied understanding of nature. Orduña's historical understanding of ritual sacrifice as an ethical act therefore suggests a contemporary cultural value for Mesoamerican metaphor and poetics.

The power of drawing as a poetic translation of the architectural imagination is a prevalent theme in the chapters by Roquet, Lending, and Zou. In the former, Nicholas Roquet focuses on the artistic persona and process of William Burges in Victorian England. Roquet looks at the cultural meanings of Burges's emulation of Villard de Honnecourt in his Vellum Sketchbook. He is primarily concerned with the impact of this adoption of a fictional persona on Burges's artistic process through drawing. Mari Lending's chapter also addresses the relationship between the architectural imagination and the narrative potential of architecture as drawing. In her exploration of the multidimensional layers of meaning in the text, drawings, and drawn-text of Stendhal's *Life of Henry Brulard*, Lending weighs in on the spatial and existential dimensions in Stendhal's fictional landscape, both for the reader and for the author. Similarly, Hui Zou considers the relationship between architecture and its drawn image in the design and representation of the imperial Garden of Round Brightness in late eighteenth-century China. Zou argues that this adoption of a Western system of representation is employed not as a formalistic device but, rather, as a culturally valuable and embodied vision of nature and the mind.

Architecture as the site of embodied interaction with the phenomenal world is at the centre of two chapters that posit an understanding of the material world at different temporal moments. In "The Sacred Stones of Saint-Denis," Jason Crow questions the established characterization of materiality in the Gothic cathedral, and in "Perceptual Unfolding in the Palace of Minos," Rachel McCann explores perceptual movement in the experience of Minoan art and architecture. Crow argues for a revised understanding of the role of light in the Gothic through a precise study of the medieval theological concepts of the material and the immaterial, while McCann looks at embodied experience and how it is overlooked in conventional appraisals of meaning in Minoan architecture. In McCann's analysis, movement becomes the experiential element that the participant encounters at the Palace of Minos, providing a communion of body and world through architecture.

The machine as a metaphorical device is the key preoccupation of several of the chapters. Although they deal deals with vastly different historical frameworks, these studies illustrate the continuous interrelation of architecture and technology. Lawrence Bird turns to the fictional space of the cinematic city in his dissection of the phenomenological meanings of the shadows in Fritz Lang's *Metropolis*. Through a detailed formal analysis of Lang's use of frame and surface in his construction of filmic space, Bird underscores the conflation of modern themes such as city, machine, and desire as a fictional response to the traumatic conditions of the modern urban subject. Jonathan Powers, in his examination of sixteenth-century definitions of utopia in Tommaso Campanella and John Amos Comenius, considers the orderly, cosmic machine as the eidetic concept of the city in the Renaissance. Meanwhile, Peter Olshavsky's playful exploration centres on the literary machines of "pataphysicist" Alfred Jarry and provides a useful exegesis on the history of architectural machines from Vitruvius to the so-called Machine Age.

The tradition of architectural theory and education provides the framework for two historical studies. In her chapter on Juan Caramuel de Lobkowitz, Maria Elisa Navarro Morales addresses the polymath's treatise on architecture, relating Caramuel's discussion of the columnar orders to his philosophical views in the fields of mathematics and theology. Focusing on eighteenth-century Italian architect and politician Andrea Memmo, Marc Neveu writes on the Prato della Valle, an enigmatic public space in Padua. Neveu's work provides a historic reassessment of Memmo's project, evaluating the Lodolian influence on Memmo's understanding of history and its emblematic role in the design process.

Provoking a dialogue with profound relevance for today's definition of architecture, Donald Kunze looks at the ideological juggernaut of sustainability and its contemporary status as a force that cannot be opposed. Kunze argues that the only way to decipher (and perhaps eventually dismantle) its mythic power within our culture is to consider sustainability within the psychoanalytic terms of fantasy. Caught by an overzealous reliance on computer technologies and aesthetics, architecture today is at a crucial turning point. A challenging and effective architectural discourse is increasingly urgent – one that re-establishes the human values of architectural practice beyond narrow technical parameters and recognizes that architecture has the potential to participate in the realm of action.

Lumen opacatum: Flesh in Fritz Lang's *Metropolis**

Lawrence Bird

Chora

> Those who consider the cinema as a discreet teller of tales will suffer a profound disillusion with *Metropolis*. What it tells us is trivial, pretentious, pedantic, hackneyed romanticism. But if we put before the story the plastic-photogenic basis of the film, then *Metropolis* will come up to any standards, will overwhelm us as the most marvellous picture book imaginable.[1]

LUIS BUÑUEL'S ELOQUENT words represent the critical response to Fritz Lang's *Metropolis* upon its first release in 1926, a response that derided the film's plot and characterization while acknowledging its visual power. Despite its indulgence in melodrama, spectacle, and a trite resolution, the film was, as Siegfried Kracauer put it, "rich in subterranean content that, like contraband, had crossed the borders of consciousness without being questioned." For Kracauer, that content was political: it referred to Germany's condition between the wars. But the film's explicit concern is more general: the subjection of citizens to a mechanized and totalizing modernity. These tensions are articulated in the architectures of the city, the body, and the film itself. These are the several fleshes that make up the pages of this "marvellous picture book."

The imagery of architecture is central to *Metropolis*, as it often is to Fritz Lang's cinematic vision. Lang himself had spent a year as an architecture student before moving into film. It was in the company of an architect, Eric Mendelsohn, that Lang and his wife and scriptwriter, Thea von Harbou, visited New York in 1924. For Mendelsohn, an eventual product of this journey would be his book of photographs, *Amerika*. For Lang and von Harbou, it would be their film and the accompanying novel *Metropolis*. The architectural vision of the film articulates a tension between Lang's experience of Manhattan and the social and political stakes of contemporary architectural discourse in Germany. One instance is the prominence of two architectural figures in Lang's cinematic city: the New Tower of Babel and the Gothic cathedral. Their presence refers in part to a concurrent debate in German architecture and planning: whether a new urban form based on the cathedral, a single massive building at the centre of each city, might offer a more appropriately German model of urban growth than the American skyscraper, an emblem of unbridled individualism and commerce. Some argue that the cathedral emerged from a building tradition with an authenticity and appropriateness to human living that no modern architecture could provide.

While *Metropolis* does not promote a critique of modern*ist* architecture, the workers' tenements in the film share the austere lines, the absence of detail, and the minimal expression of the modernist architectural projects that were beginning to emerge in Germany at the time. Lang associated such environments with the struggle of workers. The angular structure at the centre of the workers' tenements (see fig. 1.1) is based on Walter Gropius's Monument for the March Dead, which commemorates the striking miners killed during the Weimar riots of 1921. But, as elsewhere in the film, the intention is confused: the resolution of *Metropolis* brings about not a workers' revolution but its suppression and the union of a people under one father figure. The final scene shows a phalanx of workers marching with perfect precision up the steps of the Gothic cathedral. The city is reunited before the cathedral, still an emblem of community and tradition, but now with additional meanings associated with the German nation.

The architecture of *Metropolis* was understood in this way by critics such as Kracauer, for whom the film's "subterranean content" was primarily political and social. But several more fundamental "architectures" are also in play in this film: the human body and cinema itself. They imply

Fig. 1.1 Workers trudge to their dark tenements in the lower levels of Lang's *Metropolis*.

a more important deployment of space than the citation of specific buildings or styles in the service of a confused morality. A key event in the film – the substitution of the body of the maternal Maria by a robot, the False Maria – might be understood, in Benjamin's words, as an instance of mechanical reproduction with a corresponding loss of aura, of soul. I argue in the following pages that it represents the opposite. The robot's adoption of a human skin is, rather, evidence of a reversibility between human and machine that gives voice to a yearning for an existence beyond the conditions of modernity. This desire is also expressed in the spatiality of the city and in the screen's interplay and interpenetration of masses, frames, surfaces, movement, and relationships in depth.

CITY-MACHINE

Metropolis is explicitly about the city as machine. Its opening images present the pumping of pistons and the whirling of flywheels set against the immense architectures of a great city. The city-machine is divided into upper and lower parts, and the lower levels are divided further into workers' housing and machine rooms. In the machine rooms the workers attend to regimented rows of dials and panels. They are slaves to these machines, their movements dictated by the discipline of the clock. Their movement from tenement to workplace is similarly disciplined. They walk with heavy paces down long tunnels, as though chained together. Like goods, they are transported vertically by elevator. Lang illustrates the essential wrongness of modern human beings becoming cogs in a mechanism.

The lynchpin of this city, its fulcrum, is the building known as the New Tower of Babel (see fig. 1.2). It is from here that the callous autocrat Joh Frederson runs the city (although, by the end of the film, he would be transformed into a loving leader). It is the "central intersection for all traffic in the city ... all the different means of transport were to flow together in the building's lower stories, and batteries of elevators, partly visible on the outside, would also connect it to the central airport on the tip and to the halls for the machinery underground." This building, at first glance, exercises a panoptic control over the city below.

Yet the images that convey the apparatus of control suggest something more. For example, the rational grid that frames the view of the city is surrounded by darkness (see fig. 1.3). Blackness wells up in Joh Freder-

Fig. 1.2 The New Tower of Babel, lynchpin of the metropolis.

son's dark, curving desk. It pushes in from the corners where the desk sinks into the dark frame, and a dusky shadow slips down from above, even over the immense window. Thick, dark curtains frame the window and, as the scene progresses, close heavily over it. Even the whites in this image contribute to the opacity. The glass surface, for example, is a mist obscuring the view. As Frederson stands at his desk, his pale hand is poised above rows of identical white buttons, each standing at attention (see fig. 1.4). The lightness of its touch, reflected in the polished surface of the panel, emphasizes the sensitivity and the waiting potential of the controls. But the white hand is set off by the darkness that crowds the edge of the frame, creeping into the panel and around it. Indeed, the hand itself casts a long shadow that bleeds into the opaque black at the frame's border. This dark edge permeates the entire image, slipping into the shadows cast by the buttons, sliding beneath the desktop, turning the extents of panel, desk, and figure into one dark field. In another image Frederson speaks to his panicked foreman via a viewing screen; shadows seep in at the edges of this image, too (see fig. 1.5). Like the obscuring mist of Frederson's window, a pale opacity has slipped across the picture screen on which the foreman's image appears. Rather than connecting them, it acts as a true *screen* that separates them. Hence, the worker's agitation has no impact on Frederson's impassive figure; they are separated rather than united by this distant vision.

Fig. 1.3 The view from Joh Frederson's office: his window cuts up the city into a grid and holds it at a distance as shadows well up from the margins of the image.

Fig. 1.4 The pale hand of Frederson poised above the city's controls.

Fig. 1.5 Frederson's viewing screen connects but distances him from his foreman Grot.

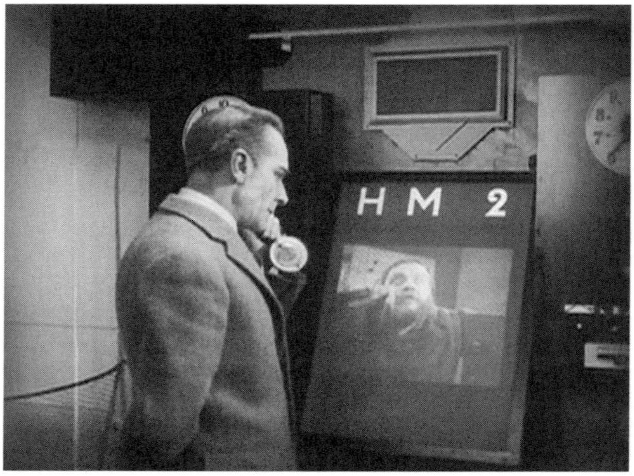

LABYRINTH

But what is the source of this darkness, this shadow lurking behind the control tower that purports to represent modern clarity? As the film plays out, we are presented with a spatial counterpoint to the Tower – its shadow. This second spatial figure is presented first in the folded pages of a map that is passed from worker to worker (see fig. 1.6). The map is covered with meandering lines, diagonals, and numbers, but they make no sense; they seem random. Even the points of the compass are skewed. These lines suggest that the rational attempt to map the city is an exercise in futility. This map undermines all maps and the optical omniscience they represent. Its dark maze of twisting passageways and tunnels is very much a disorienting labyrinth. Coiled around the city's workings, below rather than above, twisting rather than straight, hunched rather than upright, this dark tangle opposes yet insinuates itself into the city's bright spaces above.

The labyrinth suggests a specific and important relationship of frame to content. Its map actually transposes the grid of Frederson's window onto the folds of a sheet of paper. Through this gesture, Lang tears and

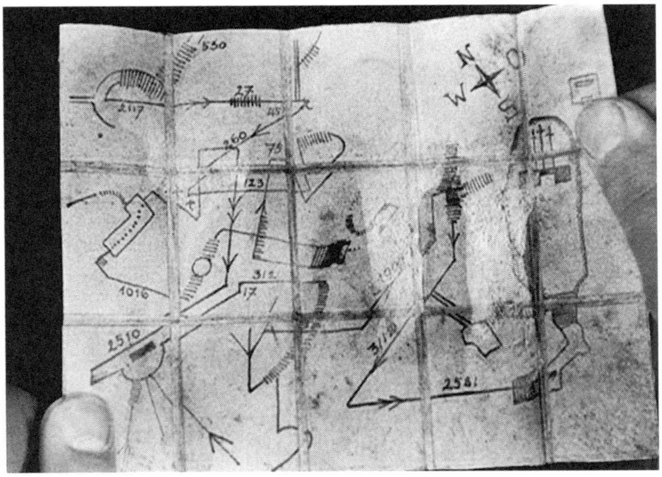

Fig. 1.6 The labyrinth.

Fig. 1.7 Rotwang trains his searchlight on Maria.

frays the rational frame; its sharp edges have become shaded pleats. In fact, the ambiguous relationship of frame to content is the rule that governs the labyrinth. Like the corrupted cells of the map, frames in the labyrinth do not simply contain: they encroach, bleed into, bend over, well up beneath, smother in labial folds, and are propped up by their contents. In turn, their contents slip out, stagger across their margins, and scatter across the torn hem of the image. In this situation, darkness and light frame each other ambiguously. Black encroaches upon white, light trespasses upon darkness: each slips into the other.

This becomes clear in a crucial sequence in which Maria is captured by Frederson's scientist, Rotwang. He lurks in the dark margins of the labyrinth to catch Maria, but it is actually through light that he traps her (see fig. 1.7). Like a weapon, his spotlight pierces the darkness, both pushing her away and pinning her in place. As she tries to flee into the shadows, her own shadow flees before her, seeking refuge in the dark, a refuge that she is denied. As this happens, there is a strange and compelling interplay – even inversion – of light and dark. Light acquires the same evil potency as darkness.

This is also the moment when the spatial frame of the labyrinth is transferred to the above-ground city, when darkness no longer laps around the edges of the machine city but penetrates it. This occurs through the body of Maria. Previously straight and upright, her body is now bent and twisted. Maria is panicked, then paralyzed, pinned in place by fear, by Rotwang's eyes, and by the glare of the spotlight. She shudders, shrinks away, twists, and recoils as she flees (see fig. 1.8). Her movement embodies the twisting labyrinth and its tortuous relationship to the light.

Fig. 1.8 Maria's flight through the labyrinth undermines any distinction between her figure and its spatial and cinematic frames.

The same can be said of other figures who move through this space. Those who are not fleeing in frenetic deviations trip in broken paces down crumbling steps or twist down spiralling staircases. As the machine-city imposed a behaviour on bodies, so does the labyrinth, but to opposite effect: rather than ordering bodies and then breaking them, it renders them chaotic, twisted, perverse. The labyrinth envelops bodies and makes their movements labyrinthine.

Rotwang's hut, to which Maria is pursued at the end of this sequence, projects the underground tunnels onto the above-ground city. The hut contains its own labyrinth, an array of identical, magical doors that trick and trap visitors. These doors are located around what appears to be a central courtyard. When Maria is caught here, her chaste and upright body again displays paroxysms of fear, adopting the twisted form of the labyrinth-within-a-labyrinth. Her terrified contortions are finally stilled when she loses consciousness. Next we see her lying prone in the machinery of Rotwang's laboratory, where he has created an artificial human being, the Machine Man, to replace the human workers of Metropolis. This creature is tall, even stately, with an other-worldly presence. Its poise resembles Maria's – until Rotwang uses his alchemical machinery to reproduce her face and skin over the Machine-Man's steel body. After this transformation, the robot becomes an exact duplicate of Maria: the False Maria. Maria herself remains prone in the workshop machinery. She has returned to her original condition: at rest, straight. Now it is the Machine Man who will be bent, presented as the False Maria to the wealthy of Metropolis at the nightclub Yoshiwara. Her double performs a perverse dance to entice and enchant the young men of the city. She twists and hunches, leers and winks asymmetrically, seducing and provoking them with movements that the true Maria's body earlier had displayed out of fear.

Thus the labyrinth is transferred via the body of Maria to the body of the robot and then to the above-ground city. The False Maria then moves through the city, instigating riots and sabotage that threaten to destroy Metropolis. She leads the people on a twisting path through the streets, first as their leader and then as their prey. The human Maria, also once a leader, is pursued by rioting workers. Over the course of the film, the two figures repeatedly overlap. Straight line and bent line change places again and again.

The interchangeability of black and white and of straight and bent is made possible by the interpenetration of frame and content noted above. This relationship of frame to content appears in many sequences in the film. In one early sequence, in which an elevator takes workers down into the depths of the city, the camera cuts from a shot of living workers against a flat backdrop to a shot of painted (flat) human figures against a (built, three-dimensional) model of the city (see fig. 1.9). As the elevator

Fig. 1.9 Workers and elevator frame the view to the underground city.

reaches its destination, the doors open and the workers pour out into a square surrounded by rigid, austere tenement dwellings.

To achieve its cinematic effects, *Metropolis* makes extensive use of painted backdrops and matte paintings, mainly for scenes of the upper city and of machinery, in which bodies are enframed by technology. But these images are of more than technical significance: they articulate a complex relationship in which frames are surfaces and surfaces are frames. Throughout the film Lang makes use of this interplay to suggest a broader ambivalence: between container and contained, man and machine, even subject and object. In Joh Frederson's window, for example, a frame is really a surface, not just in its construction but also in the milky opacity it lays over the view of the city. These frames do not frame a view of something beyond; rather, they are surfaces that separate here from there. Lang's film destroys many frames and often exchanges frames and surfaces. At the climax of the film, an act of sabotage by the workers causes the water of a subterranean river to break through the surface of the ground in the workers' city. It erupts and then spreads, becoming a surface itself before raging on to rupture other surfaces and pour through other frames. Breaking through the tenement walls, it gushes through the underground city, submerging it (see fig. 1.10).

Lang's use of frames and surfaces to mediate the relationships of light to dark, straight to bent, and subject to object can be interpreted through the philosophy of Maurice Merleau-Ponty, for whom frames and surfaces had a particular role in our understanding of depth – the dimension he privileged as the one with which human beings engage the world. A complex engagement with depth is the "plastic-photogenic basis" (to use Buñuel's term) of *Metropolis*, articulated through the manipulation of frames and surfaces. The act of framing can eliminate depth by pushing a subject away from our bodies, flattening it and disconnecting us from it. Frederson's window does this; so does the picture screen that both connects him to and separates him from his suffering foreman. These objects turn frames into surfaces but, as we have seen, Lang also turns surfaces into frames – by rupturing them. Together, these effects present an inherent ambiguity in the relationship of a frame to a surface. A frame separates us from a space but implicitly invites us to enter it; similarly, a surface denies penetration but implicitly invites rupture. This ambiguity is accentuated when frames and surfaces dissolve into each other, as they do through the action of the labyrinth. Its ambivalent gesture both deepens

Fig. 1.10 A subterranean river bursts forth, rupturing the tenement walls.

surfaces and flattens depths. Things on this side of a frame or surface interpenetrate things on the other side; our bodies and the objects before us envelop each other. Frame and surface both guard a boundary and enable us to cross it: between inside and outside, subject and object, order and disorder; between the thickness of things and its unravelling in the apocalyptic moment. The most telling example of this condition is in the imagery of the destruction of the Tower of Babel: not the New Tower of Babel – in von Harbou's novel this building was damaged, while in Lang's film it remains intact, consistent with its confused political state – but the biblical Tower.

BABEL

Maria recounts the story of Babel in a sermon to the workers in a chapel deep in the labyrinth. This incident evinces an interesting mis-telling of the Babel story, for in Maria's version, rather than God's destroying Nimrod's tower, his suffering workers overthrow it. This Babel scene is framed by radiant lines, setting it off from the rest of the film as a "tale within a tale." Within this frame, Lang presents the Tower of Babel itself but then immediately reveals that the tower before us is only a model, framed this time by the bodies of the conceivers who imagine and design the actual

Fig. 1.11 The Tower of Babel as model, framed by its architects' bodies.

Fig. 1.12 The Tower, in ruins, revealed as hollow.

tower by building a model of it (see fig. 1.11). The story continues with a series of images that illustrates the construction of the tower and the conflict that leads to its downfall, concluding with an image of the tower in ruins. But the ruined edifice again is represented to show that this is a model and not the real tower. One would expect the interior of the ruined Babel to be a honeycomb of interior spaces with many buttressed walls and internal divisions, as the perforated mass suggested by its many historical pictorial representations. Instead, Lang represents the ruined building as a hollow shell, a hollowness emphasized by the irony of the words written in the sky above (see fig. 1.12). This tower is revealed not as a tower at all but, rather, as a work of artifice, a model, a shell without contents. It is not a building but a surface: a broken wall.

The dissolution (or envelopment) of one thing into (or by) another inherent in these ambiguous frames and surfaces is evident in other works of architecture in *Metropolis*, all of which bear a relationship to the Tower of Babel. We have already been introduced to Rotwang's house, the labyrinth within a labyrinth. This bent hut, we are told, was built long ago "by a man from the East" (see fig. 1.13). It shares its provenance with the biblical Tower of Babel and metaphorically with the New Tower of Babel in the centre of Metropolis. Appropriately, the machinery of the New Tower of Babel originates here, as does the False Maria. As we have seen, the False Maria is presented to the public for the first time in the nightclub known as the Yoshiwara (see fig. 1.14). This too is an Eastern space. Yoshiwara was the name of the entertainment district in Edo, or early modern Tokyo. It was also associated with destruction, having been destroyed by fire after a devastating earthquake in 1923, the year before Lang's trip to Manhattan. The young men of the upper city gather around the body of the False Maria in this place. In parallel, the workers deep in the labyrinth gather around the body of the first Maria and then the False Maria in an underground chapel. The chapel is Christian but its labyrinthine form invokes an ancient Christianity. In von Harbou's novel this is where Maria discovers the body of the magician from the East. The chapel refers to another historical gathering place above, where the cross is also present: the Gothic cathedral. This is where the climax of the film takes place. As a medieval cathedral, this structure echoes both the biblical tower and the labyrinth. In this sense it is a double of the other building that dominates Lang's city: the New Tower of Babel. Both are upright and both are centres of the city. We have already seen that this doubling refers to contemporary debates in German architecture. The cathedral also brings us back to Rotwang's house, which is equally historical. As a half-timbered rural hut, it resonates with Goethe's definition of the hut as the predecessor of the Gothic cathedral. Finally, at the climax of the film, the central space surrounded by workers' tenements becomes another gathering space as the children of the city climb the central monument, its stepped form resembling a ziggurat.

The overlap of these architectures is emphasized by their common geometry: the pentagon. The top of the New Tower and the square surrounded by tenements are both pentagons in plan. The profile of Rotwang's hut, the entrance of the Yoshiwara, and the cathedral façade are

Fig. 1.13 As Maria escapes from Rotwang's hut, her body is framed by light and shadow.

Fig. 1.14 Revellers descend the steps of the Yoshiwara as the city begins to fall into chaos.

all based on the pentagon. A pentagram is inscribed on the doors in the maze of Rotwang's house; and a pentagram forms the backdrop to our first view of the Machine Man. The five points of this star echo the human figure. This is reinforced when Maria flees from Rotwang and her body contorts like the labyrinth, her arms folded across her chest (see fig. 1.15). The lines connecting her hands, elbows, shoulders, and face form a pentagram, bound into a pentagon by her quaking body. The bodies that move within this city share their geometry with its architecture. Thus, their corporeal and architectural forms are projected onto or through one another.

The spaces of the city intermingle, as do dark and light in the labyrinth. Together, they form the primal architectural figure: Babel, the tower/world/city that combines the upward thrust of a tower and the twisted meandering of a labyrinth. Babel also invokes various complementary but contradictory notions: the primal hut (it is the ur-building), the centre of community (it brings together a people in one act of construction), and the origin of foreignness (its fall results in the sundering

Fig. 1.15 Maria, trying to fend off Rotwang's searchlight, folds her arms into the shape of a pentagram.

of tongues and nations). Babel is the technological emblem of the city or building that anticipates its own destruction. The labyrinth was an emblematic foundation of architecture for most of European history, but here it is simultaneously intertwined with and at war with the city.

FLESH

A fundamental gesture of this film is the intermingling of the straight line and the bent line, mediated through a filmic spatiality that insists on breaking down the frames, boundaries, and surfaces of both architectural and human bodies. This ambiguity destabilizes the boundaries between dark and light, machine and human body. It leads not just to the replacement of Maria's body by the robot but also to a strange reversibility between human and machine. The covering of the Machine Man by Maria's skin implies a re-covering of her flesh: a transformation mediated by the labyrinth. As flesh transforms the robot, so the labyrinth interrupts the Cartesian drive to divide cities into levels, zones, and grids. This is achieved in a twilight in which neither light nor darkness remains pure, a space whose folds and convolutions envelop their contents and each other. Light and dark, black and white, here become something new: a *lumen opacatum* (see fig. 1.16).

Maurice Merleau-Ponty speaks of a similar material, the "flesh of the world," which is opposed to the machine and what it stands for: "Neither purely transparent nor completely opaque, the flesh is an interplay of dimensionalities, of light and shadow." The labyrinth, as both a refuge and a trap, an enveloping space in which objects no longer keep their distance, also fits Merleau-Ponty's definition of the condition that brings about hallucinations and myths: "a shrinkage in the space directly experienced, a rooting of things in our body, the overwhelming proximity of the object, the oneness of man and the world." In these conditions "every object is the mirror of all others"; the bodies and buildings of the city overlap and interpenetrate each other. Our machines are no longer merely our works: they have the potential to possess us. In so doing, they cease to be merely objects; instead, they become Things, for they now satisfy Merleau-Ponty's dictum that, in conditions of the flesh, "the things have us, and … it is not we who have the things." This is a mythic space of metamorphosis that approximates the seething Chaos of the *Theogony*, which Hans Blumenberg describes as "the pure metaphor of the gaping

Fig. 1.16 *Lumen opacatum.*

and yawning open of an abyss, which requires no localization, no description of its edges or of its depth, but is only the opaque space in which forms makes their appearance."

For Blumenberg, myth responds to what he calls the "absolutism of reality," the condition of anxiety in a world that is always a potential and living threat. Following Freud, he equates this with "the complete helplessness of the ego in the face of overwhelming danger as the core of the traumatic situation." Lang's *Metropolis* emerged in a social and political situation that was traumatic. Germany's military defeat, followed by its long period of economic instability, promoted a condition of helplessness. The film portrays human beings explicitly as victims of a more general modern technological and economic condition that can be considered traumatic. Suffering workers, for example, are forced to labour as slaves to the machinery of the city. These machines sustain the lifestyles of the city's wealthy inhabitants. Maria's imprisonment, as part of a quasi-scientific experiment and technological transformation, is another instance of this condition. She is imprisoned by Rotwang at the instigation of Joh Frederson. Frederson exercises power in part either by bestowing money upon his subjects or by denying it to them (the industrial machinery invented by Rotwang generates this wealth). Thus, the film depicts a modern city built on a collusion of technology and economics that renders the human subject powerless and vulnerable, threatening to evacuate it of its humanity. Lang's labyrinth and the robot/human body that emerges from it are responses to such conditions. They echo Blumenberg's words: "Out of the night, all sorts of awful and formless things can emerge, to occupy the edges of the abyss."

PHANTOM

Merleau-Ponty had a great interest in fantasies generated in response to trauma. He was interested in the fantasy not as a symptom of what has been lost but as an addition that suggests what survives. For him, this condition was epitomized by the phantom limb imagined by patients who lose a part of their body due to trauma. Such fantasies can be interpreted as "modalities and variations of the subject's total being." They reveal the direction or trajectory on which the subject's being is engaged as a life project or a movement towards death. One continues to pursue a life direction *through* the phantasm, despite the damage done to the body;

the phantom limb is thus a manifestation of one's intentional arc. This is evident also in the flesh recovered by Lang's robot: a flesh that emerges in the cinematic imagination to replace a flesh that has been lost, or is in the process of being lost, in the real world. This complex is also embodied in Rotwang, who lost a limb when an experiment went wrong and now has an artificial arm.

A mechanical body could be interpreted as an emblem of the Cartesian *res extensa*, the body reduced to a machine, but in this film the robot body and its intimate and incessant intertwining with human bodies has a different meaning. The strange reversibility between machine and body suggests an undiminished yearning for what has been lost due to modernity. We could even recognize this in the people's desire for the body of Maria, transposed onto the robot. This reversibility between machine and human body, and its implied overturning of the Cartesian mind/body relationship, creates a cinematic and corporeal topography analogous to what Merleau-Ponty refers to as the *chiasm*: the gap that is spanned by our experience of the world but is incomprehensible to Cartesian thought. In the chiasm lies the mystery of depth. This same mystery is implied in the space of *Metropolis*: a depth that is crossed by tides of dark and light, by frayed and broken boundaries, and by the labyrinth that enfolds these two bodies. The Tower of Babel, with its intertwining of straight and bent lines, and the city itself, machine and labyrinth, can be read in a similar way.

This condition implies a specific relationship between surfaces and depths. Merleau-Ponty speaks of the depth experienced by the new-born child and by the trauma victim whose body has been breached. He speaks of it as a primordial depth, a depth we must seek to recover:

> We have to rediscover beneath depth as a relation between things or even between planes, which is objectified depth detached from experience and transformed into breadth, a primordial depth, which confers upon the other its significance, and which is the thickness of a medium devoid of everything … a depth which does not yet operate between objects, which, *a fortiori*, does not yet assess the distance between them, and which is simply the opening of perception upon some ghost thing as yet scarcely qualified.[26]

It is a thickness that is both infinitely deep and infinitely shallow, in which surface and depth become one in the same sense that visible and invisible

Fig. 1.17 The False Maria immolated on the parvis of the Gothic cathedral.

imply each other. This is the depth of a ghost or the skin of a robot: a depth that is a mere "fraction of dimensionality." It resonates with the surfaces with which Lang plays, with Maria's skin, and with the flat silhouettes of Expressionist films from *Nosferatu* to *The Golem*. It is perhaps this concordance of depth and shallowness that enables Lang's translucent opacities, his blazing shadows, his machines with phantom flesh, to be both there and not there, the most substantial and the most insubstantial of things.

The film makes it clear that this flesh is "frightful." Any distinction between good and evil, between desire and fear, remains ambiguous. The modern disruption of the human body has been so extensive that it may be recovered only through a *malevolent* haunting. While the flesh (the images) of Lang's film proposes recovery, the film ultimately cannot stomach its own proposition. The human robot must be depicted as evil. The blurring of organic and machine is unacceptable; the plot is resolved only by eradicating all traces of humanity from the machine and by eliminating the machine from human space. At the climax of the film the robot is immolated and her human skin burns away (see fig. 1.17). The inventor, who is part machine, is also killed: thrown from on high. This purification of the city saves the community. It restores an ordered, healthy, holistic world, but it also condemns the city to the inevitable return of the crises at its heart, both in subsequent retellings of the *Metropolis* story and in the imminent unfolding of European history. The great lie here is that the fecund potential of the labyrinth can be eliminated. This is what dooms the citizenry of Metropolis – and perhaps also of Germany. The complexity and instability of our condition disavowed, we are left with both city and body purified, everyone back in their proper form. The true Maria is once again demure, upright, chaste, and radiant: without a shadow.

NOTES

* The images in this chapter are reproduced from the definitive reconstruction of *Metropolis* (1926) by the Friedrich Wilhelm Murnau Foundation: *Metropolis* (New York: Kino International/Transit Films, 2002; videorecording). Director: Fritz Lang. Screenwriters: Fritz Lang and Thea von Harbou. Actors: Brigitte Helm, Alfred Abel, Gustav Frœhlich, Rudolf Klein-Rogge. Cinematography: Karl Freund, Günther Rittau, and Walter Ruttmann. Art direction: Otto Hunte, Erich Kettelhut, and Karl Vollbrecht. Score: Gottfried Huppertz. Restoration: Enno Patalas, UFA (firm), Transit Films, Friedrich Wilhelm Murnau Stiftung, and Kino International Corporation.

1 Luis Buñuel, "Metropolis," in *Great Film Directors: A Critical Anthology*, ed. Morris Dickstein Leo Braudy (New York: Oxford University Press, 1978), 590.

2 Siegfried Kracauer and Leonardo Quaresima, *From Caligari to Hitler: A Psychological History of the German Film*, rev. and expanded ed. (Princeton/Oxford: Princeton University Press, 2004), 164.

3 During the film's production, from its conception in 1924 to its release in 1926 and its re-release in a highly edited version in 1927, Germany was mired in a debilitating economic crisis as a result of the punitive Treaty of Versailles, which brought the First World War to a close. Resentment against this condition would be one factor behind the rise of the Nazi party. Kracauer placed the film in the context of an interwar German filmography, which for

him was a clear premonition. He compared, for example, *Metropolis*'s choreographed crowd scenes and immense set-pieces to the Nuremburg rallies. There is substantial evidence in the film to support such a reading: the equation of Oriental spaces (the Tower of Babel, Rotwang's bent hut built by a magician from the East, the nightclub known as the Yoshiwara, machines inhabited by foreign and usually Eastern gods) with a lurking evil; the overtly racist tone of certain passages in scriptwriter Thea von Harbou's novel *Metropolis* (Boston: Gregg Press, 1975); the populace united as one folk beneath a father-figure; and the purification of the city through the immolation of an Other.

4 Erich Mendelsohn, *Amerika, Bilderbuch Eines Architekten* (Berlin: R. Mosse, 1926).

5 This building thus would represent a "Germanization of the skyscraper." Rainer Stommer, "Germanisierung des Wolkenkratzers: Die Hochhausdebatte in Deutschland bis 1921," *Kritische Berichte* 3 (1982): 36–54, quoted in Dietrich Neumann, "Before and after Metropolis: Film and Architecture in Search of the Modern City," in *Film Architecture: Set Designs from Metropolis to Blade Runner*, ed. Dietrich Neumann (Munich/New York: Prestel, 1996), 35. Thousands of buildings based on this principle were designed as projects in the 1920s, including Otto Kohlz's federal office building in Berlin, and Haimovici, Tshcammer, and Caroli's trade fair tower in Leipzig (both 1920). See Neumann, "Before and after Metropolis," 35–6, 102. Such projects all drew to some extent on the memory of Bruno Schmitz's Völkerschlachtdenkmal, the memorial commemoratingNapoleon's defeat at Leipzig, which also informed the design of Lang's New Tower of Babel. See Dietrich Neumann, "The Urbanistic Vision in Fritz Lang's *Metropolis*," in *Dancing on the Volcano: Essays on the Culture of the Weimar Republic*, ed. Thomas W. Kniesche and Stephen Brockmann (Columbia, SC: Camden House, 1994), 150.

6 Even one of the proponents of the Modern Movement in architecture, Walter Gropius, had expressed doubts about the use of a modern, technologized architecture: "Now, however, the ancient forms of human life, as they come to expression in household functions, have little in common with what has transpired in technology, and to seek in industrial forms a tuning fork for this aspect of life, not to mention machines, is neither particularly clever nor correctly felt on an instinctual level." See Walter Gropius and Paul Schultze-Naumburg, "What Is Right? Traditional Architecture or Building

in New Forms," in *The Weimar Republic Sourcebook*, ed. Anton Kaes, Martin Jay, and Edward Dimendberg (Berkeley: University of California Press, 1994), 444.

7 Neumann, "Before and after Metropolis," 36.

8 Joseph Goebbels would write an essay in 1928 in which he condemned the foreign pollution of Berlin's streets, opposing to it the image of a cathedral (the Kaiser Wilhelm Gedachnichtskirche). This use of the cathedral resonates so strongly with Lang's presentation that it must have been written after viewing the film. See Joseph Goebbels, "Around the Gedächtniskirche," in Kaes, Jay, and Dimendberg, *Weimar Republic Sourcebook*, 560–2.

9 More precisely, this was a "paternoster machine," an early elevator based on a continuously moving chain of cellular compartments, each carrying passengers. A few still exist.

10 Neumann, "Urbanistic Vision," 148. Von Harbou's novel makes clear what the film implies: that there is a direct vertical mechanical connection between the Tower above and the machinery below, through the paternoster machine.

11 How a house with a pitched roof can contain a courtyard is never explained to us. It is as anomalous as is the house itself, which is a vestige of the rural caught beneath the superstructures of the modern city.

12 This is only one of several Oriental spaces in the film (see note 3.)

13 Von Harbou, *Metropolis*, 55. This is yet another instance of Oriental space.

14 Hans Blumenberg, *Work on Myth* (Cambridge, MA: MIT Press, 1985), 501.

15 I take this term from Gilles Deleuze's discussion of Expressionist film. He takes it from Goethe, who takes it from Athanasius Kircher. See Gilles Deleuze, *Cinema 1: The Movement Image*, trans. Hugh Tomlinson and Barbara Habberjam (Minneapolis: University of Minnesota Press, 1986), 50–1.

16 Maurice Merleau-Ponty, "Eye and Mind," in *The Primacy of Perception and Other Essays on Phenomenological Psychology, the Philosophy of Art, History, and Politics* (Evanston, IL: Northwestern University Press, 1964), 172–3, quoted in Alberto Pérez-Gómez and Louise Pelletier, *Architectural Representation and the Perspective Hinge* (Cambridge, MA: MIT Press, 1997), 336. Though space does not allow a thorough discussion here, the congruence between Deleuze's and Merleau-Ponty's work has been explored in Elena del Rio, "Alchemies of Thought in Godard's Cinema: Deleuze and Merleau-Ponty," *SubStance* 34, 3 (2005): 62–78; and Leonard Lawlor,

"The End of Phenomenology: Expressionism in Deleuze and Merleau-Ponty," *Continental Philosophy Review* 31 (1998): 15–34.

17 Maurice Merleau-Ponty, *Phenomenology of Perception*, trans. Colin Smith (London and New York: Routledge Classics, 2002), 339.

18 Ibid., 79.

19 Maurice Merleau-Ponty and Claude Lefort, *The Visible and the Invisible* (Evanston, IL: Northwestern University Press, 1968), 194, quoted in Pérez-Gómez and Pelletier, *Architectural Representation*, 336.

20 Blumenberg, *Work on Myth*, 127.

21 Ibid., 5.

22 Ibid., 127.

23 Merleau-Ponty, *Phenomenology of Perception*, 123.

24 "What is in us which refuses mutilation and disablement is an *I* committed to a certain physical and inter-human world, who continues to tend toward his world despite handicaps and amputations and who, to this extent, does not recognize them *de jure*" (Merleau-Ponty, *Phenomenology of Perception*, 93).

25 "The life of consciousness – cognitive life, the life of desire or perceptual life – is subtended by an 'intentional arc' which projects round about us our past, our future, our human setting, our physical, ideological and moral situation, or rather which results in our being situated in all these respects" (Merleau-Ponty, *Phenomenology of Perception*, 157).

26 Merleau-Ponty, *Phenomenology of Perception*, 310.

27 Pérez-Gómez and Pelletier, *Architectural Representation*, 376–7.

28 Deleuze, *Cinema 1*, 50–1.

On Fire and the Origins of Architecture

Lian Chang[1]

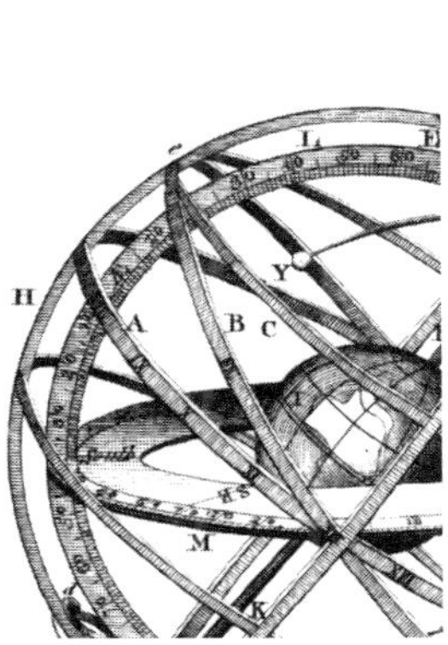

ONCE UPON A TIME, so Vitruvius tells us, men lived like animals, taking shelter in woods and caves, and foraging in the fields. One day, in a certain place where the trees were densely crowded, stormy winds caused the branches to rub together, kindling a fire. The people fled in terror, but as the flames subsided they came back and – discovering the advantage of its warmth – threw logs onto the fire to preserve it. They then brought other people, through gestures showing them the benefits of the fire. Although each person at first spoke in his or her own voice, they gradually fixed words as they came across them in their daily routines. Over time, they began to speak in sentences and to hold conversations. In this way, the discovery of fire held the origins of deliberative assembly and a life in common.[2]

Vitruvius tells this story in Book 2 of *De architectura*. It closely echoes the account of Lucretius, which also features the chance discovery of fire as a catalyst of an incremental process of civilization, in part through the development of language and architecture.[3] The Hippocratic *Ancient Medicine* also, albeit implicitly, gives fire a civilizing role in its explanation of how the craft of medicine resulted from the progressive invention of refining and cooking food to transform the rough fodder that suits animals into food that suits healthy people and – ultimately – sick people who need soup and other weak forms of sustenance.[4]

But Vitruvius's aim, of course, is not to present the origins of civilization in general or medicine in particular but, rather, to present the origins of architecture. So he continues, pointing out that, unlike other animals, humans had the gift of walking upright. This allowed them both to look upon the magnificence of the universe and the stars and to manipulate things with their hands. Some began to make shelters of leaves while others dug caves or built structures out of mud and twigs. By observing each other's homes and adding new ideas day by day, they began to produce better huts, achieving greater insight as the days passed. And when their hands were fully adept at building and their cunning had given them craftsmanship, a few industrious men declared themselves carpenters. In this way, people progressed from savagery to civilization. With lofty ideas born from the variety of their crafts, they began to build not huts but houses with foundations, walls of brick or stone, and roofs of wood and tiles. And from observations made in their studies, they were led from uncertain judgments to the stable principles of proportion (*symmetria*).[5]

Fig. 2.1 The origins of architecture, from Vitruvius, *De architectura*, Cesariano edition (1521).

As sensible as it is charming, this story does not strike us as unusual among other ancient accounts of origins. But still, we might ask, what does fire have to do with architecture? More precisely, why are these events – the chance discovery of fire, the gathering of people, the first stuttering attempts at language – given such priority that they precede the craft of building in a treatise that is just as much about extolling the importance of architecture as it is about architecture itself? How does *symmetria* become a key feature distinguishing civilized from savage buildings? And why is star-gazing so important? By considering the associations of fire in Vitruvius's Greek cultural and intellectual background –

as evinced in poetic, philosophic, political, and medical texts as well as in ritual – this chapter contextualizes Vitruvius's use of this story, centred around the origins of architecture in the chance discovery of fire.

COOKING

Necessary for the firing of pottery; for the bending, smelting, and forging of metal; for cooking; and for generally keeping warm, fire was seen as a powerful technical and civilizing force in antiquity. In the myth of Prometheus, as told by Hesiod, Aeschylus, and others, fire symbolically stands for all human *technai* (crafts or skills). Aeschylus has Prometheus boast of fire, first among the many gifts of *technai* that he has given to humankind, exclaiming that it is "teacher to mortals in every art (*technê*) and a means to mighty ends."[6] And, just as the Hippocratic author of *Ancient Medicine* distinguishes between the rough and uncooked food of animals and the refined and cooked food of civilized people, ancient Greeks more generally associated rawness and the consumption of raw food with barbaric (foreign, savage) conditions in contrast with the civilized, and therefore Greek, practice of cooking.[7]

Fig. 2.2 A *mageiros* and another man cutting and roasting sacrificial meats at a fire. Attic black-figure krater (late sixth century BCE). British Museum, London. Drawing from Marcel Detienne and Jean-Pierre Vernant, eds., *The Cuisine of Sacrifice among the Greeks* (Chicago and London: University of Chicago Press, 1986).

The act of blood sacrifice – that is, of slitting an animal's throat, properly dividing it into parts, roasting the assigned parts for human consumption, and burning the thigh bones for the gods – played a central role in this association of fire and cooking with the life of a civilized Greek. Most animals – and certainly those domestically raised for meat, such as cattle, sheep, and goats – had to be slaughtered through the ritual of sacrifice in order to be legitimately consumed. A sacrifice could be a major event for an entire city or camp during a festival or a funeral, as when the Trojans mourned Hector; or it could be a humble meal, as when Odysseus's swineherd sacrificed a piglet for a meal with Odysseus, who was disguised as an old beggar and suppliant.[8] In any case, both gods and mortals had to receive their fair share. The thigh bones were wrapped in fat and burned as offerings. The gods, who ate for pleasure rather than for sustenance, consumed their share in the form of smoke. The rest of the parts were cut up, roasted, and shared out among the people for consumption along lines that acknowledged both the ideal of equality and the need to honour particular individuals such as guests and priests.[9]

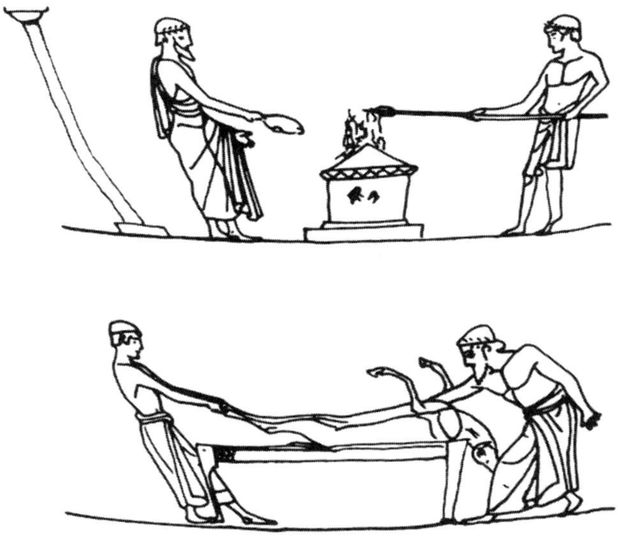

Fig. 2.3 Two scenes: (1) roasting sacrificial meat and (2) removing the *splanchna* (innards) of a sacrificed animal. Skyphos by the Euaion Painter (460–440 BCE). National Museum, Warsaw. Drawing from Detienne and Vernant, *Cuisine of Sacrifice*.

SHARING

Why did the gods receive their portion through smoke from the fire at the altar? Hesiod gives one answer in the form of a story, woven through both *Works and Days* and the *Theogony*, of a series of cunning exchanges between Prometheus and Zeus. First, the Titan god Prometheus is assigned the task of preparing a feast for gods and humans, but – always on the side of humankind – Prometheus tries to outwit Zeus. He conceals the edible meat in the ox's stomach and hide, and wraps the inedible bones in glistening fat. He then offers these doctored portions to Zeus for his selection. Zeus, never outwitted, is "angry at heart" when he sees the trick. He accepts the bones, and Hesiod tells us that mortals then had to burn the bones at their altars to the gods. But Zeus is not finished. Smouldering with anger, he "thought mischief against mortal men" and confiscated fire as a punishment.[10] This prompts Prometheus to steal fire back for humans, hiding its gleam inside a fennel stalk. His outrage renewed, Zeus then contrives woman as a final retribution and punishment: with the help of Hephaistos and Athena, god and goddess of crafts, he forms, dresses, and brings to life a "beautiful evil" named Pandora.[11]

The Greeks often compared women to leaky vessels in the insatiability of their hungers and their ability to reproduce.[12] With Pandora came a vessel from which all sorts of evils and ills escaped. She also brought the need to reproduce and to constantly toil to feed the insatiable hunger of the stomach – a fitting punishment for Prometheus's filling of the ox stomach with meat. Hesiod's tale, therefore, speaks not only about the origins of sacrifice but also of the gaps, contingencies, and imperfections of mortal life that constantly need to be bridged through cooking, medicine, and other *technai*. It also speaks about the new distance between gods and mortals: whereas before this incident, gods ate at the same table as humans – who were mortal but had an easy life without hungers and ills – the distinction became more marked, and this gap needed to be continually acknowledged and bridged through the offering of meat and through the fire that facilitated its delivery.[13]

Although the distribution of sacrificial portions emphasized the inequality and distance between mortals and gods, it was also meant to display equality between men. As Jean-Pierre Vernant famously argues, the origins of the *agora*, or open place of assembly, may be found in the circle of noble warriors coming together to make decisions during the

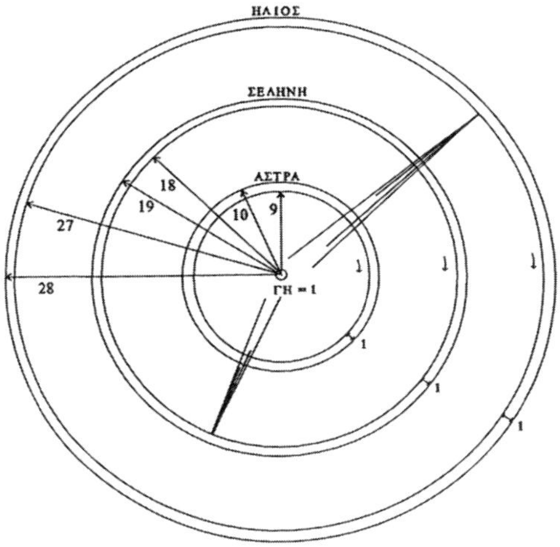

Fig. 2.4 Map of Anaximander's universe, with the earth in the centre of the circular orbits of the stars, moon, and sun. Drawing from Dirk L. Couprie, "Anaximander's Discovery of Space," in *Essays in Ancient Greek Philosophy VI: Before Plato*, ed. Anthony Preus, 23–38 (Albany, NY: State University of New York Press, 2001).

Fig. 2.5 Isonomic carving and division of sacrificial meat in preparation for cooking and distribution. Lid of a Boeotian dish (sixth or fifth century BCE). Schloss Fasanerie, Adolphseck, Germany. Drawing from Detienne and Vernant, *Cuisine of Sacrifice*.

"dark" ages between the fall of the Mycenaean civilization and the rise of the city-states. To put an issue into the forum for discussion is to place it *en mesôi*, or in the middle. Homer's poems are full of these kinds of meetings. Evoking a similar geometry, Anaximander proposes that the universe must be spherical, with each point on its circumference equidistant from the earth at the centre, in order for it to be stable.[14] And Plato in the *Timaeus* organizes the spaces of both the cosmos and the city of Atlantis on this model of political equality, or *isonomia*. Each household, or *oikos*, is rooted by its central fire, or hearth, just as the city has a central hearth, or *hestia koinê*, in the *agora* that symbolically roots and joins its members. The sanctuary spaces around sacrificial altars, where each receives his equal portion of meat, also act as symbolic centres that root and fix the bonds among citizens.

FORGING

The bonds that held together the civic body – or, indeed, any kind of body – were not idle metaphors. The work of craft, or *technê*, which characterized productive human endeavours governed by skill and a particular kind of order, was often that of forging bonds. These bonds were literal for a craftsperson who joined wood, metal, cloth, stone, or other materials, but they could also include the work of a politician or rhetorician: Plato refers to the construction of an argument in speech as a process of cutting or analyzing the material at hand and then weaving or joining it back together.[15] But the archetypical Greek craftsman, as depicted in Homer, is Hephaistos, god of fire and of the *technai* of metalworking. When Hephaistos works he stands, sweating, at his forge. His craft resides in the skilful wielding of fire's power to shape and join metal. His creations range from wheeled tripods that move of their own accord to golden handmaids who come alive to serve their master to the famous shield and other armour for Achilles. The wondrous quality of these items – each is *thauma idesthai*, or "a wonder to behold" – lies in the godly skill with which he forges their bonds and is manifest in the spark of life that these objects emit.

Fig. 2.6 Hephaistos crafting Achilles' armour as Thetis stands by. Interior of a red-figure cup by the Foundry Painter (480–470 BCE). Altes Museum, Berlin.

Fig. 2.7 Zeus hurling a thunderbolt. Bronze statuette from Dodona (early fifth century BCE). Collection of Classical Antiquities, National Museums in Berlin.

When Achilles receives his new armour in the *Iliad*, his comrades shrink back in fear of its bright clamour and are afraid to look at it, but Achilles – the son of a goddess – is not afraid as he recognizes the work of an immortal. His eyes light up, glowing "terribly from beneath their lids, like flame."[16] The fire associated with Achilles is a sign of his half-divine status as a hero; his incomplete baptism in fire literally left him mortal at his heel while rendering him otherwise impervious to harm. Before he receives his armour, he appears in the Achaean trench to frighten the Trojans, and Athena lights a gleaming fire above his head. Conjuring a fearsome power like that of Zeus's lightning, Achilles shouts from the Achaean trench three times with his "voice of bronze," and twelve of the finest Trojan warriors drop dead out of terror, "there and then … among their own chariots and their own spears."[17]

DISJOINTING

Fire and the *technai* were therefore signs not just of humans' mortality but also of their rewarding but dangerous relationship with divine powers, and their constant struggle to transcend their existence as mortal animals. Why was this constant struggle necessary? Besides the usual difficulties of human life in a time when hunger, war, and illness were a constant threat, the Greeks, as Rosemary Desjardins argues, "found themselves shadowed by an ever-present threat of de-generation, a process that we associate with entropy in which everything is in danger of sliding back into the undifferentiated soup from which it was derived."[18] They were, in a sense, particularly worried about things falling apart. It turns out that in the *Iliad*, the earliest work of literature in the West, the verb most frequently used to describe death is *luô*, "to loosen, unbind, resolve a whole into its parts."[19] When used in this sense, *luô* normally takes for its object either (and interchangeably) the *gounata*, "knees," or *guia*, which we can translate as "joints," "jointed limbs," or even "the self to the extent that it is articulated." In the *Iliad*, people die not through spillage (which suggests a body composed of container and contained) or through damage to specific vital parts (which suggests a body composed of organs) but through disarticulation.[20]

At the political level the fear of *stasis*, "factional rivalry" or "internal discord" of an individual or state, plagued the imagination of Classical Greeks. This word first appeared in the sixth century BCE after the formation of the classical *polis*, and, as Jonathan Price shows, remained tied to the notion of the *polis* thereafter. Thucydides describes *stasis* as a nightmarish situation in which "every form of wickedness arose," in which order regressed into disorder and "fathers killed their sons, people were dragged from temples and killed beside them."[21] By overturning the action of the strongest of societal bonds, *stasis* constituted a kind of disarticulation in which members of the civic body were no longer harmoniously joined but instead began to separate and struggle against each other. The notions of disarticulation and articulation were never dissociated: when Thucydides applies the notion of *stasis* to the Peloponnesian War, depicting Athens and Sparta as members that fight against each other only in "unnatural" situations, he is subtly but powerfully arguing for the coherence of Hellas, of a natural body or identity of Greekness.[22]

MIXING

Health and illness in the human body were described in similar terms. In Homer, the articulation of *guîa* stands for one's life, health, and power. The notion of *guîa* gave way in the fifth century BCE to components that were more precise but still intangible. Alcmaeon describes sets of opposing powers in the body such as wet, dry, hot, cold, sweet, and bitter, which, in illness, separate out from *isonomia*, or equality, into *monarchia*, or a tyrannical rule of one. This explicitly political view would persist in Greek medicine: Hippocratic physicians in the late fifth and early fourth centuries BCE similarly posit the notion of *eukrasia*, or good mixture, as a thorough mixing of the proper relative proportions of powers in the body. Improper proportions of powers often result in the suppuration, or separation, of powers or elements out of the mixture. These separated elements become visible as symptoms through the colour of the skin or the emission of fluids as in the vomiting of bile, coughing of phlegm, or bleeding.[23]

In a time when a flushing of the cheeks or an inappropriate discharge from the body could lead to fears of tyrannical internal discord, the language and connotations of mixing and separation, equality and imbalance, pervaded much of Greek life. In examining the politics of the *symposium*, a social institution of dinner and drinking, James Davidson finds that they were arguably even more politically charged than were the officially political banquets of public sacrifices. Whereas sacrificed meat had to be cut and cooked in a specifically sanctioned manner to fulfill religious requirements, other foods, such as fish, which were exempt from these requirements, became available as objects of culinary experimentation, connoisseurship, and sensual indulgence. As such, *symposia*, in serving wine and foods such as fish, became places for the enjoyment of the pleasures of food, drink, friendship, and sex.[24]

Far from relegating *symposia* to a realm of apolitical pleasures, this freedom made these gatherings the object of heightened scrutiny. Wine, for example, was normally consumed only after a *krasis*, or mixture, of wine and water was prepared in a special vessel known as a *krater* and the resulting mixture served to each guest in equal measures. At public gatherings, an *oinopteros*, or "wine watcher," could be employed to ensure that nobody, in their greed, drank more than the others.[25] A gluttonous appetite, whether for food, drink, or sex, was a sign that one was like a womanly, leaky vessel whose appetite was not sated with a fair portion. This attitude stands in stark contrast with our modern one, which might assume that the conspicuous consumption or over-consumption of pleasures is a sign of masculine virility or of the wealth and power necessary to furnish such luxuries. For the Greeks, to live with *sôphrosunê*, which required moderation, self-control, and *harmonia*, or the balanced integration of soul and body, was a sign of one's nobility and fittedness to rule both oneself and others. Whereas over-consumption by an individual might have led to rumours of womanly or tyrannical impulses, over-consumption by a group of aristocrats gathered in their private *symposia* ignited fears, among the masses, of bonds of friendship that were too close among too few. This inevitably raised the spectre of *stasis*, conspiracy, and revolution.[26]

One of the surest ways to over-indulge at a dinner party was to drink wine from cups that were too large and deep, to reduce the proportion of water to wine, or to drink wine straight, in its unmixed form. This last option was particularly drastic, an affront to the communality of the party and leading almost inevitably, in ancient accounts, to drunkenness and savage behaviour. It was akin to the consumption of raw meat that had bypassed the civilizing process of cooking by fire and dividing and setting out just portions. In this sense, the *krater* for mixing wine assumed a central position, like that of the fire in sacrifice.[27] In making food and drink communal through the articulating work of *technê*, the threat of private enjoyment and interests was neutralized by the equality established through proportional mixing, cutting, and divvying out.

STRUGGLING

Alongside the fear of *stasis* was an appreciation that divisive forces could never be completely eradicated and, in fact, that one could not exist without them. For example, in the fifth century BCE, Empedocles sets the binding force of Love in eternal opposition to the divisive force of Strife and sees the drama of the cosmos and all life played out in the struggle between these forces. For him, life did not exist during the strongest reign of Love but in the middle stages, when Love and Strife struggled against each other as relatively equal powers. When the binding force of Love is too great and everything binds to everything else without resistance, the world collapses into a massive, undifferentiated sphere. Life is no more possible in this state than it is during the reign of Strife, in which every element separates out, like tribal factions in a city, to reside and mix only with its own kind.

The idea that wholeness does not come easily, that it must be achieved through constant struggle, is expressed in the notion of the *agora* as the centre of Greek political life. In the *agora*, the core of the city was continually engaged in debate, and this held the people together. A fragment of Heraclitus reads: "Men do not know how what is at variance agrees with itself. It is an attunement of opposite tension, like that of the bow and the lyre."[28] This kind of tension, in cords that bind, holding the capacity for both wholeness and movement, is also expressed in a particular Homeric fascination with sinews and tendons as key sites of articulation that, when severed, bring about debilitation and death.[29] For the Greeks, articulation was not a static state but an active engagement of tension and coherence.

The word *agôn* describes such struggles, whether in the *agora* or on the battlefield. Meaning "contest, competition, or challenge," *agôn* is exemplified by debate in the *agora*; by athletic contests held at festivals, funerals, and the Olympic games (or, literally, "struggles," *olumpiakoi agônes*); and by engagement on the battlefield. These struggles could even be understood as the natural occupation of a person or city. In the *Timaeus*, Plato has Socrates say:

> Suppose, for instance, that on seeing beautiful creatures, in paintings or – better yet – alive but in repose, a man should be moved with desire to see them in motion and vigorously engaged in some struggle or conflict [*agônian athlounta*] to which their forms seem suited; well, that is the very feeling regarding the state we have described. There are conflicts which all cities undergo, and I would like to hear someone tell of our city contending against others in those struggles [*athlous*, contest or struggle for a prize] which states wage … whether in respect of military actions or verbal negotiations.[30]

In Classical Greece, combat between city-states was highly ritualized as an encounter between hoplite armies. The two armies would meet on a flat plain outside a city. Each hoplite unit was organized in orthogonal rows and would approach the opposing army squarely for a head-on clash. Each man's shield protected the man to his left, and the men – free

Fig. 2.8 Closely massed warriors, possibly depicting an early hoplite formation. Painting on shoulder of the "Chigi" vase, a Corinthian oinochoe from Monte Aguzzo (mid- to late seventh century BCE). Villa Giulia, Rome.

citizens of the same *polis* – were said to fight as equals in absolute solidarity. Because breaking rank endangered the entire unit, each phalanx aimed to retain its own formation while pushing, spearing, and intimidating men of the opposing phalanx into turning and scattering in a shameful panic.[31] Hoplite warfare was notable for its ideological vigour and tactical inefficiency. Rather than seeking to fight from high ground or other defensive positions, Classical Greek city-states deliberately chose the most exposed form of encounter in which the order and bonds between citizen soldiers were tested most directly.

HOSTING

Just as citizens symbolically bonded in a hoplite unit, or around the fire of the *agora* or the sacrificial altar, the act of inviting a stranger to take a place at the fire symbolized the integration, albeit temporary, of a guest into a household. Zeus Xenios (*xenos* meaning "stranger") protected the guest-host relationship by punishing those who did not provide hospitality to strangers.[32] The act of gracefully receiving and honouring strangers at one's hearth, and of sharing sacrificed meats in a meal, is elaborated in Homer into a motif that distinguishes the civilized and good from the savage and unworthy.

In the *Iliad*, Achilles displays his true nature as the "best of the Achaeans" not only by killing Hector in revenge but also by gracefully receiving Hector's father, Priam, in his tent when – according to custom – he came to offer ransom for his son's body. But this act of reconciliation did not come easily. Achilles' savage fury towards Hector is expressed in his initial refusal of his opponent's dying request that his corpse be returned to his parents in order for him to receive his "due meed of fire in [his] death." Achilles tells Hector, "I wish that somehow my wrath and fury might drive me to carve your flesh and eat it raw because of what you have done." He vengefully adds that Hector's corpse would never lie on a bier for a proper funeral but that "dogs and birds will devour you utterly."[33] This denial of the normal Homeric protocol of war, in which captives are ransomed and corpses exchanged to allow for funeral rites, emphasizes Achilles' uncivilized wrath. It also makes Achilles' reconciliation with Priam, as marked by the shared sacrificial fire and the fire of Hector's funeral, all the more poignant: not only do these fires mediate between mortals and immortals but they also signify the end of Achilles' wrath and his reintegration with his people. In Homer, both sacrificial and funerary fires are aptly described as the "flame of Hephaistos," evoking its role in joining and civilizing.[34]

The epics abound in examples of poor behaviour in guest-host situations. In the *Odyssey*, the suitors' occupation of Odysseus's home and their wasting of his resources through immoderate feasting is an example of poor guest behaviour that does not go unpunished. Earlier in the *Odyssey*, when Odysseus arrived at the island of the Cyclopes, he wonders "whether they are cruel, and wild, and unjust, or whether they are kind to strangers and fear the gods."[35] Unfortunately for Odysseus, the Cyclops Polyphemos is one of the worst hosts in all of Greek literature. For us, this encounter is interesting for exemplifying the contrast between raw savagery and the skilled use of fire. The Cyclopes have only minimal *technai*: they have no laws or assemblies, live in solitude, and ignore their neighbours. Their island is a naturally fertile place where wheat, barley,

Fig. 2.9 Odysseus and his men blinding Polyphemos. Interior of Laconian black-figure cup (550 BCE). Cabinet des Médailles, Paris.

and vines for wine spring up without any craft. Their harbour is shallow and protected; ships do not require the bonds of anchors and cables to stay fast. They also have no crafted architecture, as Polyphemos lives in a great cave with a rock for a door. Perhaps most viscerally, Polyphemos drinks "unmixed milk" and – disdainful of Zeus' injunction protecting guests and wandering strangers – gleefully dines on Odysseus's comrades, eating them raw.[36]

Instead of welcoming the strangers to his fire and preparing a sacrifice for a shared meal, Polyphemos greedily gorges himself on Odysseus's men and on his vintage, unmixed wine. He then passes out, covering himself with a mess of wine and bits of human flesh that he vomits upon himself in his sleep. Odysseus and his men cunningly heat a pointed stake of olive wood in the fire and, with a rapid twisting motion that Homer compares to the work of a craftsman drilling the timbers of a ship, plunge the pointed end into his single eye.[37] Of course, a simple stabbing motion would have sufficed to put out Polyphemos's eye as he lay in his drunken stupor, but in the way that Homer tells the story, the fire and the skilled twisting motion are signs of the triumph of *technê* over barbarism.[38] To the sound of the hissing, or cooking, of Polyphemos's eyeball – a sound that Homer compares to the sound of another act of *technê*, the quenching of a heated iron axe in cold water – Odysseus wields the power of Polyphemos's own fire against him.

CRAFTING

Odysseus's act is strategic and skilful, employing the *technê* of fire against a brute who failed to observe basic elements of civilized behaviour. His act even has an architectural outcome, since – when combined with the trick of binding sheep together in threes and tying one man under each of the middle sheep – it allows him and his men to elude the Cyclops's notice and escape the cave, blocked by a giant stone and by the blinded Polyphemos himself.[39] But it is a stretch to consider this act, in itself, as architectural. By returning to consider Hephaistos and the crafts that he makes in metal, we can move closer to the realm of architecture. Near the end of the famous passage describing the crafting of Achilles' armour in the *Iliad*, we also have the first mention of what today we would call an architect and an architectural project: Homer compares one of the images adorning Achilles' shield to a *choron*, or dancing floor, created at Knossos by a certain Daidalos for a certain pretty-haired girl named Ariadne.[40] Although the words "architect" and "architecture" are anachronistic in Homer, the figure of Daidalos would later become known as the first mythical architect.[41] Daidalos's *choros* is part of a set of objects called *daidala*, which exemplifies powerful, quasi-divine works of particularly fine craftsmanship in Homer and other works of Greek literature.[42] Homeric *daidala* include a dizzying array of items: helmet, breastplate, belt, shield, chariot, throne, chest, tripod, bowl, brooches, bracelets, rosettes, necklaces, earrings, clasps, crown, bed, and bedroom.[43] It is difficult to make sense of these objects when listed in this manner, but because they exist in literature we can pay attention to their characteristics and the situations in which they appear.

In doing just this, Françoise Frontisi-Ducroux and Sarah P. Morris find that, although the meaning of *daidalon* (and other words that share the *daidal-* root) is less technical than evocative, it evokes very specific and powerful associations. *Daidala* are characterized by their craftsmanship, value, luminosity, and beauty, and they are prized items in the economy of gods and heroes. Because of their wondrous appearance and their implied divine connections, they have profound effects upon those who see them. Although *daidala* include only defensive items rather than weapons such as swords and spears, the mere sight of a *daidalon* can immobilize and even kill an enemy with fright, or – when worn by a woman or a goddess – disarm and seduce a potential lover.

APPEARING

Daidala become interesting for us because they are articulate objects. By considering the archaic techniques used in making objects like the *daidala* described by Homer, Frontisi-Ducroux finds that the common characteristic – across a variety of materials, including metal, wood, and cloth – is a focus on the cutting and joining of parts.[44] We have seen how, for the Greeks, articulation characterized bodies and human-made things such as a city, a hoplite unit, or the cunningly crafted pieces of a butchered ox. For a thing to be composed of well-joined parts was for it to have health, vigour, and power. In the case of a city, it also suggested political harmony and a sense of common identity. In the case of Prometheus's cunning crafts – the meat and the fire stolen in the fennel-stalk – there was also a sense of enclosure, of providing something with a new and deceptive veneer.

These characteristics are exemplified in the most famous of *daidala*, the shield and armour made for Achilles by Hephaistos. These items appear in battle only once in the *Iliad*, but they are presaged twice: first, when Patroclus dresses himself in Achilles' armour to go to battle in his place; second, when Achilles appears in the Achaean trench to terrify the Trojans. In the first case, Patroclus borrows Achilles' armour to trick the

Fig. 2.10 Bronze sculptor's workshop: manufacture of athlete statue. Exterior of red-figure cup by the Foundry Painter (as shown in Fig. 2.6) (480–470 BCE). Altes Museum, Berlin.

Trojans into thinking that he is Achilles. Patroclus's fate is ominously foreshadowed by an implicit suggestion that he is insufficient to take Achilles' place: While dressing himself in this borrowed armour, he "took two valiant spears that fitted his grasp" but left behind the one that Achilles would ultimately carry into battle, "the spear heavy and huge and strong [that] no other of the Achaeans could wield."[45] And indeed, although Patroclus for some time plays the part of the hero and hacks through ranks of Trojan warriors, he is in the end vanquished by Hector, who strips his corpse of its borrowed armour. This event both draws Achilles into the war and makes it necessary for Hephaistos to craft a new set of armour for this purpose.

The second event that prefigures Achilles' entrance in battle occurs when he appears in the Achaean trenches without armour, but with the enhancements provided by Athena for the occasion. Taken together, the appearance of Achilles' old armour worn by Patroclus and of Achilles without his armour comprise two partial entrances of Achilles into the war. When Achilles finally dons the new armour, the full power of his heroic status is manifest through his fiery appearance. Hector's father, Priam, upon seeing Achilles approaching the city of Troy like "the star that rears at harvest, flaming up in its brilliance," begs his son not to leave the safety of the city walls. Hector leaves anyway, but when he sees Achilles, surrounded by "bronze flash[ing] like the gleam of blazing fire or of the sun as it rises," he flees in terror.[46]

Achilles' body and his armour – both of which are articulate, fiery, and powerful – mirror each other as necessary components of his identity. Achilles' armour envelopes and protects him, providing him with an impressive veneer and appearance that strikes fear in his enemies, thereby completing his identity through *technê*. In this way, the armour is to Achilles' body what a city wall is to its city.[47] But not all *daidala* operate by inspiring fear. In Hesiod, the jewellery given to Pandora has the role of seducing men. In the *Odyssey*, the marital bed built by Odysseus acts as a secret token of Odysseus' true identity as it is carved out of the massive trunk of an olive tree. The bed is covered in a deceptive veneer of ivory and other inlays, and hidden by the walls of the bedchamber, and Penelope knows that only Odysseus knows its secret: that it is immovable and rooted at the core of the house. It is this information that finally reunites them, enabling Odysseus to be reintegrated – rearticulated – into

Fig. 2.11 A master potter, a porter bringing fuel to the furnace, and a workman raking the furnace of an Attic pottery workshop. Shoulder of black-figure hydria (late sixth century BCE). State Collection of Antiquities, Munich.

his household.[48] What *daidala* have in common with what we understand as architecture is their status as archetypical works of *technê*, their equivocal nature as both protective and dangerous, and their indispensability for the struggles of humans, who can never be complete without them.

SPEAKING

Achilles' shield may have been architectural in nature, or an architectural object, but it is still removed from architecture as discussed by Vitruvius. Our last stop is Plato. Plato's *Timaeus* discusses the role of proportion in the demiurge's crafting of the cosmos, and it was an important source for Vitruvius, his interpreters, and neo-Platonic philosophers until the nineteenth century. This late Platonic dialogue therefore gives us a glimpse of the theories of proportion that, to a large extent, structured the intellectual background of this core notion in Vitruvius's *De architectura*. Over three centuries separate Homer and Plato and, in turn, Plato and Vitruvius, so the connections are suggestive rather than direct. Nonetheless, we can find in Plato a line of questioning about bodies, social life, and crafts – including what we call architecture – that persists in various forms throughout antiquity. But before we discuss the nature of craft in the *Timaeus*, it is worthwhile to consider how Plato describes his own craft – that of rhetoric.

In the *Philebus* and other dialogues, Plato describes a threefold process of dialectics that governs language, thought, and, indeed, everything that can attain beauty and virtue. One starts with the chaos of the unlimited continuum (*apeiron*), then applies a limit (*peras*) to divide the continuum into diverse elements, and finally combines these elements to generate a new whole. What is generated is an articulate compound or mixture (*to mikton*). Plato is preoccupied with this process of ordering the One and the Many; for him, dialectics governs how an individual thought is organized as well as how arguments and counterarguments come together in the active tension of their engagement. This process is, Socrates says, a divine gift that Prometheus delivered to humans together with fire.[49] Elsewhere, he sees how this process finds parallels in other *technai*. In the *Phaedrus*, Plato draws an explicit comparison between the work of rhetoric and that of preparing a sacrificial animal: he says that we must not divide the components of an argument clumsily but, rather, with skill like a *mageiros* (priest, cook, butcher of sacrifice) who cuts "where the natural joints are."[50]

Plato also often draws an analogy between the process of dialectics and that of forming language out of sound. Raw sound that comes out of animal mouths is unlimited and unordered. In contrast, humans can divide and limit the sound of their utterances through syllables, which are in turn combined to form words and sentences: this is language. The same also applies in writing, in the combination of letters (*stoicheia*, or elements) to form words. Not all combinations of sounds or letters form words, nor do all combinations of words form sentences; for example, one needs certain letters or sounds – a combination of vowels and consonants – in each word.[51] When it constitutes a "working whole," a word embodies a certain *dunamis*, or power, that is not present in its component raw sounds. A word, unlike sounds, has meaning and can describe, refer, qualify, and so on.[52] A word, in turn, acts as an element in combining with other words; again, this combination must occur in a certain way for a sentence to gain its meaning.[53]

In this way, the process of articulating sound into language successively produces compounds with generative powers greater than those of their component parts.[54] Where does this power come from? For Plato, as Rosemary Desjardins observes, it comes from the "bond" (*desmon*) that mutually modifies elements as it joins them. In various dialogues Plato discusses the bonding of letters to form words, the interweaving and bonding of opposite temperaments in a community, the bonding of limbs to form a body, the bonding of body and soul, the bonding of true opinion with causal reasoning to form knowledge, and the bonding of the four elements in the cosmos.[55] These bonds not only allow a composite body to be both One and Many but also activate and empower the component parts through an active tension, like that of Heraclitus's bow.

In the *Timaeus*, Plato describes these bonds as being forged by the demiurge as he crafts the indissoluble souls and bodies of the gods. The gods, in turn, craft mortal beings whose bonds are very strong but not dissoluble. Joined together with little pegs, mortal souls and bodies can eventually loosen and come apart, in illness and eventually in death. Plato's argument is rigorously organized and highly complex, setting out the principles by which primordial stuff is formed into fire, air, water, and earth, then into the tissues of the body and the body itself. Nonetheless, the basic premise of the Homeric poems permeates the dialogue: we are strong and alive when our articulations cohere, and weak or dead when they fall apart.

Plato frequently compares the dialectical process with the *technê* of fire. In the *Theatetus* he presents two theories, one of cosmic generation and one of perception, that follow the same pattern of undifferentiated continuum, division, and generative combination. He asks how the mutually modifying combination of two elements generates something new, and how a sense organ and a sensible thing interact to produce perception. To answer these questions, he turns to an analogy between the production of fire through the rubbing of two sticks and the generation of a child through sexual intercourse. Just as friction between two sticks changes each element by making it red-hot and fiery in order to produce something new in the flame, Plato says, so two interacting mates are changed through intercourse – one becoming a father, the other a mother – as they produce a child. Although this analogy is perhaps more suggestive than informative, it is clear that the formation of fire is, itself, an analogy for the generative process of forging bonds.[56]

STAR-GAZING

But Plato requires that things be more than just well joined. For things – bodies, arguments, cities, and other works of craft – to be beautiful and good, they must be whole and they must partake of measure. For a body to be whole, there must be no parts left out or neglected; for instance, one could not make an argument about the nature of all humankind by speaking only about barbarians, or Greeks, or men, or women.[57]

This is simple enough. But how does measure make a thing beautiful and good? It turns out that for Plato, measure – as found through geometry – is the most fitting model for dialectics. That is, measure creates the surest divisions and the strongest bonds. In the *Theatetus*, Plato describes his reasoning for this. First, the most primitive element of geometry is the line. Unlike the unit, which forms the basis for arithmetic, the line is *apeiron*, or unlimited. Second, the art of measurement serves as the basis for cutting and joining because it is by the principle of due measure that elements are determined and separated out from the continuum.[58] Third, geometry allows for the processes of squaring and cubing, of moving between one-, two-, and three-dimensionality; and this gives us the geometric mean, "the number such that, as the first term is to it, so is it to the last term."[59] For example, 8:4::4:2 expresses a geometric mean, and by continuing the ratio a string of geometric means can be extended into a chain.[60] For Plato, a chain of geometric means is held together by the most perfect of bonds because each term is modified by the terms on either side of it. In the ratio above, just as the four is to the two, so the eight is to the four; but the eight in turn serves as a bond between four and sixteen. Each number becomes both a part and a bond.

For Plato, therefore, "God is the true measure of all things," and everything that is beautiful and good is unified and whole in its order and arrangement as determined by measure.[61] Plato has his demiurge in the *Timaeus* craft the soul and body of the cosmos along these principles. First, to craft the soul of the cosmos the demiurge mixes Being and Becoming, "even though they are naturally difficult to mix." He then divides this mixture into portions corresponding to the series of the power of two and of three. Between these amounts he sets joints, further portions corresponding to the geometric and arithmetic means of each pair in the series. This sequence is musically harmonious, with the value of 3/2 representing a fifth, 4/3 a fourth, and 9/8 a tone.[62] If we are tempted to think that Plato is imagining these harmonies as an abstract series of numbers, this impression is challenged when he tells us that the next step is to split this articulated soul-stuff lengthwise, to lay the pieces across each other, bend them into a circle, and join them to themselves and to each other to form an inner circle and an outer circle. The inner circle he divides into seven – one for each of the planets – before joining the body to this soul, centre to centre. The seven planets, moving of their own accord through the regular motions of the cosmos's soul, thus circle each other, bringing into existence Time.[63]

For mortals to perceive time, the demiurge had to allow us to see these revolutions. He did this by kindling the fire of the sun to light up the whole heavens, creating night, day, months, and years. In the stars he also created a class of gods, made mostly of fire. The wandering paths of these stars, Plato professes, are more complex than are those of the planets and therefore not yet calculated; nonetheless, he asks us to believe that these wanderings are also based on measure.[64]

Mortal souls and bodies, so Plato tells us, are made with similar principles and methods as the souls and bodies of the cosmos and the gods. Our soul-stuff is less pure and the bonds holding our bodies together are ultimately fallible. As such, our bodies are subject to ills, and the revolutions of our souls are distorted at birth. But all is not lost: Plato tells us that through the gift of sight, which is the greatest good and gift that we have received, we can see day, night, months, and years when we cast our gaze towards the sun and the stars. By contemplating the harmonious revolutions of the heavenly bodies, our souls are moved to understand the nature of the universe and, thereby, are harmonized with the greater order of the cosmos.[65] And so, it is by gazing at the stars that we are able to understand and embody measure and proportion. For Plato, this is how we nurture the more divine part of ourselves. By introducing a demiurge, or divine craftsman, who creates by ordering the primordial stuff of the universe through proportion (*analogia* and *symmetria*), in the *Timaeus* Plato provides a model for the work of the architect, as in Vitruvius – and, indeed, as in architectural theorists until the nineteenth century. Creating works with well-adjusted proportions, an architect imitates the work of the divine craftsman while providing an earthly source for order and a frame for a harmonious public life.

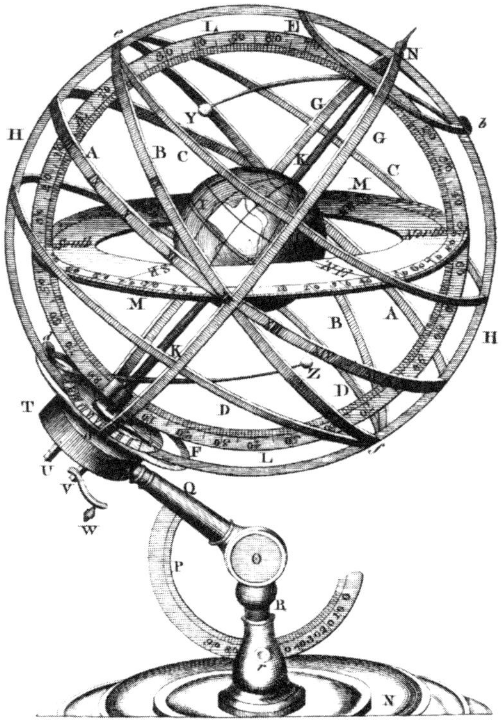

Fig. 2.12 Armillary sphere, from Plate LXXVII of the *Encyclopaedia Britannica* (1771). In Plato's description, the two circles formed by the joined soul-strips correspond to the celestial equator and the ecliptic, or the beginning of an armillary sphere.

ENDING

From a chance gathering around a fire in Vitruvius, we have made our way through ideas about cooking and sacrifice, the sharing of sacrificial portions, the forging of bonds, the disjointing of bodies and cities, the mixing of wine and water, the struggling of hoplites, the hosting of guests at one's hearth, the crafting of architectural objects, the brilliant appearing of Achilles in the Trojan War, the articulate nature of speaking, and the need for star-gazing – to this ending, where we may look again towards Vitruvius's story of the origins of architecture. I try to show how fire, with its associations of technical mastery and divine connections, its social role as a focal point for the city in both the *agora* and the ritual of animal sacrifice, and its ties to the notion of articulation – the cutting and joining of parts – lies at the centre of the Greek consciousness of language, social life, and crafts. I also consider how, alongside the social work of city-building and the dexterous work of honing the craft of building, the notion of star-gazing – of harmonizing one's soul with the cosmos – was central for Plato in explaining our discovery of measure and proportion as the key to the good life. From our vantage point, these pursuits – one social and political, one manual, and one philosophical – seem distant from each other. Nonetheless, by surrounding ourselves with the stories and ideas of Vitruvius's world, perhaps we can imagine how, for him, the work of architecture begins when we draw ourselves in, closer to the fire, and turn our gaze up to the fires in the sky while our hands remain free to play.

NOTES

1 I would like to thank Stephen Parcell for his generous help and incisive editing, Lori Riva for shepherding me through the editorial process, and Alberto Pérez-Gómez for his ongoing commitment to my survival.

2 Vitruvius, *De architectura*, 2.1.1–2. My (often loose) paraphrase of these passages is based on the translations in *Vitruvius: On Architecture*, trans. Frank Granger, 2 vols., Loeb Classical Library (Cambridge, MA: Harvard University Press, 1955); and *Vitruvius: Ten Books on Architecture*, trans. Ingrid D. Rowland and Thomas Noble Howe (Cambridge: Cambridge University Press, 1999).

3 Lucretius, *De rerum natura*, 5.1012–16. Although Vitruvius probably based his account on that of Lucretius, written only twenty-five years earlier, the original version of this story was most likely written by Democritus or the Hippocratics. Diodorus Siculus, a contemporary of Vitruvius, tells a similar story in his *Bibliotheca historia*, 1.7–8. See W.A. Merrill, "Notes on the Influence of Lucretius on Vitruvius," *Proceedings of the American Philological Association* 35 (1904): xvi–xxi; C.A.R. Sanborn, "An Emendation of Vitruvius," *Harvard Studies in Classical Philology* 20 (1909): 166; Benjamin Farrington, *Greek Science: Its Meaning for Us* (Harmondsworth, Middlesex: Penguin Books, 1944), 82–5; Arthur O. Lovejoy and George Boas, *Primitivism and Related Ideas in Antiquity: Contributions to the History of Primitivism* (New York: Octagon Books, 1965), 374; Karl Reinhardt, "Hekataios von Abdera und Demokrit," *Hermes* 47 (1912): 492–513; and Stephen Frith, "A Primitive Exchange: On Rhetoric and Architectural Symbol," *arq* 8, 1 (2004): 39–40.

4 Hippocrates, *De vetere medicina*, 3.

5 Vitruvius, *De architectura*, 2.1.2–3, 6–7.

6 Aeschylus, *Prometheus vinctus*, 110–11. As translated in *Aeschylus*, trans. Herbert Weir Smyth, vol. 1 (Cambridge, MA: Harvard University Press, 1926). See also Arthur D. Kahn, "Every Art Possessed by Man Comes from Prometheus," *Technology and Culture* 11, 2 (1970): 137–8.

7 For example, the Greek word for "raw" (*ômos*) also means crude, uncooked, or undigested as well as savage, fierce, or cruel.

8 Homer, *Iliad*, 24.801–3; Homer, *Odyssey*, 14.72–9.

9 For a thorough discussion of animal bodies in Greek sacrifice, see Jean-Louis Durand, "Greek Animals," in *The Cuisine of Sacrifice among the Greeks*, ed. Marcel Detienne and Jean-Pierre Vernant, 87-118 (Chicago and London: University of Chicago Press, 1986).

10 Hesiod, *Theogony*, 551–4. As translated in *Hesiod, Homeric Hymns, Epic Cycle, Homerica*, trans. Hugh G. Evelyn White, Loeb Classical Library (Cambridge, MA: Harvard University Press, 2002).

11 Jean-Pierre Vernant, *Myth and Society in Ancient Greece* (New York: Zone Books, 1996), 193–7.

12 James Davidson, *Courtesans and Fishcakes: The Consuming Passions of Classical Athens* (London: Fontana Press, 1997), 270–2.

13 Vernant, *Myth and Society in Ancient Greece*, 198–201.

14 Jean-Pierre Vernant, "Part Three: The Organisation of Space," in *Myth and Thought among the Greeks*, trans. Janet Lloyd (New York: Zone Books, 2006), 201–7.

15 Plato, *Phaedrus*, 265d–e; Plato, *Statesman*, 287c3–4.

16 Homer, *Iliad*, 19.13–23. Quotations from the *Iliad* are as translated in Homer, *Iliad*, trans. A.T. Murray, revised by William F. Wyatt (Cambridge, MA: Harvard University Press, 1999).

17 Homer, *Iliad*, 18.212, 230–11.

18 Rosemary Desjardins, *Plato and the Good: Illuminating the Darkling Vision*, ed. Michael Krausz, Philosophy of History and Culture (Leiden and Boston: Brill, 2004), 110.

19 Guillemette Bolens, *La logique du corps articulaire: Les articulations des corps humain dans la littérature occidentale*, ed. Hervé Martin and Jacqueline Sainclivier, Histoire (Rennes, Switzerland: Presses universitaires de Rennes, 2000), 40.

20 Ibid., 10–12. For the role of the drama provided by the visibility of blood and wounds in the *Iliad*, see Brooke Holmes, "The *Iliad*'s Economy of Pain," *Transactions of the American Philological Association* 137, 1 (2007): 45–84.

21 Thucydides, *History of the Peloponnesian War*, 3.81.5, 3.83.1. As translated in Jonathan Price, *Thucydides and Internal War* (Cambridge: Cambridge University Press, 2001), 8–11. See Price, *Thucydides*, 30–1.

22 Ibid., 77.

23 For an incisive discussion of the notion of the symptom and the emergent concept of a "body" in Greek medical thought, see Brooke Holmes, "Interpreting the Symptom: The Body between Misfortune and Mastery in Archaic and Classical Greek Thought" (PhD diss., Princeton, 2005).

24 Davidson, *Courtesans and Fishcakes*, 14–18.

25 Ibid., 47.

26 Ibid., 278–83, 290–2.

27 Ibid., 49–52, 63–9.

28 Heraclitus frag. 51. As translated in John Burnet, *Early Greek Philosophy* (Whitefish, MT: Kessinger Publishing, 2003).

29 Bolens, *La logique du corps articulaire*, 22–7.

30 Plato, *Timaeus*, 19b–c. Quotations from the *Timaeus* are as translated in Plato, *Timaeus, Critias, Cleitophon, Menexenus, Epistles*, trans. R. G. Bury (Cambridge, MA: Harvard University Press, 1929).

31 For the strategies and ideologies of hoplite warfare, see John Carman and Anthony Harding, eds., *Ancient Warfare: Archaeological Perspectives* (Phoenix Mill: Sutton Publishing, 1999); Hans Van Wees, "The Homeric Way of War: The 'Iliad' and the Hoplite Phalanx," *Greece and Rome* 41, 1 (1994): 1–18, 131–55; and Hans van Wees, *Greek Warfare: Myths and Realities* (London: Duckworth, 2004). For a literal image of *agon* as a joint, see the wrestling scene between Odysseus and Aias in Homer, *Iliad*, 23.710–20.

32 For example, when the swineherd welcomes the disguised Odysseus into his home, he refers to the fact that all strangers are from Zeus and therefore must be welcomed. Homer, *Odyssey*, 14.56–8.

33 Homer, *Iliad*, 22.337–55. For a treatment of the coherence of the uses of fire across a spectrum of religious activities, including sacrifice and funeral rites, see William D. Furley, *Studies in the Use of Fire in Ancient Greek Religion*, ed. W.R. Connor, Monographs in Classical Studies (Salem, NH: Ayer Company, 1981), 33. See also C.J. Mackie, "Achilles in Fire," *Classical Quarterly*, n.s., 48, 2 (1998): 332.

34 Homer, *Iliad*, 2.426; Homer, *Odyssey*, 24.71. For the power of fire to purify through sacrifice and funerals, and the need to keep fire separate from polluting activities such as the discharge of sexual fluids, see Robert

Parker, *Miasma: Pollution and Purification in Early Greek Religion* (Oxford: Clarendon, 1983), 77, 227–8.

35 Homer, *Odyssey*, 9.174–6. As translated in Homer, *Odyssey*, trans. A.T. Murray, revised by George E. Dimock (Cambridge, MA: Harvard University Press, 1995).

36 Homer, *Odyssey*, 9.216–317.

37 As Athena is a goddess of craft, and the olive tree was her gift to Athens, the use of olive wood emphasizes the *technê* of this act.

38 Homer, *Odyssey*, 9.318–402.

39 Ibid., 9.420–63.

40 Homer, *Iliad*, 18.590–2.

41 Stephen Parcell, "Four Historical Definitions of Architecture" (PhD diss., McGill University, 2007), 31–3. See also Alberto Pérez-Gómez, "Chora: The Space of Architectural Representation," in *Chora 1: Intervals in the Philosophy of Architecture*, ed. Alberto Pérez-Gómez and Stephen Parcell, 1–34 (Montreal and Kingston: McGill-Queen's University Press, 1994).

42 These objects are named through a series of words that share the root *daidal* and include nouns, adjectives, verbal participles, or – in the case of the *choros* – the proper name "Daidalos."

43 Françoise Frontisi-Ducroux, *Dédale: Mythologie de l'artisan en Grèce ancienne* (Paris: Librairie François Maspero, 1975), 24; and Sarah P. Morris, *Daidalos and the Origins of Greek Art* (Princeton, NJ: Princeton University Press, 1992), 4.

44 Frontisi-Ducroux, *Dédale*, 24.

45 Homer, *Iliad*, 16.139–44.

46 Ibid., 18.202–38, 22.25–366.

47 Also like a city wall, other *daidala* – particularly those in the later tradition attributed to Daidalos, such as the cow for Queen Pasiphaë, the labyrinth to house the resulting Minotaur, and the wings constructed to escape the labyrinth – share a similar set of traits with regard to how they envelop, help construct an appearance, and endow humans with unusual and powerful abilities.

48 Homer, *Odyssey*, 23.175–215.

49 Plato, *Philebus*, 16c. The process of dialectics is described at 15d4–6, 16c2–3, 16c9, 17a3–4, and 26b1–7.

50 Plato, *Phaedrus*, 265e. As translated in *Plato*, vol. 9, trans. Harold N. Fowler (Cambridge, MA: Harvard University Press, 1925). See also *Cratylus*, 387a2–8, and *Statesman*, 287c3–4. Elsewhere, Plato also draws com-

parisons with weaving and potting. See Desjardins, *Plato and the Good*, 103.

51 Plato, *Sophist*, 252e9–253a6. See also Plato, *Phaedrus*, 268a8–269c3, 276e4–277c6; and Plato, *Theatetus*, 163b9–c3, 203b1–204a3. Desjardins, *Plato and the Good*, 97–8.

52 Plato, *Sophist*, 247d8–e4. See also Plato, *Theatetus*, 202e6–203c6.

53 Plato, *Cratylus*, 424e4–425a3.

54 Desjardins, *Plato and the Good*, 98. At *Theatetus*, 210b1–2, and *Philebus*, 64e1–3, Plato argues against the notion that such bonding could be the result of simple aggregation and juxtaposition.

55 For the bonding of letters, see Plato, *Sophist* 253a4–5; of temperaments, *Statesman* 309b7, 309e10, 310a4; of limbs, *Timaeus* 74b5, 84a–b; of body and soul, *Timaeus* 73b4, 84a1; of true opinion and knowledge, *Meno* 98a3–4; and the four elements, *Timaeus* 32b7. Desjardins, *Plato and the Good*, 86, 101.

56 Rosemary Desjardins, *The Rational Enterprise: Logos in Plato's Theatetus*, ed. Anthony Preus, SUNY Series in Ancient Greek Philosophy (Albany, NY: State University of New York Press, 1990), 39. Desjardins observes that Plato has anticipated this comparison between fire-producing friction between two objects and generative combination through "overtones (perhaps both literal and sexual) of 'kindling' and 'being kindled.'" See Desjardins, *Rational Enterprise*, 221n16. See also Plato, *Theatetus*, 154b1, 154.

57 Plato, *Statesman*, 311c3–6; Plato, *Timaeus*, 32c7–8.

58 Plato, *Statesman*, 284b1–2, 284c1–2, 284d1–8, 285a1–c2; Plato, *Philebus*, 26d7–9. Desjardins, *Plato and the Good*, 105–6.

59 Plato, *Timaeus*, 31c3–32a1.

60 A geometric mean between two numbers is also the length of the side of a square whose area is equal to that of a rectangle whose sides are of the lengths of those two numbers.

61 Plato, *Laws*, 4.716c4–5; Plato, *Gorgias*, 506e1–4; Plato, *Philebus*, 64d9–65a5, 66a6–7. See also Plato, *Laws*, 4.716c4–5. Desjardins, *Plato and the Good*, 106.

62 Andrew Gregory, *Ancient Greek Cosmogony* (London: Duckworth, 2007), 145.

63 Plato, *Timaeus*, 35a–37e.

64 Ibid., 38e–39e.

65 Ibid., *Timaeus*, 46e–47c.

The Sacred Stones of Saint-Denis

Jason Crow

Chora

IN THE MIDDLE OF THE twelfth century, Abbot Suger (1081–1151 CE) renovated the abbey church at Saint-Denis, located just north of Paris. His renovations recreated the church as a hierurgic equivalent to the physical and theological properties of his precious stones (see fig. 3.1). Today we perceive the church as a light-filled form representing the sacred. This modern understanding of the abbey church is indebted to the writings of Otto von Simson.[1] However, through von Simson's overemphasis on form, we have lost the material understanding that enabled a twelfth-century visitor to experience the immaterial nature of God within the church. The renovations to the church manifested Suger's twelfth-century Christian Neoplatonic understanding of the theurgic relationship between material and immaterial, which focuses on light.[2] The present study examines the twelfth-century immaterial light of God in the material of the church – its sacred stones – as the phenomenal and imaginative vision given by the church.

OTTO VON SIMSON'S GOTHIC CATHEDRAL

Interpretations of Suger's renovations that focus on Saint-Denis' light-filled form as a symbolic representation of an immaterial God are consistent with modern understandings of the Gothic cathedral (see fig. 3.2). However, the cosmological belief system of twelfth-century monks and pilgrims would not have bifurcated the experience of light from the material reality of the church. This standard interpretation of Saint-Denis as a light-filled form is most indebted to the writings of Otto von Simson, who argued strenuously that light was the primary element of the Gothic. It is largely from his work that the Gothic is understood as "transparent, diaphanous architecture."[3] His seminal text, *The Gothic Cathedral: The Origins of Gothic Architecture and Medieval Order*, declares that the originality of the Gothic style is to be found in "the use of light and the unique relationship between structure and appearance."[4] He immediately qualifies this introduction to his subject by saying that when he speaks of light he is discussing its relationship "to the material substance of the walls."[5] In the following pages of his book, however, von Simson's lack of consideration for the material nature of the walls is quickly apparent. In his analysis the walls of the Gothic cathedral become transparent, invert gravity, and deny the "impenetrable nature of matter."[6] They are

Fig. 3.1 The abbey church at Saint-Denis, west façade. Photograph by Martin Bressani.

reduced to the formalism implicit in his "geometrical functionalism."[7] Deep in his discussion of the twelfth-century renovations of the abbey church, von Simson encapsulates his understanding of the Gothic as the abbot's Dionysian-inspired "invention." He states that "Suger was the first to conceive the architectural system as but a frame for his windows, and to conceive his windows not as wall openings but as translucent surfaces to be adorned with sacred paintings."[8] Strip away the sacred paintings and von Simson's interpretation of Saint-Denis resembles the Crystal

Palace of 1851, despite the radically different philosophical and historical contexts of these two buildings. In reducing the Gothic light-containing church to a discussion of form, von Simson overlooks the twelfth-century understanding of matter. As a result, the materiality of the church is discarded, along with the imaginative potential for vision that the stones of the church offer. In short, the church loses its stones.

SUGER'S LIGHT MYSTICISM IN THE CONTEXT OF NEOPLATONIC THEURGY

For Abbot Suger, the light mysticism of Pseudo-Dionysius the Areopagite, a fifth-century Christian Neoplatonist, resolved the split between the material and the immaterial. In medieval cosmology the terrestrial realm was an imperfect material reflection of the immaterial celestial realm. The split between the two realms posed a significant conflict for twelfth-century theologians. Believing that the material realm was in a corrupted state after the fall of Adam, twelfth-century theologians asked how Christ could exist in this corrupted world. In 431 CE the Chalcedon Council had indoctrinated a dual nature for Christ, both human and divine. The council distinguished between the material and the immaterial but stated that the dual-natured Christ was of one substance that bridged the two realms. Following Pseudo-Dionysius, Suger believed that this bridging was manifested in Christ as light.

In the twelfth century, the fifth-century mystic Pseudo-Dionysius the Areopagite was conflated with both the founder of the abbey at Saint-Denis and the convert of Saint Paul mentioned in Acts 17:34.[9] The light mysticism of Pseudo-Dionysius was a Christian interpretation of an earlier Neoplatonic emanationist theory of light. For Pseudo-Dionysius, God was an invisible light from which the immaterial and the material realms were created. After forming the heavens, angels, stars, and planets in an immaterial light, he condensed that light as it descended from the heavenly bodies into the material substance of the earthly realm. Importantly, Pseudo-Dionysius believed that one could ascend mystically to a union with God. Angels associated directly with God, as they were equally immaterial and required no mediation. However, those on earth could ascend mystically only through the materiality of the world. The necessity of materiality was evident in the theurgic rituals of earlier Neoplatonism, which relied on gems, bowls of water, mirrors, and other brilliant

Fig. 3.2 Nave. Photograph by Martin Bressani

matter to ascend to a union with God. However, because of a prevalent perception that theurgy in the Dionysian corpus was incompatible with Christrine doctrine, theurgy has been largely overlooked in Neoplatonic Christian studies.[10] Theurgy was understood as God's direct action in the terrestrial realm. It was complemented by hierurgy, humans' ritual re-enactment of God's work. The relationship between theurgy and hierurgy is evident in the Dionysian understanding of Christ and the Eucharist.[11] Christ was God's divine work in the material realm, while the Eucharist was a ritual re-enactment of that gift, in which bread was the material key that enabled humans to ascend to God. For Pseudo-Dionysius and for Suger, the Eucharistic bread was not a symbol for the body of Christ: it was literally the material of Christ. Christ was the material bridge who connected the terrestrial realm to the celestial realm.

While the Eucharist is the ultimate material in the Dionysian cosmology, the bright and shining matter of earlier Neoplatonism did not disappear from the theology of the fifth-century mystic or the twelfth-century abbot. In Suger's writings the most direct connection to Dionysian theurgy emphasizes the hierarchy of light in relation to his church. The material bridge of Christ was made of light. Erwin Panofsky is typically credited with identifying Suger's light metaphysics with those of Pseudo-Dionysius.[12] Panofsky translated portions of two texts, *De administratione* and *De consecratione*, in which Suger justifies his enlargement of the abbey church. Panofsky emphasizes the role of Pseudo-Dionysius in the references to light and the *anagogicus mos* (anagogical manner) as a means of ascending from the material to the immaterial. Panofsky's discussion became the starting point for Otto von Simson's interpretation of the Gothic cathedral. For Suger, the light of Christ was the middle figure in a hierarchy, with light on earth at the base and the light of God at the summit. The light of Christ was understood as a bridge between the two other lights, one material and one immaterial. In *De administratione*, Suger describes this hierarchy of light in a poem inscribed on the new golden doors leading into the church.

> Whoever thou art, if thou seekest to extol the glory of these doors,
> Marvel not at the gold and the expense but at the craftsmanship of
> the work.
> Bright is the noble work; but being nobly bright, the work

Should brighten the minds, so that they may travel, through the true
lamps [*lumina vera*]
To the True Light [*verum lumen*] where Christ is the true door.
In what manner it be inherent in this world the golden door defines:
The dull mind rises to truth through that which is material
And, in seeing the light [*luce*], is resurrected from its former
submersion.[13]

The poem distinguishes among three different types of light: *lux* is the immaterial light that is God; *verum lumen* is the perfect material light that is Christ; and the *vera lumina* are the material lights of lamps. Suger later hints at the Dionysian source of his hierarchy of light in *De administratione* in the inscription added to Saint-Denis to consecrate its new choir.

Once the new rear part is jointed to the part in front,
The church shines with its middle part brightened.
For bright is that which is brightly coupled with bright,
And bright is the noble edifice which is pervaded by the new light
[*nova lux*]
Which stands enlarged in our time,
I, who was Suger, being the leader while it was being accomplished.[14]

In this inscription the immaterial light of God pervades the church by joining its multiple and varied lights to manifest the new light of God. The unification of light described by Suger is comparable to the unification of light described by Pseudo-Dionysius. In his *Divine Names*, Pseudo-Dionysius explains how the physical phenomenon of material light could enable one to experience the immaterial light of God.[15] As an illustration, he describes how light from multiple lamps joins together within a house. Individual lamps can be taken away or added without lessening the brighter, unified, and more perfect light that transcends their individuality. As with Suger, there is a hierarchy of three lights in the Dionysian example. The light from the lamps is the material light of the *vera lumina*. The brighter, unified light inside the house is the *verum lumen*. Because the *verum lumen* is not changed by adding or subtracting material lamps, its brightness points to the invisible *lux*, which we can experience and understand but not rationalize. The *verum lumen* enables us to understand *lux* through the experience of brightening and through a new understanding of interior light that is independent of physical lamps. This creative apprehension of *lux* is the mystical experience of "the dull mind ris[ing] to truth through that which is material," leading to a new vision beyond the material reality of the house and its lamps.

Returning to Christ as the middle term, we can understand how Suger reconciled Christ's dual nature and single substance. The substance of Christ is the *verum lumen*. In the terrestrial realm, Christ has a material covering that functions like a house. In the celestial realm, Christ has no need of a material covering: he is simply the light as substance. Just as the *vera lumina* are lights with material coverings, so Suger understands humans as likenesses of God in material form.

THE SACRED STONES OF SAINT-DENIS

It remains to be seen how Suger understood the materiality of his church. Perhaps the most quoted and discussed passage from the writings of Abbot Suger is the *anagogicus mos* passage from *De administratione*. It clearly shows Suger's fascination with gems, and, for Panofsky, it is the strongest tie between Suger and the light mysticism of Pseudo-Dionysius.[16]

> Often we contemplate, out of sheer affection for the church our mother … sighing deeply in my heart: "Every precious stone was thy covering, the sardius, the topaz, and the jasper, the chrysolite, and the onyx, and the beryl, the sapphire, and the carbuncle, and the emerald." To those who know the properties of precious stones it becomes evident, to their utter astonishment, that none is absent from the number of these (with the only exception of the carbuncle), but that they abound most copiously. Thus when – out of my delight in the beauty of the house of God – the loveliness of the many-colored gems has called me away from external cares, and worthy meditation has induced me to reflect, transferring that which is material to that which is immaterial, on the diversity of the sacred virtues: then it seems to me that I find myself dwelling, as it were, in some strange region of the universe which neither exists entirely in the slime of the earth nor entirely in the purity of Heaven; and by the grace of God, I can be transported from this inferior to that higher world in an anagogical manner.[17]

Unfortunately, little has been said about the theurgic qualities of Suger's precious stones.[18] In the twelfth century, the stones theologically and physically would have been similar to the house in the Dionysian story mentioned above, understood as material coverings for visible and invisible light. Suger was drawn to the light contained within the stones, like the *verum lumen* of Christ. That light pointed to the special properties of the stones, which could be contemplated to reveal the presence of the invisible light of God. To Suger, the precious stones were theurgical. They were literally the work of God and had mysterious, god-like powers. Suger would have understood the renovations at Saint-Denis as a hierurgical equivalent of the stones. The stones from which the church was made were sacred. The joining of the stones made them more sacred, like the joining of individual lights within a house. As such, the stones of Saint-Denis would have been understood as a perfect material. The renovated Saint-Denis would have been understood as a perfect material covering for substantial light, equivalent to the body of Christ. Suger's poem and his inscription on the door help us understand the materiality of his renovated church through their references to precious stones and light mysticism. As in Neoplatonist theurgy, anagogical ascension relies on the stones of the church.

From antiquity to the Middle Ages, stones – particularly gems – were believed to have magical powers. Hildegard of Bingen (1098–1179 CE) explains in her *Physica* that the power in stone comes from the fire that it contains.[19] Dionysius claims that the material substance of fire is the origin of light in the atmosphere.[20] Thus, the power in stones is understood to be light. Marbode of Rennes (1035–1123 CE) wrote extensively on stones and their properties. In addition to his major book on stones, *De lapidibus*, he wrote three shorter texts that explain the properties of biblical gems in symbolic and medicinal terms.[21] Of particular interest to the light mysticism of Suger is Marbode's description of Chalcedony. In his short medical lapidary work, Marbode notes that stone is brightened and warmed in the sun. As it is warmed, the stone attracts chaff. He notes that this property of the stone is reflected by the faithful who do good works in secret. This is because

> [they are] breathed upon by the radiance of the true sun, that is, Christ, or handed and warmed by the fingers, that is by the gifts of the Holy Ghost, by

the word of their preaching and by the example of their goodness, they draw the chaff, that is sinners, to themselves, and they ally [sinners] to themselves and they admonish them to persevere in good works.[22]

According to Marbode, this biblical stone functions by containing and passing along the light of God. This ability of a material to contain and convey the light of God is at the core of the twelfth-century understanding of Christ, the precious stones of Suger, and the renovated church.

Two passages in Suger's *De consecratione* explicitly connect his renovation of Saint-Denis to hierurgy. The first associates his precious stones with the actual stones of the renovated church. The second describes the stone walls of the church as a construction of Christ's materiality and regards the stones reused from the existing church as sacred relics.

Deliberating under God's inspiration, we choose – in view of that blessing which, by the testimony of venerable writings, Divine action had bestowed upon the ancient consecration of the church by the extension of [Christ's] own hand – to respect the very stones, sacred as they are, as though they were relics.[23]

Robert Ousterhout, writing about the use of *spolia* in the ongoing renovations of the Church of the Holy Sepulchre, draws on this very quotation. He argues that both the reused stones and the entire material church were understood as sacred relics.[24] Suger follows his comment about relics with a statement that Christ unifies the stones of the church – a statement that is similar to the Dionysian description of the house, with material and immaterial implications:

Jesus Christ Himself being the chief cornerstone which joins one wall to the other; in Whom all building – whether spiritual or material – groweth unto one holy temple in the Lord. In whom we, too, are taught to be builded together for an habitation of God[25] through the Holy Spirit by ourselves in a spiritual way, the more loftily and fitly we strive to build in a material way.[26]

Panofsky notes that this passage originates in Ephesians 2:19–22; however, Suger changes the original biblical text by adding that the joining of walls is performed by Christ and that it occurs in both a spiritual manner and a material manner.[27] This is a direct reference to the Dionysian belief in the dual nature of Christ as material and immaterial. It reveals the strong connection between the material construction of the church and the immaterial light of the church.

THE MYSTIC'S IMMATERIAL VISION

Suger believed in two modes of vision: material and immaterial. Similarly, he believed that Christ, as the mediator between *lumina* and *lux*, was the bridge between material vision (the eyes of the body) and immaterial vision (the eyes of the heart). Although the eyes of the body could be associated with our modern concept of eyesight, the meaning of light in Suger's material vision requires twelfth-century theories of optics to be taken into account. Suger describes immaterial vision not only as the eyes of the heart but also as the eyes of the mind. Although this type of vision could be associated with modern intellectual imagination, Suger does not understand the eyes of the heart as a rational construction of the world, imperfectly seen through the medieval eyes of the body. The unified Dionysian light is not seen literally by the eyes of the body; instead, one's experience of unified light implicitly enables the heart to understand the immaterial light of God as being present. This implicit understanding is critical, as the immaterial light is recognized not by rationally measuring the luminosity of combined individual lights but by understanding, through inspiration, that immaterial light exceeds measurable luminosity.

For Suger, our ability to see relies on both the power of the eyes and the light of Christ. The eyes send out a ray of light to apprehend an object; however, the eyes alone are too weak to see in darkness and cannot fully illuminate the object. When the sun brightens the world, its rays of light strengthen the power of our visual ray and increase our capacity for vision. Suger believed that the light of the sun is Christ; therefore, it is Christ who makes our vision possible. In a similar manner, our ability to understand is strengthened by the wisdom of Christ. For Suger, understanding is an internal vision that most closely resembles the imagination, which he calls "the eyes of the heart."[28] Our corporeal eyes enable us to experience the world but do not give us wisdom. We can experience God only when the wisdom of Christ strengthens our immaterial vision of the eyes of the heart. This immaterial vision is the key to Suger's cryptic reference in his poem on the golden doors of the church. It explains how the materiality of the church resurrects the monk or pilgrim into a unity with Christ on the verge of ascending to heaven. This refers both to the Dionysian concept of the sacrament of Illumination and to the iconography of the golden doors. The doors teach us how the threshold can be crossed by relying on our internal vision, assisted by the abbot of the church. The abbot's light strengthens the internal vision of his faithful parishioners in a way that is analogous to Christ's gift of sunlight.

The twelfth-century understanding of eyesight, the operation of the eyes of the body, was based on the Platonic extramission theory of sight and Galenic theories.[29] In extramission, light issues from the eye instead of being received by the eye. In Suger's time, William of Conches (1080 ca.–1150 CE) combined the two theories in his belief that vision requires three things: an interior light, an exterior light, and an opaque object. A process of refinement within the body creates an interior light that can be sent out from the eye to the object. To receive impressions of objects, the light of the eye is combined with the light of the sun. This mixing overcomes an inherent weakness of the eye alone. The stronger, combined light becomes extended and diffused over the object to assume its shape and colour. Finally, this unified light returns to the eye, carrying the impression of the object to the soul.[30] William's unified power of sight resembles the Dionysian unity with God. The light of the sun, equated with the *lumen* of Christ, enables the light sent forth by the eye to receive the impression of material objects in the world. The unification of light and material is critical.

Pamela Blum proposes that the triple figures in the outermost archivolts of the left portal of Saint-Denis show the bishop (abbot), sponsor, and initiate before and after the initiate's ritual death to sin and divine rebirth (see figs. 3.3 and 3.4). The three figures represent stages of the sacrament of Illumination that Pseudo-Dionysius describes in *The Ecclesiastical Hierarchy*.[31] This sacrament conflates baptism with a reenactment of the death and resurrection of Christ. Pseudo-Dionysius describes the sacrament as the gift of sight.

Fig. 3.3 Left portal. Photograph by Martin Bressani.

Fig. 3.4 Detail of outermost archivolt of the left portal, with the bishop, sponsor, and initiate following the sacramental Illumination. Photograph by Martin Bressani.

> It is the same with regard to the sacred sacrament of divine birth. It first introduces the light and is the source of all divine illumination. And because this is so we praise it, giving it the designation of what it achieves, that is, illumination. It is true of course that all the hierarchic operations have this in common, to pass the light of God on to the initiates, but nevertheless it was this one which first gave me the gift of sight. The light coming first from this led me to vision of the other sacred things.[32]

For Suger, the vision of "other sacred things" is the sight of the new light in the church. The light that is immaterial can be seen only with immaterial eyes. Suger gives light through the bright and shining materiality of the doors and through the brightened interior of the church. However, as he notes in his poem, it is noble brightness that leads to the true light that implies Christ. He points out that the immaterial light that pervades the new church comes not from the literal brightness of the doors that is seen by the eyes but, rather, from an understanding of the narrative depicted on the doors that brightens the mind.

Paula Gerson, in her analysis of the iconography of the central portal, explains that the golden doors include eight medallions that depict the passion, crucifixion, resurrection, and ascension of Christ.[33] Arranged in pairs ascending the door, the lower four medallions likely depict Christ's material life on earth, while the upper four medallions likely depict the crucifixion, the resurrection, the supper at Emmaus, and the ascension (see fig. 3.5). An image of Suger kneeling is included in the medallion with the scene of the supper at Emmaus, a story told in Luke 24:1–35. Suger also directly refers to the supper at Emmaus in *De consecratione* when he discusses the stones of the church as relics.[34] After the resurrection, two disciples of Christ are travelling to the town of Emmaus. Along the way, Christ joins them. The disciples convince Christ to eat with them at the village before he travels onward. When Christ gives them bread during the meal, their eyes are opened and they recognize him. He then disappears from their sight. Christ has left the earth, finally giving up almost all of his material covering. The scene portrays Christ following the resurrection in a most perfect material state, in his last appearance on earth.[35] The sight given by Christ is the same wisdom of the eyes of the heart that Suger offers his followers: a direct vision of the immaterial Christ. In this scene Abbot Suger, like the disciples on their way to Emmaus, is represented as experiencing a direct vision of God. As abbot, he can give this vision hierurgically to his followers. The gift of vision is the subject of the Illumination sacrament depicted in the archivolts of the left portal. The capacity for sight represented on the doors is remembered by the disciples of the Emmaus story as a burning in their hearts. As such, it is an actual phenomenon that can be experienced, like the light in the Dionysian house. It is the operative power of God as light that gives sight. The same power exists within stone, where Suger's fascination with gems indicates the power of the immaterial light within a material covering. He constructs the church to give immaterial light through wisdom. The light-filled church fills the bodies of the faithful with an immaterial light that contains the hidden wisdom of God. While knowledge can be seen with the eyes of the body, wisdom can be seen only with the eyes of the mind. The lamp, the body, and the church are material coverings for this light-wisdom.

CONCLUSION

In the opening of this chapter, I note that Otto von Simson's understanding of Suger's abbey church as a light-filled form disregards the fact that the church is made of impenetrable stone. I try to show that Suger's relationship between the immaterial and the material is not a dialectical opposition but, rather, different degrees of perfection based on vision as a phenomenal experience. This is a direct result of Suger's understanding of the material with which he built his church. For Suger, the light of the world was God's gift of our bodily sight, understood experientially as a mystical vision of the eyes of the heart. For twelfth-century vision, the immaterial presence of God was the light both within the church and within the body. In von Simson's interpretation, the materiality of the church disappears in a discussion of form, and the stone of the church vanishes as it loses its theological grounding. This is why von Simson's concept of Saint-Denis as an architectural framework for translucent surfaces can be transferred so easily to the 1851 Crystal Palace or a modern glass-encased high-rise. This reduction denies us their rich historical and philosophical contexts.

Fig. 3.5 Centre portal. Photograph by Martin Bressani.

Jennifer Bloomer discusses a similar bias against materiality and matter in "The Unbearable Being of Lightness," in which she traces the desire to make architecture immaterial to the criminalization of matter, gravity, and ornament in the discourse of modern architects (such as Adolf Loos's "Ornament and Crime"). Bloomer believes that a different relationship between the material and the immaterial is evident in the example of the child floating weightlessly in the womb of its mother.[36] In his article on the Gothic, Peter Fingesten evokes something similar in a medieval analogue of this bodily experience by comparing the interior of the Gothic cathedral to the womb of Mary.[37] Provocatively, Suger himself evokes the church as mother to introduce the precious stones in his passage on the *anagogicus mos*. If Bloomer's critique of modern formalism offers a different bodily way of thinking about the immaterial, Suger's twelfth-century understanding of material and immaterial could be relevant to situating it historically.

NOTES

1 In particular, see Otto Georg von Simson, *The Gothic Cathedral: Origins of Gothic Architecture and the Medieval Concept of Order*, 3rd ed. (Princeton, NJ: Princeton University Press, 1988).

2 Suger's texts are not sophisticated theological or literary works. Conrad Rudolph suggests that Hugh of Saint-Victor, the twelfth-century theologian, may have provided the iconographic program for Saint-Denis. Grover Zinn also argues Hugh's influence on Suger, although without the direct attribution that Rudolph assumes. See Conrad Rudolph, *Artistic Change at St.-Denis: Abbot Suger's Program and the Early Twelfth-Century Controversy over Art* (Princeton, NJ: Princeton University Press, 1990); and Grover A. Zinn, "Suger, Theology, and the Pseudo-Dionysian Tradition," in *Abbot Suger and Saint-Denis: A Symposium*, ed. Paula Gerson, 33-40 (New York: Metropolitan Museum of Art, 1986). However, I would argue that Suger's program for the renovations should be seen in the light of a common material culture of the twelfth century, and I would not assign a specific influence to Suger. The position of Rudolph, in particular, belittles Suger's artisanal contribution. I use "material culture" as an extension of Paula Findlen's "scientific culture." Findlen uses the term to describe a broad,

commonly held body of knowledge that exceeds the contemporary limitations of what we would call disciplines. See Paula Findlen, *Possessing Nature: Museums, Collecting, and Scientific Culture in Early Modern Italy* (Berkeley/Los Angeles/London: University of California Press, 1994).

3 Simson, *Gothic Cathedral*, 4.

4 Ibid., 3.

5 Ibid.

6 Ibid., 4.

7 Ibid., 8.

8 Ibid., 122.

9 See Erwin Panofsky, "Introduction," in Abbot Suger, *Abbot Suger on the Abbey Church of St.-Denis and Its Art Treasures*, 2nd ed., 1–38 (Princeton, NJ: Princeton University Press, 1979).

10 Gregory Shaw notes the exclusion of theurgy in Pseudo-Dionysian literature and examines Paul Rorem's translations of the Dionysian corpus as an exemplar. See Gregory Shaw, "Neoplatonic Theurgy and Dionysius the Areopagite," *Journal of Early Christian Studies* 7, 4 (1999): 573–99. Sarah Klitenic Wear and John Dillon discuss theurgy and its complement, hierurgy, extensively. Their understanding of theurgy and hierurgy is paraphrased in the following paragraphs. See Sarah Klitenic Wear and John M. Dillon, *Dionysius the Areopagite and the Neoplatonist Tradition: Despoiling the Hellenes* (Aldershot, UK/Burlington, VT: Ashgate, 2007).

11 Pseudo-Dionysius, Colm Luibhéid, and Paul Rorem, "The Ecclesiastical Hierarchy," in *Pseudo-Dionysius: The Complete Works*, 218–23 (New York: Paulist Press, 1987).

12 See the introduction to Suger, *Abbot Suger*, 1–38.

13 Suger, *Abbot Suger*, 46–49.

14 Ibid., 50.

15 Pseudo-Dionysius, Luibhéid, and Rorem, "The Divine Names," in *Pseudo-Dionysius*, 61–2.

16 Suger, *Abbot Suger*, 19–25.

17 Ibid., 63–5.

18 To my knowledge, nothing has been written about theurgy in relation to Suger.

19 Priscilla Throop, *Hildegard von Bingen's Physica: The Complete English Translation of Her Classic Work on Health and Healing* (Rochester, VT: Healing Arts Press, 1998), 137–8.

20 Pseudo-Dionysius, Luibhéid, and Rorem, "Divine Names," 62.

21 Marbode, *Marbode of Rennes' De lapidibus: Considered as a Medical Treatise with Text, Commentary, and C. W. King's Translation, Together with Text and Translation of Marbode's Minor Works on Stones*, trans. John M. Riddle (Wiesbaden: Steiner, 1977). The shorter texts being discussed are on pages 119–20 and 125–9 of this translation.

22 Marbode, *Marbode of Rennes*, 126.

23 Suger, *Abbot Suger*, 100–1.

24 Robert Ousterhout, "Architecture as Relic and the Construction of Sanctity: The Stones of the Holy Sepulchre," *Journal of the Society of Architectural Historians* 62, 1 (2003): 4–23.

25 See Suger, *Abbot Suger*, 241. Panofsky notes Suger's modifications to the text of Ephesians 2:19–22 in the commentary he appends to his translation.

26 Ibid., 105.

27 Ibid., 241.

28 Gordon Rudy discusses the two levels of the senses, the bodily and the spiritual, in *Mystical Language of Sensation in the Later Middle Ages* (New York: Routledge, 2002). In medieval mysticism, a hierarchical structure of the senses usually culminates in eyesight as the highest material sense. Even higher is the spiritual sense of sight, often called the "eyes of the heart" in reference to Ephesians 1:17–18. This spiritual sense of sight was also called the "eyes of the mind," but in the twelfth century this would not have been an intellectual understanding.

29 David C. Lindberg, *Theories of Vision from al-Kindi to Kepler* (Chicago: University of Chicago Press, 1976), 91–2.

30 Ibid.

31 Pamela Blum, "The Lateral Portals of the West Façade," in *Abbot Suger and Saint-Denis: A Symposium*, ed. Paula Lieber Gerson, 199-228 (New York: Metropolitan Museum of Art, 1986).

32 Pseudo-Dionysius, Luibhéid, and Rorem, "The Ecclesiastical Hierarchy," in *Pseudo-Dionysius*, 210.

33 Paula Gerson, "The West Facade of St.-Denis: An Iconographic Study" (PhD diss., Columbia University, 1970), 107–11.

34 See Suger, *Abbot Suger*, 100–1, where Suger paraphrases the beginning of the Emmaus story in Luke: "We communicated this plan [to enlarge the church] to our very devoted brethren, whose hearts burned for Jesus while He talked with them by the way."

35 In the Bible, after the dinner at Emmaus, Christ appears as a ghost or a spirit.

36 Jennifer Bloomer, "The Unbearable Being of Lightness," *Thresholds* 20 (2000): 12–19.

37 Peter Fingesten, "Topographical and Anatomical Aspects of the Gothic Cathedral," *Journal of Aesthetics and Art Criticism* 20, 1 (1961): 3–23.

(Why No One Can Be) Against Sustainability: Traversing the Fantasy of Sustenance and the Topology of Desire

Donald Kunze

Chora

> By nature, sustainability must claim a monopoly of belief: as a "belief" it cannot admit an opposite belief is equally valid. It is a consistent and universalist world-view, *Weltanschauung*. Its adherents act in accordance with one general principle: that it should be accepted by all persons. In practice, too, there is common action for sustainability, by governments, non-governmental organisations, loose groups of activists, and industry. The ability to unify diverse groups also suggests sustainability is an ideology, in a negative sense.
>
> – Paul Treanor[1]

IT'S OFTEN THE CASE that a good idea is not an idea at all but simply a way of seeing the world that excludes others by appearing to have an unquestionable rational basis. In a sense, it is more accurate to say that reasons emanate from conclusions rather than the other way around. For this reason, sustainability – arguably architecture's most compelling contemporary aspect and a central component in nearly every educational program – should be regarded technically as a fantasy.[2] This is not intended to diminish sustainability as a topic or, even less, to detract from the compelling environmental, social, political, ethical, or other (real) reasons for doing the things that march under the flag of sustainability. The term "fantasy" is the only means available to theory to approach sustainability in order to examine its grounds, its existence as a "human thing *par excellence*."

A fantasy is, first and foremost, a means of stabilizing discourse. Anglo-American uses of fantasy emphasize its fictional and individual nature. In this sense even fantasy is subject to a political agenda directed towards subjectivity. But, historically and culturally, fantasy is just the opposite: a collective construct that is not only publicly accessible but also essential to maintaining one's position in any network of symbolic relations. A fantasy is like a free magazine subscription that, if refused, justifies a criminal investigation on the part of the postal service. There are things we "must believe in" to be regarded as sane and moral. Questioning such things is impossible without serious consequences, for the simple reason that they are points of view rather than logical arguments. The subject must cover any logical gaps silently, obediently, in order to sustain the power of the point of view. As in the fable of the Emperor's New Clothes, sustainability is a signifier that organizes other signifiers, a logic that works as long as it is not scrutinized too closely. The purpose of this chapter is to look into sustainability as a fantasy without detracting from its effectiveness as an inspirational theme. This is intended as an archeology in the spirit of the "old Foucault," in hopes that discourse, now foreclosed by the ideological role of sustainability, can develop a broader knowledge of the subject's real condition.[3]

Why is there instability in discourse – instability that must be settled by fantasy? There is a slogan in psychoanalysis: "Anxiety never lies!" The problem, of course, is that anxiety never says what it really means. Its terms are chosen to obscure the real source of its concerns, so that, when anxiety speaks, you can be sure something's wrong, but the language of its warning is purposefully misleading. Fantasy comes into this situation to compensate for anxiety's inability to speak directly. Every fantasy involves a recto and a verso version that relates directly to the function of anxiety: a positive fantasy that is the public relations script and, beneath that, a kind of anamorphic implant, what Slavoj Žižek calls the "dirty fantasy," to exploit anxiety's asymbolic dimensions.[4] For example, the 1990s "rhetoric" of the sport utility vehicle touted its indestructibility and power features as acceptable compensation for its greater susceptibility to accidents due to its large, poorly balanced bulk. Although SUVs were more likely to generate accidents, the dirty fantasy was that it was better to kill the other driver, the real source of anxiety. Hence, the anxiety about the Other of the road is translated into the silent directive, "kill the Other first!" This is only an unofficial translation; the asymbolic dirty fantasy can be realized only through images and double entendres. In the case of the SUV, anxiety's inability to say what it means can thus be described in terms of an official fantasy of sophisticated dashboard controls, reinforced steel frames, air bags, and so on, and a set of vague undertones about the dangerous drivers "out there." The subject is free to fill in the blanks of this dirty fantasy regarding who those drivers are specifically.

Architectural theorists are not invulnerable to the lure of twinning positive and dirty fantasies. In her anthology *Architecture of Fear*, Nan Ellin and other authors catalogue the threats, and some of the recommended defensive actions, facing modern city dwellers.[5] Without overly challenging the idea of fear itself in true Rooseveltian fashion, the book accepts that bad things are really bad and that we must do something to protect ourselves. The problem, the dirty fantasy, is Other People. Thanks to television, film, and other popular culture propaganda about Los Angeles, "we" are more or less aware of who those Others are.

With the smuggling of an anamorphic dirty fantasy inside the Trojan horse of the positive fantasy, anxiety moves into the category of ideology. As in the Steven Spielberg's film *Jaws* (1975), the shark becomes a means for organizing all of the "free radicals" floating about in the popular consciousness.[6] Is a rogue shark a sign of human incursion into the natural realm? Is it retribution for the greed of businesspeople intent on keeping the beaches open at all costs? Who knows? The shark, at first a contingent feature of life in a seaside town, ends up as the root of all evil; and, as such, it must be eradicated. The ideological efficiency of *Jaws* lies in its combination of enunciation with the *point of view*. Like the New Age endorsement of multiculturalism, the real claim is to be in the *position* to confer value-equality on other cultures. But how has this privileged position been appropriated? What is the "perspective of perspectives" that has exempted it from being one of the cultures to which it confers acceptability? In *Jaws*, the townsfolk adopt the generic identity of the simple peasants in search of Frankenstein's composite monster, justified in their vigilante action by the very essence of the monster-as-monster.

FROM SUSTAINABILITY TO SUSTENANCE

There is a torch-and-pitchfork aspect of sustainability as well. Consider why no author in his or her right mind would entitle an article or book "Against Sustainability." There is no rhetorical space for negative views once a topic has become ideology. This is why knifing apart the uncut pages of the sustainability book is important: on these pages are written the account of sustenance and its subversive role in the pre-ideological career of sustainability. Sustenance is not, as sustainability has been regarded, a coming-to-terms with nature: *it is a use of nature in the subject's own coming-to-terms with the human*. Sustenance offers a supplement to the ideological appeal of sustainability because it promises to keep open the *gap* that lies at and defines the heart of sustenance, which is the subject's involvement with the world *as subject*, not simply as a consumer in need of protection from threats real and imagined.

Sustenance is a congeries of terms and ideas. Sustenance involves, for its own positive fantasy, an ideology of purpose and accomplishment against a background of human actualization. Sustenance in its positive form promotes the fundamental notion of nourishment, the idea of security, the promise of "extra benefits" of happiness and tranquility. Virgil's long poem, *The Georgics*, is possibly the first major Western work to give voice to the positive fantasy of sustenance.[7] The gods have left the human scene, and humans are left behind to manage. We have to help the bees make the best honey, assist the vine in its destiny to produce top-quality wine, manage the fertility of the earth and the purity of the water. There is no evil to combat, except possibly insects, storm damage, and other obstacles dropping into the space opened up by the departing gods.

The dirty fantasy beneath Virgil's recto might be, for many, the neo-evangelical version of "Left Behind."[8] This is the X-rated version of the dirty fantasy of sustenance that forces us to have it out with the Others, with those whom we knew all along were the root of our troubles but, because of imposed rules of political correctness, were unable to exterminate when we had the chance. Now, with not just God but his righteous believers out of the way, we are free to enter into a Darwinian winner-take-all struggle. It is time for the secularists, who had refused religion, to face the music and realize that there is "real evil" out there. The challenge is to avoid making it appear as though we have a choice between the nice fantasy and the nasty fantasy and, instead, to see the two fantasies as structurally related. The structure, in fact, is created at a level of consciousness that might be considered fundamental; and an archaeology of sustenance, as a structure combining two apparently opposed fantasies, might lead us back to some theoretical perspective on the otherwise ideologically compelling subject of sustainability.

THE GAPPED CIRCLE

Here follows a conjecture that could at any point be so crammed with citations that following the footnotes might deter the reader's necessary participation as an imaginative co-author of the discussion. Diagrams, especially ones that suggest several interpretations, invite the kind of scepticism required for the reader to act as a *bricoleur*, as Claude Lévi-Strauss might have put it. The diagram able to invite the reader into an imagination experiment is that of the gapped circle.

The statement "demand exceeds need" would be an appropriate motto to place over the door of the human condition. Shelter, food, and procreative success – this triad of most species' sustainability formula, *zoe* – is "never enough" for cultures that, through their symbolic capacities (*bios*), invent anxieties that differ from animal fear. A minimum definition of that difference might be that humans are able to separate the function of use value from that of exchange value. "Use" is the direct material response to a need, an engagement, a transaction; "value" is what allows use to become a part of a network of symbolic relationships. Value would be like a price tag except that the vector is asymbolic and "silent." The price is not listed. Separating use and value results in the totem and the fetish. Another part of that network is the well known reassignment of everything – sex, food, appearance, behaviour, and so on – to "accounting systems" that place subjects within networks of symbolic relationships.[9] Subjects find their places within roles invented to support the use-exchange system. Demand, an excess going beyond the needs of sustainability, depends on anxiety as a fuel. Ideology inserts value into every use. Like a fractal or virus, this insertion converts nature into culture. A diagram preceding the gapped circle would be that of two vectors, use and exchange, bound by an orthogonal hinge. The ninety-degree angle keeps open the silent relationship between the two: the price of something is never fixed by use; rather, it is always redefinable by culture, subject to flux, to repricing.

This gap is held open because there is no "fixed price menu." Use becomes symbolic not by setting a price but by concealing value. There can be no clearer example of this than the example of "silent trade," practised widely in antiquity and still used in parts of Asia. The parties of a trade never meet. One leaves an object at a designated site, another replaces it with an object of equivalent value. If the value is perceived to be unequal, adjustment is made in the next trading cycle. The insertion of uncertainty into the valuing of use (= domestication of need) creates an opening, which is filled (symbolically) by the dimensions of space and time that "register" optional outcomes in terms of a charged field-of-play. This is not to argue for an "idealist" theory of reality per se but, rather, to use

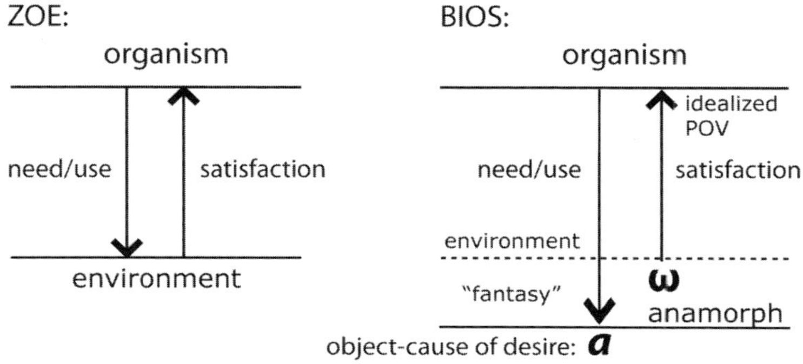

Fig. 4.1 When demand exceeds need, a space opens up that is held open by the "orthogonal" relationship between use value and exchange value. Here, humans perceive in nature an anamorphic surplus – "more than meets the eye."

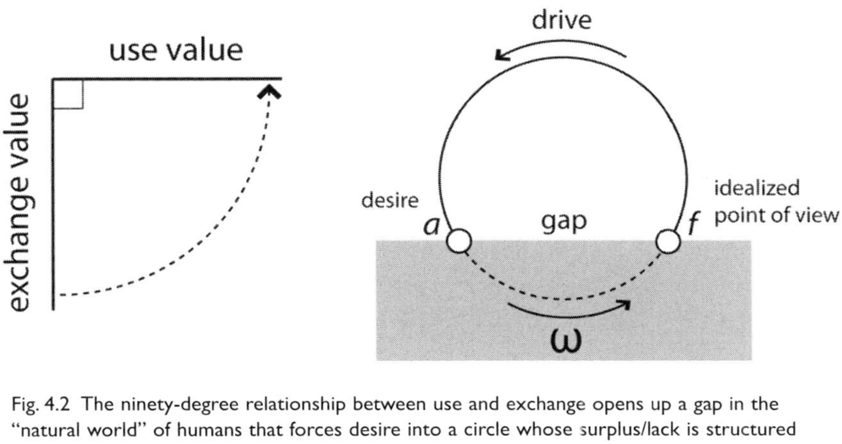

Fig. 4.2 The ninety-degree relationship between use and exchange opens up a gap in the "natural world" of humans that forces desire into a circle whose surplus/lack is structured in visual and narrative ways.

the Wittgensteinian point that *this* space and *this* time is the specificity of time and space, grounded on the contingency set out in advance by cultural directives and subjective adaptations.[10] It may be that only the specific case exists and that the general does not – that the abstractions we regard as the guarantors of objective reality are, like the idea of credit, convenient fictions.

The orthogonal angle between use value and exchange value opens up and specifies dimensions of a space and time for humans who perceive it as the "givens" of material reality. The orthogonal element keeps the circle from being closed, as it would be for animals who communicate using signifiers fixed (mostly) to their referents.[11] This opening locates the dirty fantasy whose job is not to close or cross it but, rather, to keep it permanently open by inserting a space within a space that, concealed (as is the exchange value, the hidden price), exhibits a striking architecture that can be recognized in cultures from ancient times to the present. The gapped circle creates a subsegment of space and time materialized by the motion of a quest, puzzle, exile – a "journey of discovery" structured by coincidences, symmetries, *Doppelgängers*, and clues. It is the liminal space-outside-of-space used by cultures for instruction, initiation, meditation, and sacred isolation. The curse (= "course," or circle) best describes its geometry and its magic affiliations; the spell (cf. G. *Spiel*) denotes its extension in a time and space structured by narrative.

In the ancient Greek house, the hearth was this place sustained by secret narrative, presided over by the women of the household who were the representatives of Hestia, "wedded to the flame" as were the Vestals of Rome, responsible for the conversations (paid for in burned fat) with the dead ancestors (*manes*) who protected the home. The hearth was shielded from the view of strangers. Alternatively, it may have been that the secular life of the family needed protection from the *manes*' volatile gaze.[12] True to the "silent" role of exchange (Hermes, the god of commerce, is typically shown with his finger to his lips), the gap was invisible from any point outside. Its perceptual dimensions could be opened only with verbal formulae – passwords – accompanied by some token gift (hence, the role of the offering).

This cursed surplus space had the property of converting from inside to outside.[13] The Roman Forum, for example, began its life not as a civic centre but as the periphery to the seven tribes who used it as a common

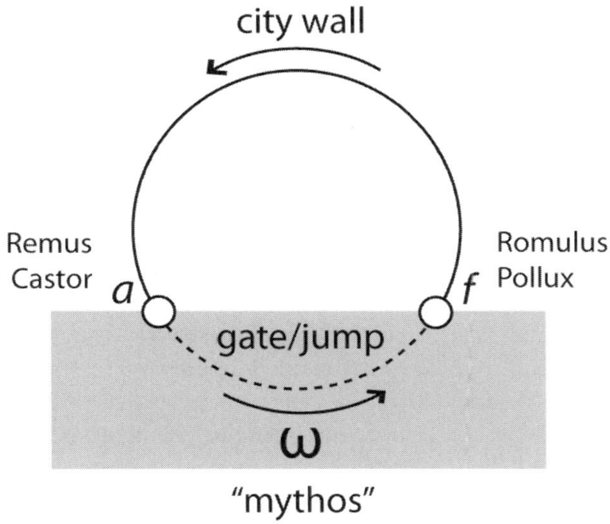

Fig. 4.3 The "anamorphosis" of the gap can be materialized in visual or narrative ways. Here, it is an approach to myth using the "stereognostic" theme of twins. Rome was founded by twins (Romulus and Remus) and later protected by the twin Dioscuri, Castor and Pollux. The use of twins to structure the gapped circle is "stereognostic" – a puzzled relationship between two minimally different parts.

burial ground. It was marginal to "all" taken one at a time but central to "all" realized as a unity in the act of the foundation of Rome. The particulars of that narrative involve the theme of twins, Romulus and Remus; the element of sacrifice (Remus's murder); the creation of a symmetrical space coincident with religious spells; and – last but not least – the inclusion of gaps (gates) as Romulus lifted the plough to allow the connection of inside and outside. Although this latter feature would seem to be just a convenience item, it was itself a complex restatement of the whole act of foundation. Traditions surrounding the gate as the consummate example of what Lacan would christen "the extimate" (an out-of-doors version of intimacy) consistently link the function of passage with verbal formulae, uncanny in-between-ness, and mortification. The astute Michelangelo was able to capture the irony of the gate in his Porta Pia, a fractal of the city, a building turned inside out.

Compared to the "life" of ordinary space and time, the gap of the gapped circle becomes, in literature, the death narrative, a quest for the *gnosis* of the dead. The tradition of sibyls, who sat at the edge of this space, gives the clue that this *gnosis* could be uttered only in riddle or irony. The Oracle at Delphi presided over a flame regarded as the centre of the world (*omphalos*), symbolized by a conical stone statue derived from the practice of shaping the ashes of the night fire in preparation for the next day. The relation of the oracle to language gives a clue: the sibyl spoke "outside" the denotative and connotative functions of ordinary speech. Hers was a "voice" empowered by ventriloquism, a voice that is a resistant kernel of non-meaning inside language's phonemic semiotics. This kernel, in all cultures, becomes the official voice of the dead.

The marginal-yet-central placement of the gap lays bare the function of placement itself. The "where" of the gap is a nowhere, but it is also a central nowhere. In Jean-Paul Sartre's famous story about looking for the tardy friend, Pierre, in a restaurant, Pierre is *not there* in a way that makes the negative into a positive force field. Guests in the restaurant are summoned to a screen, asked to stand apart from the ground as the figure, Pierre, but they fail and fall back into the ground.[14] This spectral summons is more than a failed experiment: it is a Hegelian "tarrying with the negative," which is to say that the negative *is* this experience of tarrying, duration, in the absence of conventionalized meaning, space, and time. It is the "hard time" of prison, the slow architecture of exchange described so well by Kafka in his pivotal novels *The Trial* and *The Castle*. It is the "feel free to go anywhere" space of Piranesi's *Carceri*, the imaginary prisons of infinite extent. These matters of placement, voice, extimacy, and curse are brought together in the ultimate sustenance narrative, the biblical story of the Garden of Eden.

EDEN TOPOLOGY: TEMPLE OR LABYRINTH?

In the Garden of Eden (see fig. 4.4), God is only marginally present. His footsteps can be heard rustling from time to time, but he has by and large left Adam and Eve alone to enjoy their fully furnished sustainable home – the ultimate green architecture. In a sense, this returns us to our original concern about anxiety always telling the truth but not in terms we readily understand. Eden's use value is more like the legal term of usufruct: "You can use it as long as you don't waste it." The exchange value is the covenant's codicil, "Don't eat from the tree of knowledge!"

Fig. 4.4 Lucas Cranach the Elder, *Adam and Eve* (1526). Oil on panel, 80 cm x 117 cm. ©The Samuel Courtauld Trust, the Courtauld Gallery, London. Reproduced by permission from the Courtauld Institute of Art, London.

The space and time of Eden are held open through the "moment" between the two statements. An uncertain circularity develops. We are given a space and time to "think about it" before exchange collapses into use (the vectors will coincide once the serpent makes his argument, that the true value of Eden is this one fruit). The space and time of Eden circulate around its own "impossible-Real" condition, the Tree of Knowledge. The circle has a gap, just as the serpent, cousin to the Uroboros whose self-referential credentials are well known, is a boundary with a face, a rule with an exception.

We know the story. Eve is, according to her initial creation and later role in converting Eden to Wilderness, "extimate," a "subjective object." In some ways, Eve and the serpent are roommates in the sense that, through the partnership of knowledge and space, they keep open the gap that allows free choice, motility, and all that is based on them – which, incidentally, the labyrinth represents as a meandered boundary.

Virgil's margin is in most ways the same as the *zimzum* of Yahweh's evacuation.[15] Whether it is the invisibility of God in the garden or the subsequent more radical absence, it is a margin to be completed by humans. Virgil is optimistic. We can fill the margin with the arts of husbandry, of taking care of the earth (this is the positive fantasy of sustainability). The Bible and, hence, the evangelicals of the "left-behind" school see it as a neurotic space. The term "stereognosis" comes closest to describing how this space challenges knowledge with its puzzle of minimally differentiated "halves." Adam-Eve, Castor-Pollux, the Dioscuri, and so on are really parts of an "anamorphosis system" that supplies content to the gap created between disguise/blindness and gnosis. The evangelical left-behind version is more vivid than Virgil's: it involves what René Girard calls the unavoidable violence of semblance.[16]

How can the two fantasies be reconciled? According to ecologists in the tradition of Howard Odum, sustenance is a circle that must be completed. Inputs and outputs, in terms of both energy and material, must add up to zero. Any remainder is passed on to the next system of equilibration, until finally the universe balances the books. New Age sustainability enthusiasts frequently point to accounting to underscore the idea of the zero-sum game, which, in theological terms of *zimzum*, means no presence without an absence.

My speculation may have made it seem as if sustenance is a subjective issue, not the imposed condition of limited resources and unstable global conditions that forces us to respond creatively to discover some workable new arrangements. Global warming, resource shortages, and geo-political inequities are not illusions, unfortunately. But, the terminology we use to frame and define complex issues that are barely understandable is not only "in our head," it *is* our head: it *is* our way of thinking that establishes our collective political agenda. Sustainability fills the role of a "master signifier" that, like the shark in *Jaws*, organizes loose details and unproved assertions. What is striking is that sustainability, as an argument for duration, is the classic form of the circular drive: an aim that purposefully *keeps its goal empty* in order to sustain its motion. There is no ideal that sustainability seeks, but this lack provides the plenum of structure that connects narrative traditions, cuisine, foundation traditions, and modern practices based on contemporary anxieties. Sustainability, to put it plainly, is the temporal aspect of our cultural neurosis. Its lack of an assigned object ("Sustainability of ____?") keeps open its perennial ideological potential.

The structure of the gapped circle creates highways between the points of the constellation of the human subject. Perhaps this is why sustainability can be so personally felt and, at the same time, be a common cause connecting diverse large groups and even nations. The role of the double (the two fantasies, theme of twins, "stereo-gnostic" elements, etc.) should alert us, however, to the concealed dimensions of ideology. The dirty fantasy will not go away: its unnameability is what keeps the gap open, what allows the field of perception its durability. Public policy tends to delude itself about the dirty fantasy's existence; nonetheless, those in the way of its materializations will, like the Others of the SUV, continue to die.

NOTES

1 Paul Treanor is a Dutch freelance political blogger who questions the ethical basis of sustainability. See http://web.inter.nl.net/users/Paul.Treanor/index.html.

2 At the root of sustainability's theoretical problem is its (unintended) presumption that there is a unity of motive behind "unsustainable" practices,

against which the opposite motive can be argued. "The unsustainable" is, of course, not a set of coordinated practices but, rather, a characterization that frames a number of unrelated phenomena from a new point of view that is retroactively projected onto historical practices that have been, in retrospect, sustainable or unsustainable.

3 This chapter's position will be mistaken for ideology, too, unless the reader understands the proper meaning of fantasy. Anglo-American psychology has been dominated by "ego-psychology," the theoretical opposite of Lacanian psychoanalysis more broadly understood in Europe. The fantasy of the individual, for ego-psychology, inevitably refers to delusion, and treatment aims to dispel delusion. The spiritualistic New Age attitude of self-help is then able, on this account, to merge with its antipode, theoretical physics. Both isolate the subject as a unit of discursive decisiveness. Lacanian approaches give fantasy its due, so to speak, and help the subject identify with his/her social relations. The bias against fantasy in Anglo-American literature has hampered its incorporation into theory and trivialized such topics as imagination and the dream.

4 Slavoj Žižek, Rex Butler, and Scott Stephens, *Interrogating the Real* (New York: Continuum International Publishing Group, 2006), 60.

5 Nan Ellin, *Architecture of Fear* (New York: Princeton Architectural Press, 1997).

6 Fredric Jameson aptly observes: "The vocation of the symbol – the killer shark – lies less in any single message or meaning than in its very capacity to absorb and organize all of these quite distinct anxieties together. As a symbolic vehicle, then, the shark must be understood in terms of its essentially polysemous function rather than any particular content attributable to it by this or that spectator. Yet it is precisely this polysemousness which is profoundly ideological, insofar as it allows essentially social and historical anxieties to be folded back into apparently 'natural' ones, both to express and to be recontained in what looks like a conflict with other forms of biological existence." See Fredric Jameson, *Signatures of the Visible* (New York: Routledge, 1990), 26–7.

7 Virgil (Vergilius Maro), *The Georgics of Virgil*, trans. David Ferry (New York: Farrar, Straus, and Giroux, 2005).

8 Tim LaHaye and Jerry B. Jenkins, *Left Behind: A Novel of the Earth's Last Days* (Wheaton, IL: Tyndale House Publishers, 1998).

9 The discovery of the inexplicable valuation of trivial objects marks the

beginning of modern anthropology. Marcel Mauss's study of the fetish nearly coincided with Freud's study of the totem, laying the groundwork for Claude Lévi-Strauss's groundbreaking study of food customs, *The Raw and the Cooked*, trans. John and Doreen Weightman (Chicago: University of Chicago Press, 1983). Triviality, these studies agree, is the essence of the unconscious. In this sense, anthropology and psychoanalysis coincided with art's turn to the trivial in Surrealism and Cubism.

10 This point requires a distinction between the abstract idea of space and time and specific "contingent" experiences of space and time, the notion of "event," or "encounter." The analogy in linguistic theory would be to argue for merging the "Chomskian" view of universal structures and the "Whorfian" idea of adaptability based on cultural differences. Ludwig Wittgenstein anticipated the need for such a blended theory in his *Philosophical Investigations*, trans. G.E.M. Anscombe (Oxford, UK: Blackwell, 1967).

11 Lacan emphasizes that signifiers refer not to concrete things but, rather, to other signifiers. This reverses Ferdinand de Saussure's idea of the signified by showing how signifiers form chains of meanings that slide until they are "quilted" in a process that retroactively revises meaning in a final act of "punctuation." Lacanian quilting calls attention to the "anamorphic" role of quilting and its relation to the gapped circle as a means of using fantasy to compensate for the gap between desire and need. See Jacques Lacan, "The Instance of the Letter in the Unconscious, or Reason since Freud," in *Écrits: The First Compete Edition in English*, trans. Bruce Fink (New York: W.W. Norton, 2002), 416.

12 It would be more accurate to say that, in mythic thought at least, blindness and invisibility are more or less interchangeable. Since one and the same barrier accomplishes both the concealing of the hearth from the visitor's view and the concealing of the visitor from the hearth's view, the real function may be to exchange invisibility for blindness or vice versa.

13 The theme of the uncanny looms large in sustenance's gapped logic because it is, as Mladen Dolar notes, at its heart a blurring of the distinction between inside and outside. See Mladen Dolar, "'I Shall Be with You on Your Wedding-Night': Lacan and the Uncanny," *October* 58 (Autumn 1991): 5–23.

14 Jean-Paul Sartre, *Being and Nothingness*, trans. Hazel Barnes (New York: Philosophical Library, 1956), 9–10.

15 The term "zimzum" is the name in the Jewish mystical book, *The Zohar*,

describing God's necessary contraction to make room for creation, popularized by Harold Bloom in his book *Kabbalah and Criticism* (New York: Seabury Press, 1975).

16 René Girard, *Violence and the Sacred* (Baltimore: Johns Hopkins University Press, 1979).

Writing a Life from the Inside of a Drawing: Stendhal's *Vie de Henry Brulard*

Mari Lending

Chora

"WHEN I ARRIVE IN a city, I climb the highest steeple or tower to have a view of the whole before seeing the individual parts, and when I leave I do the same in order to fix my ideas," Montesquieu confides to his readers in his *Voyage en Italie*, from the late 1720s.[1] A perfect hermeneutic formula is thus captured in the travelling French philosopher's bodily and conceptual movement between the presumed whole and the experienced detail. The Olympic panorama, the unlimited outlook from above that proliferated in eighteenth- and nineteenth-century aesthetic culture, is a familiar literary topos. It occurs also in the famous opening scene of Stendhal's autobiography, *Vie de Henry Brulard*, composed by Henri-Marie Beyle (1783–1842) during a few months in the mid-1830s and published posthumously under his pen name Stendhal in 1890.

Stendhal's captivating first scene takes place early one morning outside San Pietro in Montorio at the Janiculum Hill. "What a magnificent view!" his alter ego Henry Brulard exclaims, surrounded by the panoramic beauty of Rome (see fig. 5.1).[2] His thoughts, however, immediately start to wander. He recalls that Raphael's *Transfiguration* was admired for 250 years in the church behind him before it was buried, as he puts it, in the Vatican. The reader, still on page 1, is given many hints that Stendhal's evocative rapture of places, times, and events differs radically from Montesquieu's well-ordered ascension and descension, with its perfect hermeneutic sequence. Stendhal identifies details in the whole, zooms in and out, and lets personal memories and historical events conflate. Whenever he is exposed to a panorama, his gaze turns inward; every outlook results in introspection. The fate of Raphael's painting leads him to the melancholic fact that his fiftieth birthday is rapidly approaching. This inward movement will later be reversed when the self-investigating subject redirects his gaze outward, towards the world around him.

The lavish description of Rome in the opening scene leaves no doubt that this is a text on architecture, cities, and landscapes, but it is also an effort by Stendhal to capture his very personal and double-pseudonym self in writing. As it turns out, his self-examination also becomes a prism for understanding the built world around him. "Have I been a witty man? Was I sad by nature then?" Stendhal contemplates, posing in front of his potential readers. The possibilities opened up by his many questions, however, are far more important than the actual answers. He continues: "Whereupon, not knowing what to say, I began unthinkingly to admire

Fig. 5.1 Lorenzo Suscipi, "Rome, Panorama from San Pietro in Montorio" (daguerreotype), 1841. Courtesy of SSPL/National Media Museum. Suscipi's view from the Janiculum Hill was captured only six years after Stendhal praised the same view in the opening scene of *Vie de Henry Brulard.*

once more the sublime sight of the ruins of Rome and of its modern grandeur: the Coliseum facing me and beneath my feet the Farnese Palace with the arches of Carlo Maderno's lovely open gallery, the Corsini Palace beneath my feet."[3] The subject asks and the world responds. His autobiographical inquiries into his own character become transformed into external views of buildings, places, cityscapes, nature, history, and contemporary phenomena of many sorts.

The rhapsodic associations that unfold on the steps of San Pietro in Montorio between dawn and dusk on 16 October 1835 can be read as a *mise en abyme* of Stendhal's method of remembering times past and presenting his double-pseudonym self. The same sublime effect is evident in the abundant drawings in his extraordinary memoir.

Natural and urban landscapes are profoundly important in the writings of Stendhal. His fictional and non-fictional textual corpus includes unforgettable buildings, cities, places, and landscapes. It is a universe of geographies and topographies as well as topologies. These landscapes are historically and topographically specific, explored through local distinctions in dialects, habits, psychology, and climate. Indeed, Stendhal's wonderful *De l'Amour* (1822) includes a whole theory of climatic and cultural variations.

"The name Parma, one of the towns I most desired to visit after having read *La Chartreuse,* appears compact, smooth, violet and soft, ... because I imagined it only by this heavy syllable in the name of 'Parme' where no air is circulating, and by all I had made it absorb from the Stendhalien sweetness and the reflection of the violets," the protagonist of *À la recherche du temps perdu* contemplates.[4] In Marcel Proust's novel, this lingering on Parma as a name and an imagined place may be interpreted as a greeting from one outstanding portrayer of places, spaces, and landscapes to another. Proust – a prominent member of the ever-increasing circle of "the happy few" to whom Stendhal dedicated *La Chartreuse de Parme* – obviously is emulating Stendhal's writing, including his obsession with invoking, creating, and recreating real and fictional places. Clearly, the rare ability to make places seem real invests certain works of literature with almost magical qualities of *evidentia* that blur the boundaries between experienced spaces, dreamt spaces, and spaces we imagine through the pleasures of reading.

To me, one of Stendhal's most vivid and memorable descriptions is of a battlefield during the Battle of Waterloo, in *La Chartreuse*. Fabrice del Dongo, the young hero of the novel, is present at this battle, which later would be considered an especially meaningful event in history. Stendhal's exposition of this event, however, is utterly chaotic, almost absurd. As a highly realistic depiction of war, it stands in stark contrast to the historian's well-ordered, bird's-eye view of the past. In Stendhal's narrative the place collapses and dissolves into so many small, meaningless fragments and misunderstandings that not even the protagonist can explain with any precision where he had been and what he had experienced. "'What he had seen, was it a battle?' Fabrice asks himself, 'And if so, was it the battle of Waterloo?' For the first time in his life he takes pleasure in reading newspapers and battle chronicles, hoping to find descriptions that might help him recognize the places he had passed through."[5] Clearly, this passage presents an ironic palimpsest. First, it is impossible not to read it as a distorted parody of the historian's desire for order and overview. Stendhal's memoirs also distinguish between the "impartial historian" and the individual who cannot separate historical facts from personal experiences. It is equally ironic that a current reader can imagine this place so clearly that it seems real, although Fabrice could not grasp it, despite being present at the battle. Stendhal thus enabled his readers to experience the historic site of Waterloo far more vividly than did most descriptions of places in European literature.

❖

Architecture, space, and place are inexorable foundations in literature: thematically, compositionally, structurally, associatively, and metaphorically. In *The Life of Henry Brulard* the architectural discourse is unusual, due to its emblematic juxtaposition of landscape, architecture, and remembrance. By describing cities, buildings, public places, landscapes, and interiors, Stendhal strives to capture his own fragile identity. The text's spatial and existential dimensions are even more evident in the remarkable sketches that are included in this autobiography. Through a synthesis of writing and drawing, a double process of remembrance and reconstruction is unfolded. Actually, there are three parallel discourses at work: the writing, the drawings, and the highly significant handwriting on the drawings – as well as the captions that are included under the sketches in modern editions. This stratified arrangement enables Stendhal to develop the narrative from within the drawing, using it not only to help him remember and reconstruct the past but also to create a *place* of remembrance. Referring to a modest sketch (see fig. 5.2), he announces, "I found myself at point H, between the main road and the Isère."[6] This "I" is projected *into* the drawing, and the point "H" – H is for Henry – functions as a viewpoint, similar to the one outside San Pietro in Montorio in the opening scene. Here, as in many other situations, the drawing provides a pivotal point that permits the view to be changed. Initially the author adopts an aerial point of view to look down at his former self, situated in the drawing, virtually on a piece of paper. Then he constructs new or lost perspectives – perhaps a vista of a landscape or a familiar urban or interior scene – that might enable him to recall something that took place there.

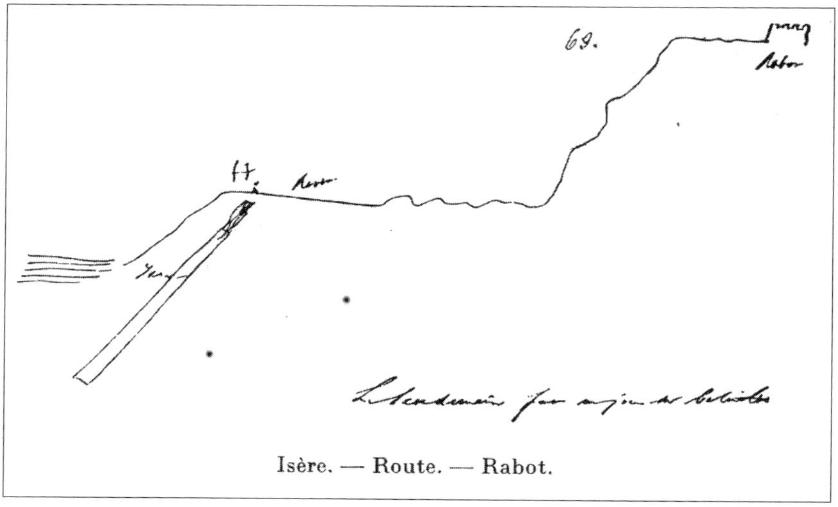

Fig. 5.2 The point H – H is for Henry – provides a viewpoint within a lost landscape. From Stendhal, *Vie de Henry Brulard*, vol. 1, in *Oeuvres Complètes*, vol. 20 (Geneva and Paris: Slatkine Reprints, 1986), 88.

The architectural dimension of the text is defined less by its description of buildings and places than by the author's world that is represented in the drawings. Stendhal's visual-narrative discourse strives to represent the past accurately and truthfully, relying heavily on his attempts to draw how he *thinks* he remembers the landscapes, buildings, and interiors of his life. The drawings in *The Life of Henry Brulard* include plans of private buildings, public buildings, and urban quarters with blocks, streets, and squares. Landscape scenes are presented in various versions and with different scales and qualities: loose sketches, terrains that allude to maps, and complex cartographic schemes. They include cross-sections of both terrains and interiors, sometimes juxtaposed in surprising ways, as well as diagrams of socio-spatial arrangements. There are also sketches of minor details, significant objects, and doodles. One sketch shows a post in a balustrade that the very young Stendhal imagined as perfect material for spinning tops. Another is a beautiful sketch of Sancho Panza (see fig. 5.3), which may have been a source for Pablo Picasso's famous drawing of Don Quixote (1955). Stendhal occasionally depicts other pictures, including artworks, anticipating his remarkable aesthetic reflections on landscape painting.

Fig. 5.3 Sancho Panza, as imagined by the young Stendhal. From Stendhal, *Vie de Henry Brulard*, vol. 1, in *Oeuvres Complètes*, vol. 20, 137.

This collection blurs the distinction between objective representation and subjective experience, evoking what Giuliana Bruno describes as "emotive geography": "Sensuously associative in connecting the local and topographical to the personal, it enhanced the passionate voyage of the imagination."[7] By presenting panoramic tableaus and lingering on details, the autobiographer invites his readers into the real and imaginary spaces in the text and the drawings. Perhaps the most fascinating trait in Stendhal's drawings is his challenge to perspective. His drawings are almost primitive and they appear to have been done hastily, but they are not primarily things to look at; rather, they are places to look from. As such, the drawings are not illustrations: they are sites of remembrance and spaces of associations, places to occupy, to observe, to contemplate, and to recall what might have happened. This enables a simple drawing of an interior to suggest what happened not only *inside* but also *outside* that space. Thus, a plan of an interior can evoke a lost *vue magnific* that may be available only from that very site – from inside the drawing.

The autobiographer declares, first and foremost, that "a drawing has to resemble nature!"[8] While his drawings often depict nature, they never resemble nature. Stendhal unabashedly brags that his drawing skills effortlessly capture the essential character of an object, a room, a street scene, or a landscape, but his drawings are anything but mimetic. On the contrary: despite their variety of subjects, the drawings are characterized by a single striking feature – their abstracted, diagrammatic qualities. What may seem at first to be a realistic, topographic sketch – a landscape, a plan of a house, or an urban context – may turn out to be a diagram that provides dimensions and determines relationships between things: objects, persons, events, buildings, or places. This attention to dimensions and relations also explains Stendhal's fascination with architectural scale models, discussed in his *Mémoires d'un touriste* (1838), which describes being astonished by a collection of cork models in Nîmes. He claims that the abstract models enabled him to grasp the comparative sizes of monuments in a way that real buildings never could.[9] "In a landscape the human eye can form an environmental image of an object, but from the point of view of the perception of phenomena, the model encouraged theoretical, relational reflection," architectural historian Renzo Dubbini observes.[10]

In Stendhal's autobiography the distinctive diagrammatic displays of landscapes and architecture have certain rare and remarkable phenomenological implications. "The drawing is a map," the narrative claims, referring to a Baroque radial city plan. This map, however, does not refer to an existing urban location. It is a diagram of social and existential possibilities, formulated as "roads" of past and future prospects. The caption names the roads on the so-called map: "Road to madness. – Road to the art of getting oneself read. – Road to consideration: F(élix) Faure makes himself peer of France. – Road to a fortune made through trade or job-seeking. – A. Moment of birth."[11] A reader who is familiar with the social distinctions in Proust's increasingly destabilized high society will be thrilled by this fascinating juxtaposition of picture and text as the diagram can be read as an early form of a fundamental sociospatial arrangement in *À la recherche du temps perdu*. Stendhal's diagram anticipates the shock that Proust's elderly narrator experiences when he finally recognizes that there is not only a connection but also a shortcut between the road to Guermantes and the road to Méséglise.

The "road to" formula presents different courses of life as if they existed in the same domain, although the reader subsequently realizes that they are based on spiritual, political, literary, and historical idiosyncrasies. The same formula, along with the location of the moment of birth at a point called "A," is repeated later in a more complex and multilayered variation (see fig. 5.4):

> Road of madness. –L. Road to getting oneself being read: Tasso. J.-J. Rousseau, Mozart. R. Road to public regard. –P. Road of good prefects and councilors of State: administrators: Messrs Daru, Roederer, Français, Beugnot. – Road to money: Rothschild.
>
> A. Moment of birth. –B. Roads taken at age seven, often without knowing it. It is supremely ridiculous at the age of fifty to try to leave road R or road P for road C. Frederick II hardly got himself read yet [*sic*] from the age of twenty had been dreaming of road L.[12]

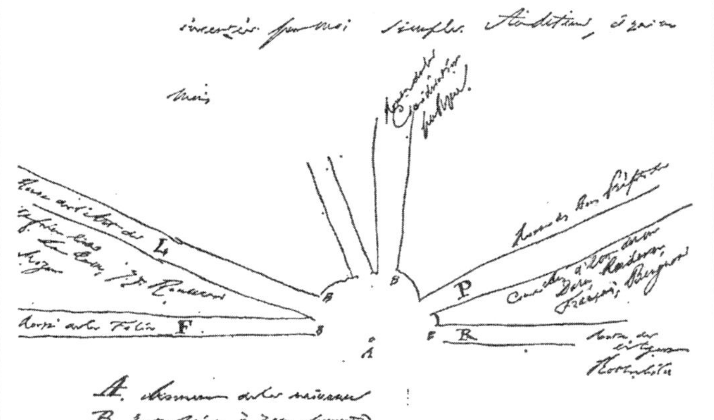

A. Moment de la naissance. — B. Routes prises à 7 ans, souvent à notre insu. Il est souverainement absurde de vouloir à 50 ans laisser la route R ou la route P pour la route C. Frédéric II ne s'est guère fait lire et dès 20 ans songeait à la route L. — Route de la considération politique. — Route de l'art de se faire lire: le Tasse, J.-J. Rousseau, Mozart. — Route de la folie. — Route des bons préfets et conseillers d'état: MM. Daru, Roederer, Français (de Nantes), Beugnot. — Route de l'argent: Rothschild.

Fig. 5.4 A diagram of social and existential possibilities, presented as a Baroque radial city plan. From Stendhal, *Vie de Henry Brulard*, vol. 2, in *Oeuvres Complètes*, vol. 21, 137.

The two types of text in the drawings – the obscure handwriting and the well-ordered caption – demonstrate Stendhal's philosophical and political wit. However, these drawings are not really maps but existential diagrams in the form of town plans. Their spatial and urban associations illustrate Stendhal's process of remembrance. As diagrams, their primary aim is to provide dimensions, to define temporal or spatial sequences, or to describe relationships between objects, persons, buildings, or places. This logic is evident even in the drawings that closely resemble architectural drawings. This may explain why his plans of buildings do not suggest a real physical presence. They present relations and dimensions but have no mimetic ambition whatsoever.

The diagram is a paradigm of Stendhal's method, which aims to recall memories by placing something in relation to something else. In these special constellations of places, events, and persons, points indicate possible occurrences and experiences. A simple and exquisite example is a drawing of an urban square (see fig. 5.5). Rather than referring realistically to the real world, it describes a relationship between buildings and people moving in space. Another diagram (see fig. 5.6) presents a more complex urban situation, with a mountain cross-section and a flagpole as vertical elements. Even a passionate love story is unveiled through coordinates in a diagram. The older Stendhal recalls how he, as a young man desperately and secretly in love with a beautiful mademoiselle, almost ran into her (see fig. 5.7). "I was at H, I caught sight of her at K," the caption reads. The accompanying narrative describes his anxiety at spotting her on the street: "I took flight, as if the devil were bearing me off along the line of railings F; she, I believe, was at K, and I was lucky enough not to be spotted by her."[13] As readers, we expect this description to develop into a love story, elaborated in detail. Stendhal, however, places the beloved one at a point in a diagram, equipped only with a letter (relieved of both her name and her physiognomy). This schematic translation of lived experiences into formulae, numbers, and letters might seem to avoid what we conventionally expect from literature, especially from memoirs. The effect, however, is the exact opposite. As an anti-Proust – Proust, of course, would have expanded fragments of this underplayed scene into a comprehensive narrative in time and space – Stendhal refers briefly and precisely to the points, lines, and patterns of movement on the map. This under-communication of the event's literary potential causes a tremendous effect. "So much to say for anyone with the patience to describe accurately!" the auto-biographer exclaims.[14] Nevertheless, he prefers to sketch a diagram, offering a line and two letters instead of a painstaking description. The result is peculiar, striking, and spectacular. Stendhal's spatial diagrams mapped his "living spaces and acted as icons of his states of mind and social and sexual relations," Anthony Vidler observes.[15] In the diagram of the scene with his beloved, the drama emerges through the tensions between the drawing, the handwritten comment, and the narrative. Together, they establish a literary space in which the passionate and elliptical love story can take place.

❖

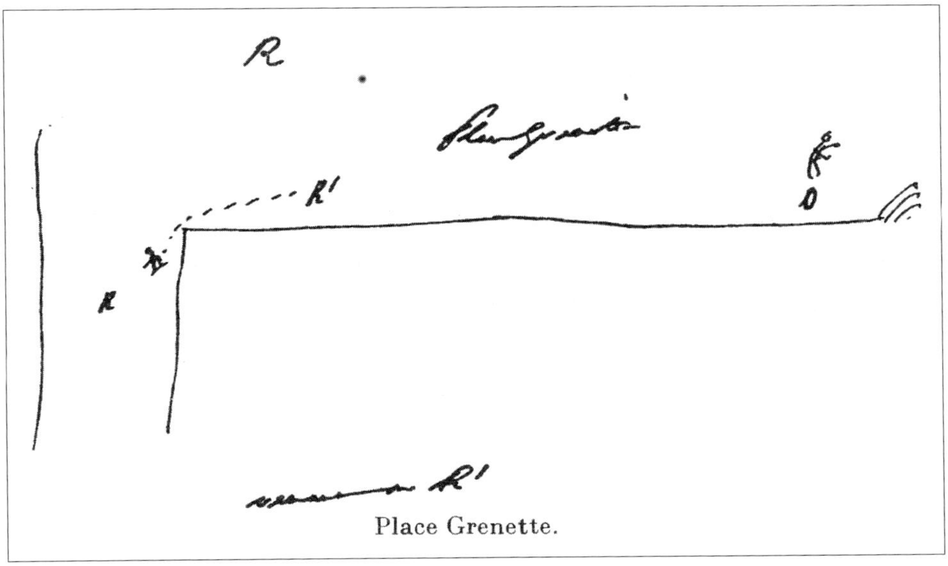

Fig. 5.5 A relationship between buildings and people moving in space. From Stendhal, *Vie de Henry Brulard*, vol. 1, in *Oeuvres Complètes*, vol. 20, 84.

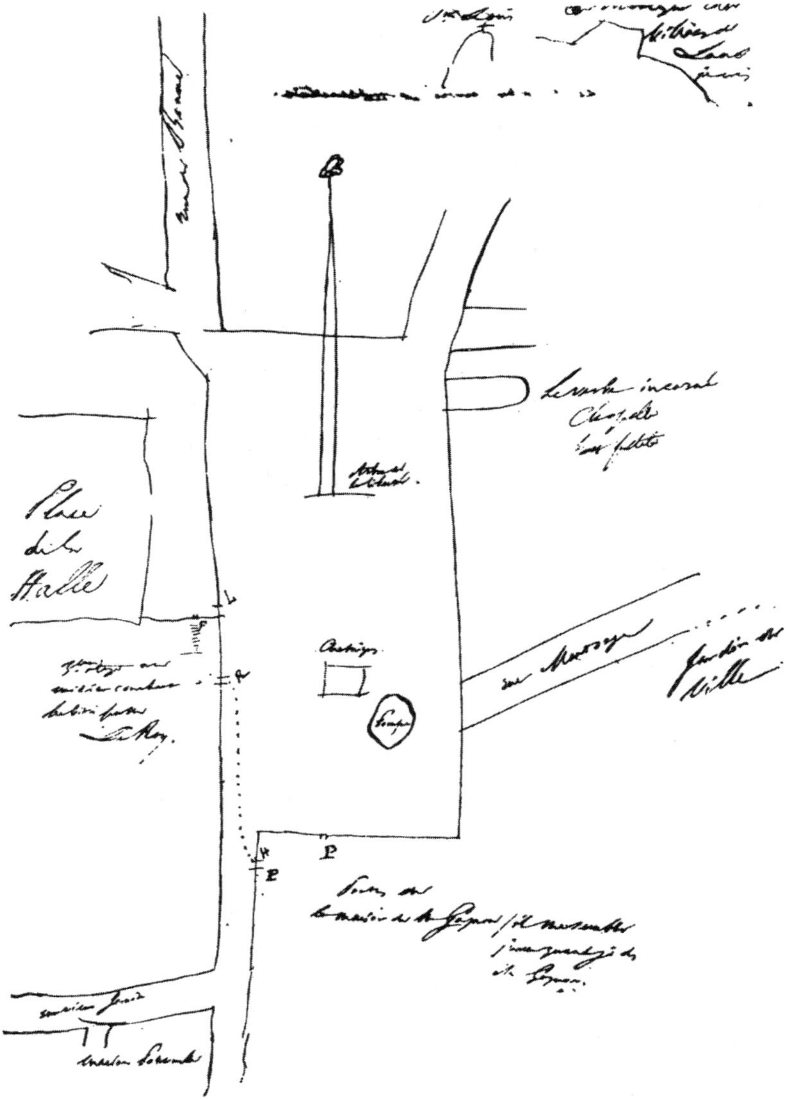

Rue de Bonne. — S[ain]t-Louis. — La montagne du Villard-de-Lans, je crois. — Place de la Halle. — Arbre de la liberté. — Le Verbe incarné. Chapelle fort petite. — Troisième étage au midi et couchant habité par M. Le Roy. — Châtaignes. — Pompe. — Rue Montorge. — Jardin de Ville. — Rue Vieux-Jésuites. — Maison paternelle. — Portes de la maison Gagnon (il me semble jurer quand je dis M. Gagnon).

Fig. 5.6 A complex urban situation with three-dimensional elements. From Stendhal, *Vie de Henry Brulard*, vol. 1, in *Oeuvres Complètes*, vol. 20, 227.

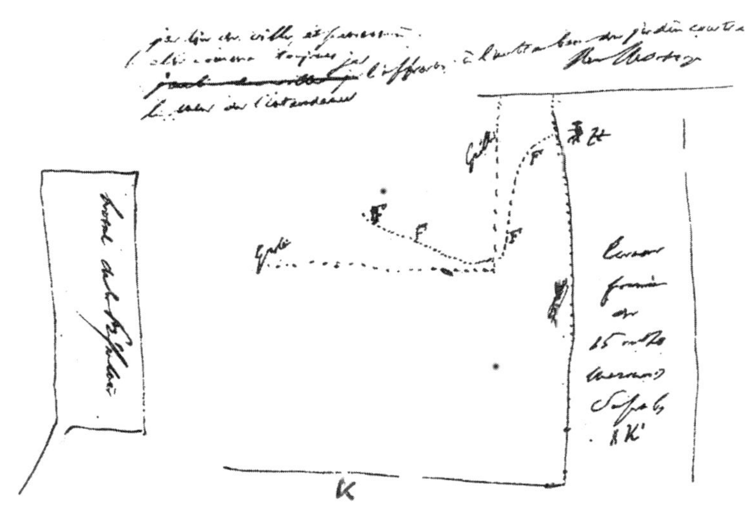

Hôtel de la Préfecture. — Grille. — Grille. — Rue Montorge. — Terrasse formée de quinze ou vingt marronniers superbes K'. — J'étais en H., je l'aperçus en K.

Fig. 5.7 A passionate love story captured in a diagram. From Stendhal, *Vie de Henry Brulard*, vol. 2, in *Oeuvres Complètes*, vol. 21, 61.

Stendhal uses the visual-poetological metaphor of a fresco to describe the act of remembrance and the reconstruction of time lost. He compares the fragmented story of his life to "large fragments of frescos on a wall, long since forgotten and suddenly appearing, and next to these well preserved fragments there are, as I've several times said, large gaps where only the brick-work of the wall is to be seen."[16] This fresco metaphor is given a twist as he tries to remember a certain place but says: "Here is the setting for the scene which I can see as clearly as if I had left it a week ago, though not its physiognomy."[17] Physiognomy, a favoured nineteenth-century literary-urban mode of reflection, becomes a metaphor for the features he cannot recall. As a spatial notion, physiognomy refers to what is not immediately accessible but must be conjured. In composing his autobiography, Stendhal relied equally on drawing and writing to reclaim the physical features of a site where something took place. As with architects, his drawings helped him think. They offered an autonomous field for reflection that enabled him to grasp and formulate particular insights.[18]

As conscientious parts of his process of remembrance, the drawings not only served a literary purpose but also *became* literature. Hence, any attempt to privilege the written memoirs over the images would be denied by the very existence of the story *in* the drawings, an existence with its own reality that encourages reflections, perspectives, and reminiscences. Stendhal occasionally identifies more closely with his drawings than with the reality they represent. Thus, the drawings cannot be regarded merely as a scaffold that supports the process of remembrance, to be removed when the memories have been identified and captured as text.[19] Stendhal uses both drawing and writing as an intertwined enterprise to uncover fragments of his past.

This dynamic unfolds in complex and lovely ways throughout *The Life of Henry Brulard*. For example, a plan of a Grenoble neighbourhood depicts streets with names, a church, a schoolyard, and a school with rooms for chemistry, mathematics, Latin, and so on (see fig. 5.8). This geographic description is contrasted abruptly with a caption that refers to point C: "On the first floor, second classroom, where I won first prize ahead of seven or eight pupils admitted one month later to the Ecole Polytechnique."[20] Situating his memory at this point, in this room, the autobiographer develops the story within the drawing. In fact, the diagram *is* the story; amazingly, it becomes narrative. The same logic is evident in a drawing that conflates a topographical sketch of a tract of land and a topological diagram of significant places in the landscape. The caption recommends: "See M. de Bourcet's map of the Dauphiné (it was in the drawing-room on the terrace to the left)." Here, the author of a work-in-progress uses the drawing to remind himself of something that may turn out to be important. Stendhal's drawing points to another drawing, an existing map to which he may return later to clarify memories and events. Likewise, in a beautiful drawing of a landscape painting (see fig. 5.9) – a picture of a picture – the text refers to point A as "Tall trees such as I like them."[21]

Plans, maps, and diagrams are normally assumed to be factual forms of representation. In Stendhal's drawings, distinctions between objective and subjective realities collapse as personal experiences frequently rise from conventional spatial projections. A highly detailed plan shows a closet in which linen was stored with "some sort of respect." A handwritten caption next to a staircase reads: "Window giving poor light, opening onto the staircase, but very big and very handsome," disclosing

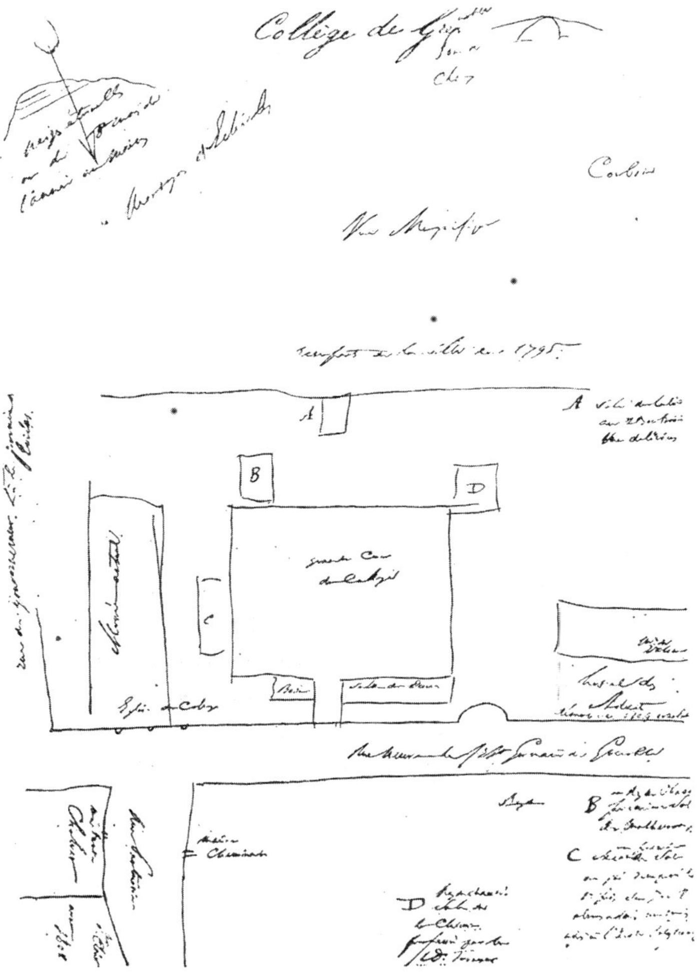

Collège de Grenoble. — Pont de Claix. — Neiges éternelles ou de huit mois de l'année au moins. — Montagnes d'Echirolles. — Comboire. — Vue magnifique. — Remparts de la ville en 1795. — Rue du Gouvernement. Là, la Journée des tuiles. — Église du Collège. — Musée actuel. — Grande cour du Collège. — Bosse. — Salle de dessin. — Salle de latin au second ou troisième. Vue délicieuse. — Mme de Valserre. — Hôtel des Adrets démoli vers 1804 et rebâti. — Rue Neuve, le faubourg S[ain]t-Germain de Grenoble. — Ma tante Chalvet. — S[ain]te Claire avant 1802. — Rue Pertuisière. — Maison Cheminade. — D. Rez-de-chaussée, salle de la chimie professée par M. Trousset. — Beyle. — B. — Au rez-de-chaussée, première salle des mathématiques. — C. Au premier, seconde salle où j'ai remporté le premier prix sur sept ou huit élèves admis un mois après à l'École polytechnique.

Fig. 5.8 A plan of a neighbourhood, with a specific childhood memory that turns the diagram into a narrative. From Stendhal, *Vie de Henry Brulard*, vol. 2 , in *Oeuvres Complètes*, vol. 21, 20.

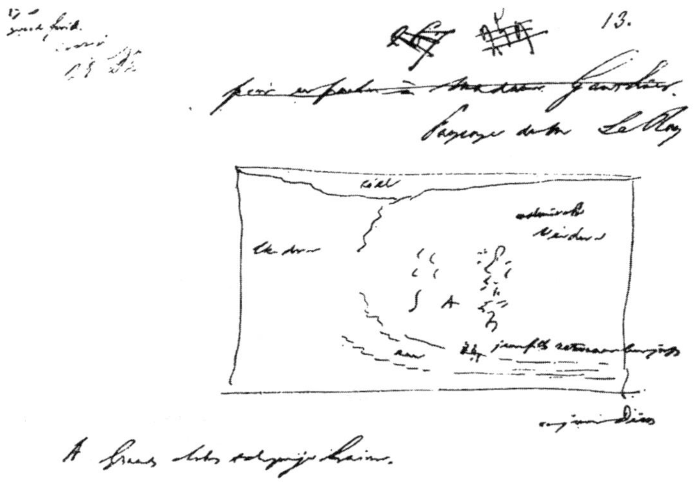

Fig. 5.9 A drawing of a landscape painting. From Stendhal, *Vie de Henry Brulard*, vol. I, in *Oeuvres Complètes*, vol. 20, 239.

a memory that invokes the virtual presence of a subject who is sensually experiencing the dimensions of a room and its light conditions. In a map, the text accompanying point R describes a significant place in the elliptical style that is so characteristic of Stendhal: "Country house which played a very big part in my childhood, which I revisited in 1828, sold to a general."[22] A highly dramatic event is presented as a simple cross-section, where point H (Henry) represents *moi*: "H. Me. Point from which I saw the black carriage pass bearing the remains of the M[aréch]al de Vaux, and what's worse, point from which I heard the guns go off two feet away from me."[23] Despite his strict father's strong dislike of the theatre, his beloved maternal grandfather occasionally brought him along. During a performance of *El Cid*, the lead actor was almost blinded during a fencing scene, and Stendhal's drawing provides a comical and touching perception of the incident from a child's perspective (see fig. 5.10). Point H denotes "Henri B, not yet six years old," while point A marks where "The Cid injures himself." A map sketch (see fig. 5.11) contains much information that one must assume is trustworthy. Point D, however, refers to a completely subjective experience: "Horribly muddy lane

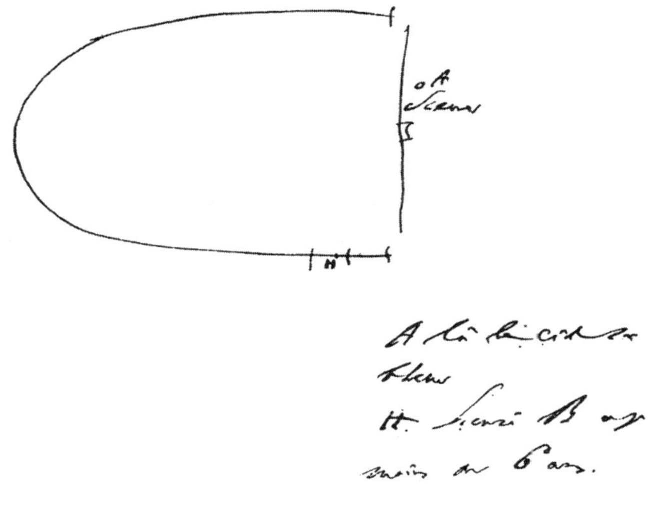

Fig. 5.10 A childhood recollection of an incident in a theatre during a staging of *Le Cid*. From Stendhal, *Vie de Henry Brulard*, vol. 1, in *Oeuvres Complètes*, vol. 20, 67.

known as Les Boiteuses," reads the caption, illustrating Roland Barthes' later distinction between *studium* and *punctum* in photography.[24] A child's memory of mud is a detail, a point that may seem trifling but that is sufficiently meaningful to stand out from the whole. This is what enables Stendhal to think in and through drawing. His particular integration of drawing, handwriting, and transcribed captions enables the images and text together to become literature.

This relationship between drawing and text is radicalized in a map-like topological diagram that includes a section of a mountain, a plan of a villa, an urban fragment, a park, a garden with a bench, and room interiors (see fig. 5.12). With Stendhal's characteristic dry sense of humour, it even includes an aesthetic judgment on his grandfather's interior preferences.

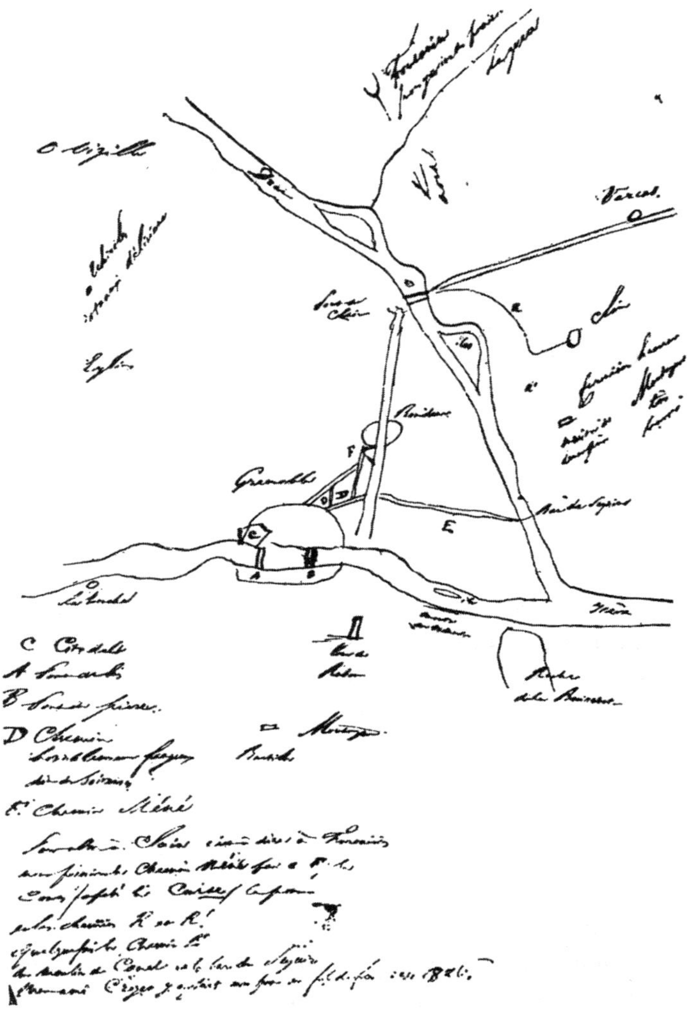

Fontanieu; nous y avions des prairies. — La Gresse [a]. — Vizille. — Drac. — Nord. — Echirolles [b]. Coteaux délicieux. — Eglise. — Pont de Claix. — Varces. — Ile. — Claix. — Rondeau. — Furonières. Hameau. — Maison de mon père. — Montagne très haute. — Grenoble. — Bac de Seyssins. — La Tronche. — Ile. — Montée de S[ain]t-Martin [le Vinoux]. — Rocher de la Buisserate. — C. Citadelle. — A. Pont de bois. — B. Pont de pierre. — D. Chemin horriblement fangeux dit des Boiteuses. — F. Chemin Méné. — Pour aller à Claix, c'est-à-dire à Furonières, nous prenions le chemin Méné par O F, le Cours (appelé le Cour*se*), le pont et le chemin R et R'; quelquefois le chemin E du Moulin de Canel et le bac de Seyssins. Mon ami Crozet y a fait un pont en fil de fer vers 1826.

[a] *Ms :* Grèce.
[b] *Ms :* Echiroles.

Fig. 5.11 A memory of mud recalled in a map sketch. From Stendhal, *Vie de Henry Brulard*, vol. 1, in *Oeuvres Complètes*, vol. 20, 230.

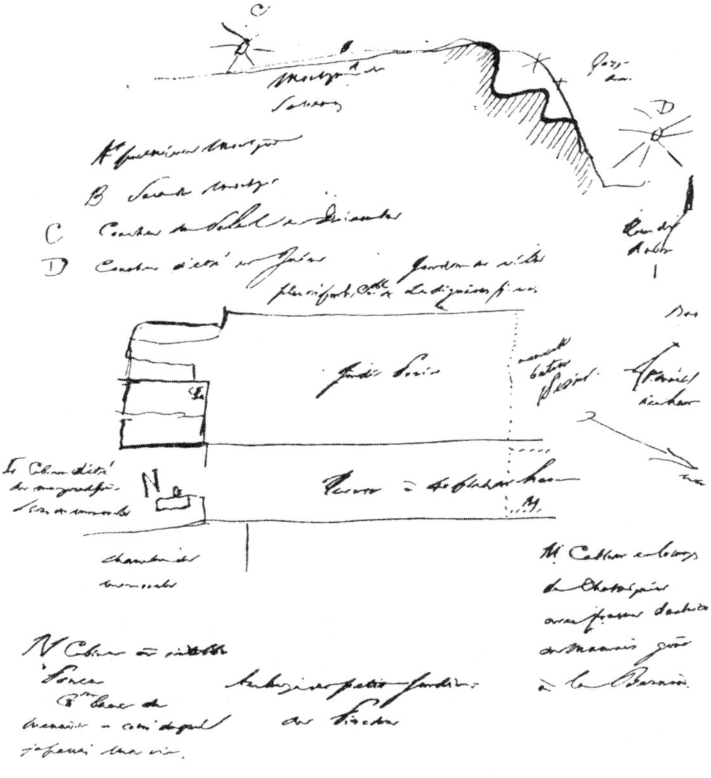

Montagne de Sassenage. — Gorges droites [a]. — A. Première montagne. — B. Seconde montagne. — C. Coucher du soleil en décembre. — D. Coucher d'été en juin. — Jardin de ville planté par le c[onnéta]ble de Lesdiguières, je crois. — Tour de Rabot. — Jardin Périer. — Nouvelle bâtisse Périer. — Bastille. — S[ain]te-Marie-d'en-Haut. L. Cabinet d'été de mon grand-père. Livres de mon oncle. — Terrasse à quarante pieds de haut. — Nord. — Chambre de mon oncle. — M. Cabinet en losanges de châtaignier avec forme d'architecture de mauvais goût, à la Bernin. — N. Cabinet où s'établit Poncet. — G. Banc de menuisier à côté duquel je passais ma vie. — Auberge et petit jardin de Pirodon. — Le pauvre Mantion.

[a] *H. Martineau:* ouvertes.

Fig. 5.12 Sunsets in December and June from a lost landscape in the author's childhood. From Stendhal, *Vie de Henry Brulard*, vol. 1, in *Oeuvres Complètes*, vol. 20, 249.

Pointing to the letter M, the caption reads: "Cabinet paneled in chestnut wood reminding one of tasteless architecture à la Bernini." By capturing the sky as well as his uncle's bookshelf, this drawing presents the same multifaceted dynamic as the initial scene outside San Pietro in Montorio. In a split second – and from inside an image – the focus changes in time and space.

At the top of the drawing, the two suns in orbit above the cross-section of the mountain is what makes this diagram so breathtaking. Points C and D indicate the positions of the sun in December and June, while a connecting line marks the sun's change in altitude. However, it is not the different positions of the sun throughout the seasons that is being depicted but the *sunset* in December and June, seen from Stendhal's childhood village. This destabilizes the distinction between objective reality and subjective experience. As is well known, the sun never actually "sets," but from any subjective point on earth, the sun appears to disappear below a point on the horizon. This very point may be marked objectively, and Stendhal does so. The aesthetic effect of light colouring the evening sky and accentuating the horizon – the phenomenon we call sunset – is captured boldly as points in a diagram, somehow materializing the immaterial. The diagram shows two sunsets over a mountain, a house, a bench, and a collection of books as Stendhal remembers them. It is the relationship between them that Stendhal turns into literature.

Architectural drawings are normally about space, not time; they are static rather than dynamic. This convention is shattered by the fact that time actually passes in Stendhal's drawing. Temporality is marked not by the seasonal movement of the sun but by a series of previously experienced sunsets. His unusual use of diagrams to capture memories of sunsets results in strong poetic effects with the same literary qualities as the narrative in his writing. The diagrammatic features in Stendhal's drawings and his generous use of letters and mathematical formulae could lead a reader to believe that Stendhal is quantifying and rationalizing his experiences. The spatial and textual sensuality of these drawings, however, enables both quantities and qualities to arise from the lost landscapes of his childhood. This interrelation of textual and visual narrative embodies a particular mode of reflection. Existential, experiential, and physical landscapes are captured paradoxically in diagrams that are as real as is the view from San Pietro in Montorio.

NOTES

1 Quoted in Renzo Dubbini, *Geography of the Gaze: Urban and Rural Vision in Early Modern Europe* (Chicago: University of Chicago Press, 2002), 76.
2 Stendhal, *The Life of Henry Brulard*, trans. John Sturrock (New York: New York Review of Books, 2002), 4.
3 Ibid., 6.
4 Proust, *Du côté de chez Swann* (Paris: Gallimard, Folio classique, 1988), 381. My translation.
5 Stendhal, *La Chartreuse de Parme* (Paris: Garnier, 1961 [1839]), 72. My translation.
6 Stendhal, *Life of Henry Brulard*, 65.
7 Giuliana Bruno, *Atlas of Emotion: Journeys in Art, Architecture, and Film* (New York: Verso, 2002), 202.
8 Stendhal, *Life of Henry Brulard*, 248.
9 Stendhal, *Mémoires d'un touriste*, vol. 2, in *Oeuvres Complètes*, vol. 16 (Geneva and Paris: Slatkine Reprints, 1986), 146. My translation.
10 Dubbini, *Geography of the Gaze*, 159.
11 Stendhal, *Life of Henry Brulard*, 155.
12 Ibid., 317. In French, this last sentence reads: "Frédéric II ne s'est guère fait lire et dès 20 ans songeait à la route L." See Stendhal, *Vie de Henry Brulard*, vol. 2, in *Oeuvres Complètes*, vol. 21 (Geneva and Paris: Slatkine Reprints, 1986), 137.
13 Ibid., 261.
14 Ibid., 341.
15 Anthony Vidler, "Diagrams of Utopia," in *The Activist Drawing: Retracing Situationist Architectures from Constant's New Babylon to Beyond*, ed. Catherine de Zegher and Mark Wigley (Cambridge, MA: MIT Press, 2001), 87.
16 Stendhal, *Life of Henry Brulard*, 141.
17 Ibid., 148.
18 See, for example, Edward Robbins, *Why Architects Draw* (Cambridge, MA: MIT Press, 1994).
19 Peter Eisenman in some sense supports this premise by promoting the diagram as rational as well as mystical, criticizing Freud's idea that only subjects and not diagrams can recollect and reconstruct the past. See Peter Eisenman, *Diagram Diaries* (New York: Rizzoli, 1999), 35.

20 Stendhal, *Life of Henry Brulard*, 234.
21 Ibid., 174.
22 Ibid., 97.
23 Ibid., 68.
24 Roland Barthes, *Camera Lucida: Reflections on Photography*, trans. Richard Howard (New York: Hill and Wang, 1981), 25.

Perceptual Unfolding in the Palace of Minos

Rachel McCann

Chora

THROUGH A PROGRESSION of thought that began in ancient Greece and reached a watershed with Descartes, Western culture came to conceive the world as divided into mutually exclusive categories of mind and matter, subject and object. These dualities still configure the way we conceive and act in relation to the world around us, including architecture. We gain intellectual clarity about our natural and built surroundings by reducing the aspects under consideration, and nothing more completely escapes the confines of the Cartesian mind than its purported antithesis, dumb matter. To grasp the material world, we commonly attempt to circumscribe it in language, but, as Elaine Scarry contends, language reaches its limits when confronted with the profoundly abstract and the profoundly concrete.[1] Thus confounded by the material and spatial complexity of the natural and built world, the philosopher – and the architectural historian – can achieve certainty only by reducing this complexity to a manipulable mental construct: to language, geometry, or idea. It is only then, as Martin Dillon points out, that "the philosopher may speak with absolute assurance, but not about the world."[2]

When examining any architecture, its materiality and spatiality exceed our attempts to circumscribe it in words. When examining ancient architecture, we are faced with acts of building that preceded rational dualism, and our conventional historical methods are called into question. For example, Minoan architecture manifests the Minoans' immersion within their natural environment, an immersion unaffected by the rational bifurcations that characterize our own architecture and our methods for understanding it. French phenomenologist Maurice Merleau-Ponty's phenomenology of perception, which recasts Cartesian subject and object as cooperative participants in a dynamic process of perceptual unfolding, offers a means for understanding architecture that draws from our shared embodiment with it and with the natural world, and thus offers a particularly fruitful means for understanding ancient architecture in general and Minoan architecture in particular.

Merleau-Ponty's focus on embodied experience stems from an awareness of our shared corporeity with the world and thus allows us to find significance in architecture's material and spatial aspects rather than dismissing them as meaningless excess. An approach that accords such significance to the body of architecture takes advantage of an immense source of knowledge that often remains unconsidered in architectural history. Focusing on intercorporeal experience, this approach provides a valuable complement to historical approaches that focus primarily on human ideation.[3]

Attunement to embodied experience slows down the rush to meaning, allowing us to dwell attentively in the murky depths of embodied perception. Contrary to the quest for certainty that fuels so many of our human activities, this slowing down recalls us to a dimension too long ignored in the history and theory of architecture. In our rush to have Minoan architecture *mean* something, we concentrate on symbolism and iconography. Even historians such as Mircea Eliade and Henri Frankfort suggest that ancient cultures imitated ideal city forms in their religious architecture, and Minoan scholarship focuses largely on the symbolic associations of its religious rituals, art, and architecture.[4] Yet the Minoans, perhaps more than any other culture, grounded these acts and artefacts in embodied movement and in the dynamic unfolding of natural and human-crafted phenomena.

MOVEMENT IN MINOAN RITUAL AND ART

The Minoans formed their ideas of the divine in response to the dynamic qualities and sensuous presence of their environment. Their rituals, art, and architecture, until the last phase of the great temple-palace at Knossos, the Palace of Minos, show the culture's deep immersion in a world of unfolding phenomena that reveals the invisible structure of the transcendent. Their religion centres on a kinetic form of epiphany: their detailed nature frescoes achieve coherence through pattern and movement, and their labyrinthine architecture downplays hierarchy and goal in favour of corporeal and temporal experience. All these acts manifest the Minoans' attunement to the dynamic qualities of their world and their own dynamic responses to those qualities.

The dynamism of the Cretan landscape infused the Minoans' beliefs and actions. They worshipped nature deities, whom they associated with mountains, trees, mythical and earthly animals, and plant forms such as poppies and lilies. The rituals associated with these deities employ various forms of rapid and vigorous movement: we see images of adorants bending trees, curling over to embrace upright stones, dancing wildly (see fig. 6.1).[5]

Fig. 6.1 Minoan seals showing ritual activity. Author with Justin Taylor, after Arthur J. Evans, *The Palace of Minos: A Comparative Account of the Successive Stages of the Early Cretan Civilization as Illustrated by the Discoveries at Knossos*, 4 vols. (London: Macmillan, 1900).

Rapid movement summoned deities into the human realm in a kinetic form of epiphany, activating and sacralizing a previously void centre. It is believed that priestesses and priests, by donning sacral garments, acted as surrogates for the deities during these epiphanic rituals. The divine arrival was effected by a priestess, clothed as a goddess, moving through ritual space to arrive at the sacred centre and superimposing the divine realm spatially and temporally onto the human realm. When the goddess arrived, sacred space sprang up around her, encompassing the ritual participants.

It is significant that, in the Minoan culture, epiphany required a moving, human surrogate for invisible truths. The invisible was made visible not in static, frontal, conceptual form, as one might address an idol in a shrine, but in a dynamic way that pulsed with the rhythms of the cosmos. Minoan art developed conventions for indicating rapid movement and distance perspective, two perceptual cues that emphasize the dynamic relationship between the perceiver and the perceived. A gold ring from the tomb at Isopata (see fig. 6.2) shows a goddess descending into the middle of a group of worshipping priestesses. The scene takes place among blooming lilies. The goddess is shown twice, first at a distance and then at the moment of arrival. The distant goddess is small and positioned high within the composition. Her hair, denoted by a series of dots, flies up

Fig. 6.2 Gold ring from tomb at Isopata. Author with Justin Taylor, after Evans, *The Palace of Minos*.

behind her, indicating motion, and her toes are pointed downward. The arriving goddess has one hand down towards the priestesses and the other raised in a gesture of benediction. Although she has not reached the ground, her feet are flat, indicating that she has stopped descending, yet her hair is flying, indicating motion. She seems to have been drawn at the precise moment of arrival.

The Minoan preoccupation with movement is emphasized in a number of carved scenes where figures are caught in mid-gesture as a moment of ritual action frozen in time. A gold signet ring from Vapheio (see fig. 6.1, top) aptly illustrates this point: the figure on the left is pulling a tree downward, and the central figure is dancing with enough vigour to send her hair flying horizontally. Objects float in the air, filling the depicted space in dynamic relationship to the moving figures.

H.A. Groenewegen-Frankfort characterizes Minoan art mainly in terms of movement, identifying movement as one of the principles that gives this art its coherence. The expression of movement may take the form of dramatic ritual, of abstract spirals or whirling motifs, or of patterns whose motion "can be followed in all directions."[6] Minoan art exhibits antithetical movement, torsion, intricate and dynamic patterns, and movement around a void centre.

This attunement to movement led Minoan artists to manipulate depicted forms so that pictorial rendering and structured narrative are both subordinate to the depiction of movement. Minoan art often depicts "antithetical movement," where figures move in two directions simultaneously to achieve an ultimate state of dynamic counterbalance (see fig. 6.3). A deer may turn its head backwards while leaping forward; a dancing figure may twist in two directions at once. This duality of movement emphasizes the act of moving itself rather than the ultimate goal of the movement. Dancers are caught up in the immediacy of the moment; running animals are not necessarily fleeing a hunter;[7] plant stalks sway in response to a world continually in motion.

Torsion, in the forms of opposed curves and spirals, is a primary motif in Minoan art. These opposed, organic shapes are evident in many of the plant and animal forms featured in Minoan art, including the lily, papyrus, cuttlefish (octopus), and argonaut.[8] Even the characteristic Minoan double axe (see fig. 6.4) is formed by opposing curves. Minoan architecture, with its twisting corridors and stairs, parallels these artistic motifs.

Minoan art derives coherence from its complex relations of movement and form. Its organic life forms are completely integrated with the larger surfaces they occupy, as tendrils curve around and swell out in sympathy with the bulging of clay vases and vegetation wraps around to embrace the curving edges of sealstones. This coherent complexity is one of the distinguishing characteristics of Minoan art, as relations among elements, contours, and edges take precedence over narrative structure.[9]

Groenewegen-Frankfort writes of the "absolute mobility" exhibited by animals and people in Minoan art: dancers with dangling feet, seated figures with no visible support.[10] As she describes it, "Figures appear to float – by no means *in vacuo* – but, as it were, suspended, caught, like a patch of colour in the centre of an intricate design."[11] The overall pattern unifies the surface into one immanent whole in which

> there is no near, no far, barely up and down. Such separable entities as occur in the form of single beasts, plants, and stones – though plants frequently seem to merge into one another – are caught in the web of a living world that has indefinite orientation and indefinite multiple relations.[12]

In this dynamic relational state, figures are related not to one element of the landscape but to the environment as a whole, and the depiction of unity through movement is more important than attachment to any one surface. Thus the dynamic movement of unfolding phenomena and the coherent web of relationships between perceiver and perceived are vividly embodied in the pattern of Cretan art.

Fig. 6.3 MM III seal. Evans, *The Palace of Minos*.

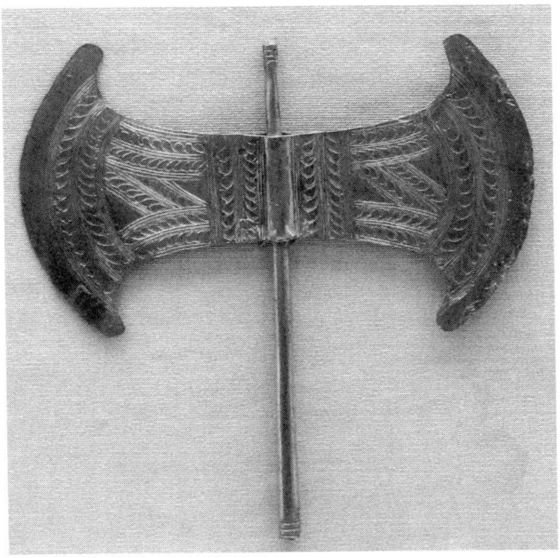

Fig. 6.4 Minoan double axe.

MOVEMENT IN MINOAN ARCHITECTURE

The relation between the variable and the stable, between the immanent and the eternal, must be negotiated constantly by every culture. John Dewey, in *Experience and Nature*, writes of the seduction of the eternal: "The permanent enables us to rest, it gives peace; the variable, the changing, is a constant challenge."[13] As evidenced by their art and architecture, the Minoans embraced this challenge, defining a stable, sacred centre defined in relation to the dynamic elements around it. Dewey's description of classical philosophy stands in marked contrast to the Minoan focus on movement:

> Classic philosophy says so much about unity and so little about unreconciled diversity, so much about the eternal and permanent, and so little about change …, so much about necessity and so little about contingency, so much about the comprehending universal and so little about the recalcitrant particular.[14]

It is precisely the emphasis on the diverse and the changing, an embracing of the "recalcitrant particular," that defines the spirit of Minoan art and architecture. Minoan religion invokes the eternal by focusing on the immediacy of the spatio-temporal present. Their sealstones depict ritual characterized by exuberant action. Their landscape frescoes show the immediate, vital presence of nature. The dynamic motifs in their art focus on movement and relationships. Their labyrinthine architecture, with its constantly changing foci, relates inevitably to the open nucleus of a central court. Their lustral basin sanctuaries, approached by descending and turning, connect the human and chthonic realms through spiralling movement.

In *Phenomenology of Perception*, Maurice Merleau-Ponty characterizes sensory experience as both spatial and communicative. It is spatial in that sensory experience inheres us in our setting and sets up an immediate preconceptual relation between us and what surrounds us. It is communicative in that our surroundings elicit responses from us that engage both body and mind. We respond to the beckoning of a thing or a place first in a primal, inarticulate way and then, after an interval, conceptually. The immediacy of the world for us, according to Merleau-Ponty, is

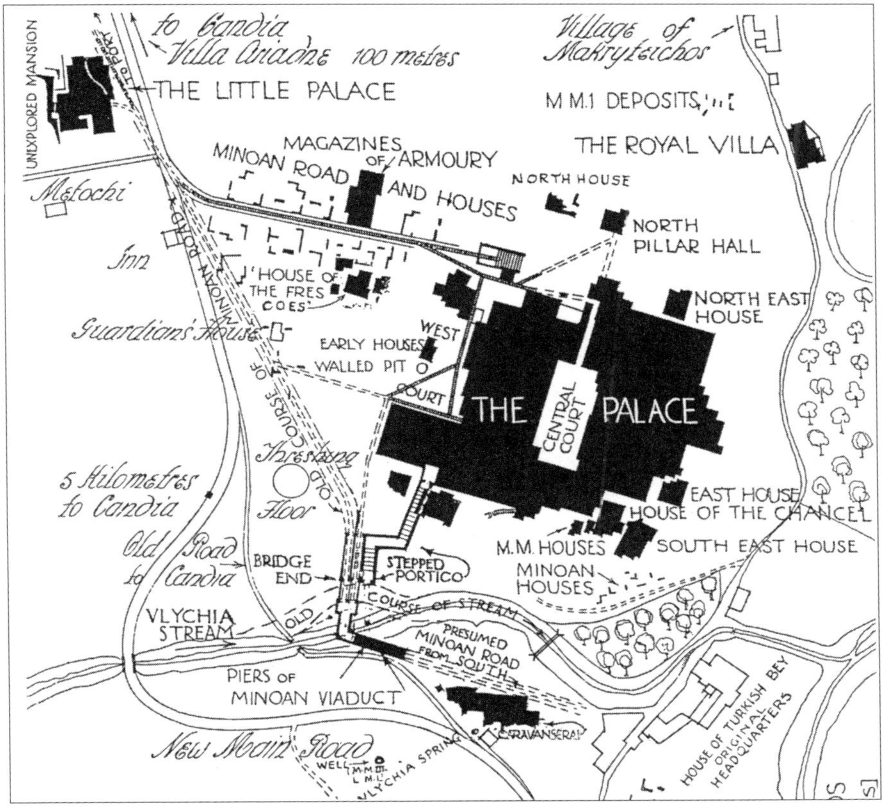

Fig. 6.5 Site plan of the Palace of Minos, with north at the top. Evans, *Palace of Minos*.

predicated on the imperceptible lag between our bodily response to a situation and our conceptualization of it.[15]

The Palace of Minos (see figs. 6.5 and 6.6), unearthed and partially restored by Sir Arthur Evans in the early twentieth century, draws out this interval by de-emphasizing the organizational and formal elements that are most readily subsumed into mental constructs. Confounding our ability to categorize and summarize, the palace's labyrinthine arrangement, ambiguous spatial boundaries, and manipulation of light delay conceptualization and demand a corporeal response to the architecture.[16] The Minoan de-emphasis on frontality, hierarchy, and overt order, and a concomitant emphasis on movement and changing viewpoints, privilege immediate experience, enfolding participants within each unfolding moment of the architectural encounter and resonating with Merleau-Ponty's description of perception as communion, even coition, of our body and the world.

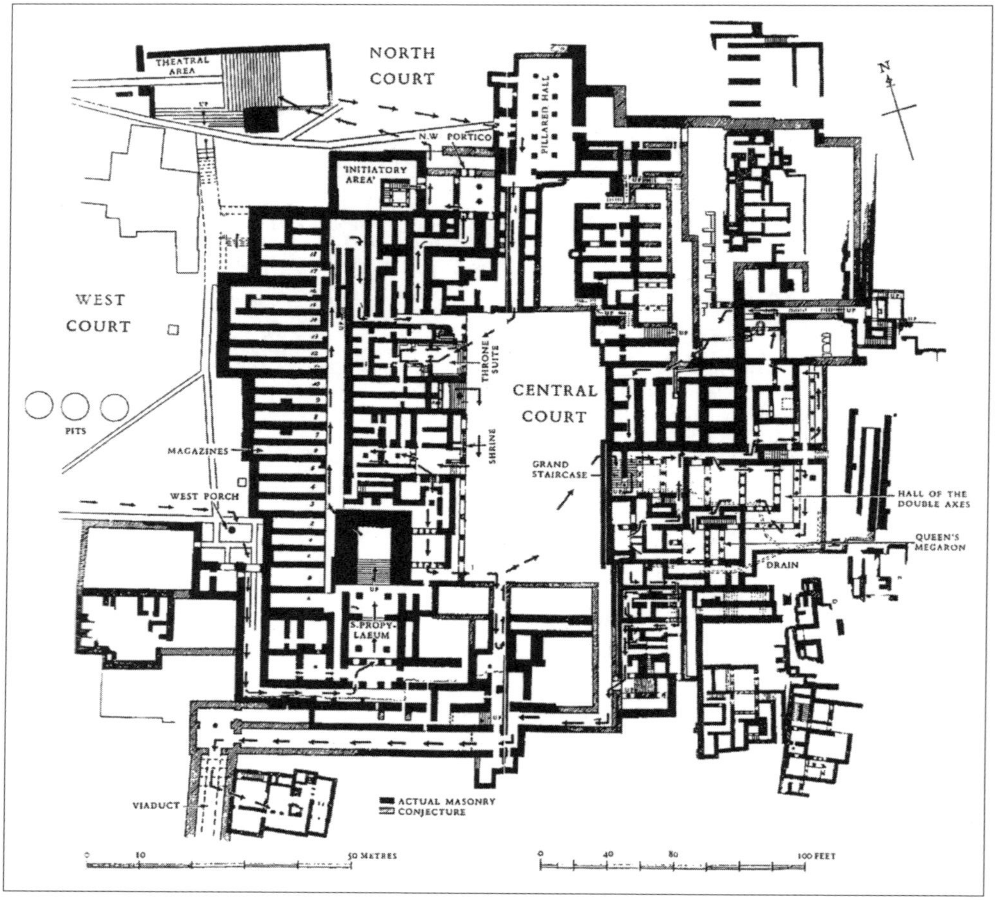

Fig. 6.6 Plan of the palace. J.D.S. Pendlebury, *A Handbook to the Palace of Minos at Knossos* (London: Macmillan, 1933). The West Porch is just below the southeast corner of the West Court. The Throne Room (labelled "Throne Suite") is near the northwest corner of the Central Court.

The Palace of Minos embodies the experiential richness of Minoan art, and its labyrinthine arrangement produces the experiential equivalent of the frescoes' complex, patterned relationships. The architecture denies vistas; engages the body with turns, changing horizons, and layered space; juxtaposes frontal and oblique views of important architectural elements; and distributes itself around a number of void centres. The temple consists of discrete groups of rooms and passages that relate ineluctably back to the central court, just as the dancing worshipers on the Isopata ring relate to the hierophanic space around which they have gathered. Thus the variable is opposed to the stable, the temporal to the eternal, deepening the character of each.

APPROACHING THE THRONE ROOM BASIN

The principal approach to the Throne Room sanctuary begins in the West Court (see figs. 6.6 and 6.7): either from the west, approaching the west façade directly while approaching the West Porch from the side (see figs. 6.8 and 6.9), or from the north, approaching the porch frontally while travelling alongside the west façade (see figs. 6.10 and 6.11). Either way, one of these two important elements is experienced obliquely while the other is confronted head-on, juxtaposing a corporeal experience and a symbolic one.

Contrary to a frontal view, where symbolic articulation presents itself as a visual whole, an oblique perception is mainly corporeal. We pass too

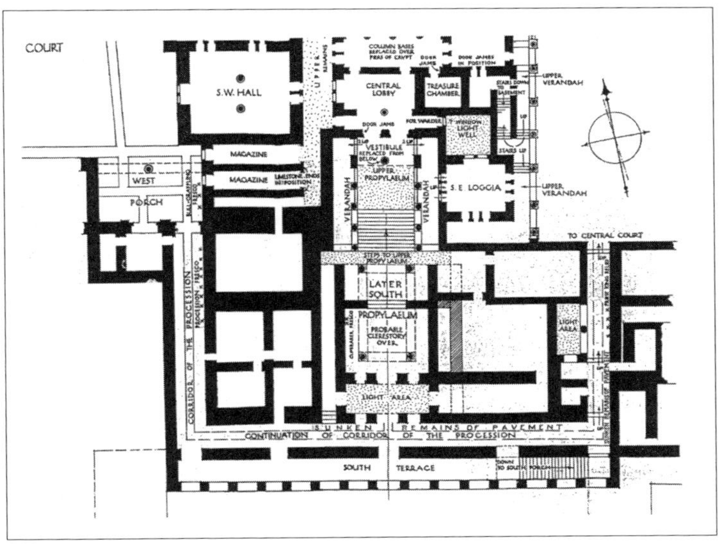

Fig. 6.7 Partial plan of palace showing West Porch and Corridor of the Procession. Evans, *Palace of Minos*.

Fig. 6.8 Top: Extant oblique approach, from the west, to the West Porch. Photograph by author.

Fig. 6.9 Bottom: Conjectural restoration of oblique approach. Author with Justin Taylor.

Fig. 6.10 Top: Extant frontal approach to the West Porch. Photograph by author.

Fig. 6.11 Bottom: Conjectural restoration of frontal approach. Author with Justin Taylor.

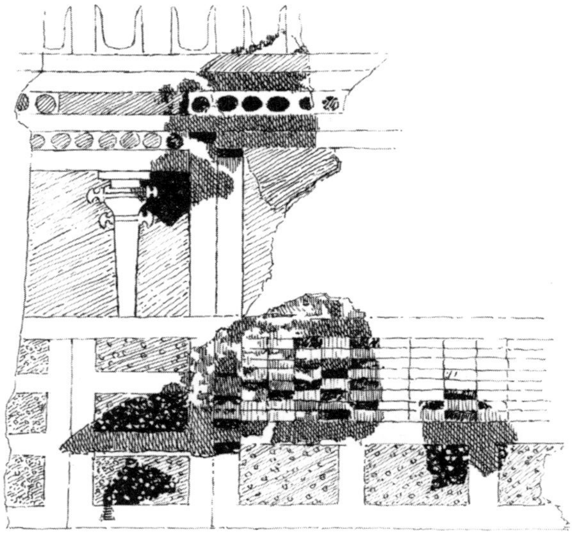

Fig. 6.12 Drawing of fresco fragment from Thirteenth Magazine at Knossos, showing façade detail thought to correspond to the west façade of the Palace of Minos. Evans, *Palace of Minos*.

close to the wall to form an overall picture of it, to grasp its elements simultaneously and apprehend their compositional relationships; instead, we experience each element sequentially. Spatially repeated elements on a frontally viewed façade become temporally repetitive events along our path. Small offsets that appear frontally only as generators of shadow lines take on discernible depth as we approach them obliquely and their depth folds out from inconsequence into perceptually inhabitable space. Conversely, windows collapse into vertically attenuated rectangles that no longer connect visually beyond the wall. From afar, a frontally perceived façade presents itself principally as a set of related shapes, whereas an obliquely perceived wall presents itself spatially and materially from the onset of our experience of it. As we approach a façade frontally, it slowly grows larger, and previously unnoticed levels of detail emerge. Conversely, the obliquely experienced wall changes at every step, opening and closing, advancing and receding. From either path to the West Porch, the pictorial experience of the frontal view forms a constant contrast to the spatial experience of the wall at our side.

A highly detailed Minoan façade (see fig. 6.12),[17] with rhythmic solids and voids, is perceived quite differently from different viewpoints. In a frontal view, pictorial and symbolic relationships are paramount. We perceive all the elements simultaneously, grasping the spatial and hierarchic relationships among them. The deep, shadowed, open porches recall the interiority of Minoan sanctuaries; Minoan columns enframe these spaces with the splendour of the goddess, and the vertical horns of consecration stand majestically against the open space and bright light of the sky. These symbolic, spatial relationships are made stable and eternal by the loss of temporal experience when viewing all the elements simultaneously.

In an oblique perception, visual symbolism collapses into temporal, rhythmic experience, and the approach to the West Porch plays one against the other. While simultaneously focusing on the façade ahead, we encounter the adjacent wall corporeally (see fig. 6.11). Hovering at our shoulder, it recedes and advances at intervals, forming an irregular spatial counterpoint to the straight line of our advancement towards the porch and providing a temporal and corporeal translation of the visual composition of the façade ahead. The massive presence of the wall at our side echoes our footsteps, throws us into shadow, lowers the ambient temperature, and radiates the smell of stone. It exceeds and demands constant readjustment of our visual focus by looming upward out of sight and by rhythmically opening and closing pockets of space as perspectival relationships adjust in response to our movement through the space. Decorative patterns of stone and tilework become sequential events, one leading us to the next. Columns stand out in spatial relief against the side walls of their porches, capturing space rather than marking points.

The nature of the approach to the temple is characteristic of its experience as a whole, as dynamic perceptual unfolding complements static viewing, illuminating the stable through variable experience. We see this relationship repeated in the West Porch, where the corporeal experience of the central column interferes with the visual experience of the bull fresco. We see it again in the Corridor of the Procession, where the labyrinthine effect of a corridor with multiple turns is complemented by the relentless forward focus of celebrants in the frescoes that line its walls. We see it yet again in the Throne Room, where the focus on the heralded west door is interrupted by the cross-axial relationship between the basin and the throne.

The West Porch's open north side is divided into two bays by a central wooden Minoan column, while the porch's interior east wall features a fresco of a life-size spotted bull "in violent action"[18] (see figs. 6.13 and 6.14). Approaching from the north, the figural location of the column overwhelms an oblique view of the fresco (see fig. 6.15). From the west, the column cleaves a frontal view of the fresco down its very middle (see fig. 6.16). In either approach, the column disrupts the experience, interrupting both the view of the fresco and the physical act of crossing the porch.[19] The experience is similar to Minoan ritual: as in bull jumping, dancing, or violently shaking a tree, corporeal experience takes precedence over visual, and the divine is experienced primarily through movement.

Fig. 6.13 Plan of West Porch, with north at the bottom. Evans, *Palace of Minos*.

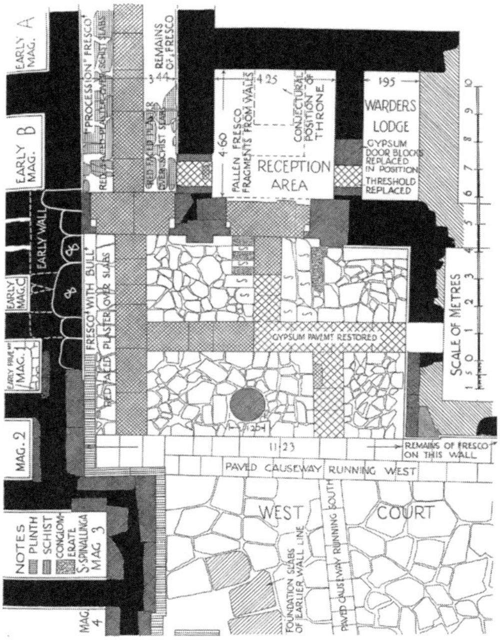

Fig. 6.14 Perspective of West Porch, with central column cut away. Evans, *Palace of Minos*.

Fig. 6.15 Top: Conjectural restoration of frontal approach at porch. Author with Justin Taylor.

Fig. 6.16 Bottom: Conjectural restoration of oblique approach at porch. Author with Justin Taylor.

In each of these instances, constantly changing physical relationships reveal the divine and eternal through the variable and momentary.

The bull fresco in the West Porch is perceived in constantly changing reference to the single column and other elements. To reach the Corridor of the Procession, we follow a zigzagging path through the porch indicated by rectangular gypsum paving stones. This path directs us south, east, and south again, channelling us between the column and the west wall to face a small, importantly placed chamber, turning us and filling our view momentarily with the bull fresco as an uninterrupted tableau, and turning us yet again to enter the corridor (see figs. 6.17, 6.18, and 6.19).

Four elements within the porch – the column, the bull fresco, the votive room, and the corridor entrance – combine in an experience wherein focus and orientation are constantly shifting. We perceive the column and the fresco simultaneously in shifting relations to each other as we proceed through the porch. We first confront the column blocking the fresco, then turn away from the fresco to experience the spatial push of the column as it channels us through the entrance, then turn to confront the fresco again, this time with the column hovering in the periphery. A detour towards the votive room relegates both column and fresco to the periphery; then we retrace our steps to confront the column and fresco sequentially before turning into the Corridor of the Procession. The spatial sequence weaves a series of abrupt turns and simultaneous focal points in shifting relationships, intertwining visual foci and corporeal presence into a dynamic, patterned process of perceptual unfolding.

The labyrinthine nature of movement through the porch is further enriched by the porch's ambiguous spatial boundaries and manipulation of light. Although the porch has solid walls on the east and west, the east wall is dematerialized by the bull fresco. Two doorways in the south wall function as a dithyron,[20] transforming the south wall into an ambiguous spatial boundary, and the north side is completely open except for the centrally placed column. At most times, the open north boundary admits only indirect light, putting the entire porch in shade, although it is probable that the doorway to the Corridor was emphasized by southern and western light coming from beyond it.[21] But late in the day between spring and fall equinoxes, the sun strikes an angle through the porch, illuminating different parts of the bull fresco as it moves, sinking and angling progressively towards the doorway to the Corridor of the Procession.

Figs. 6.17, 6.18, and 6.19 Conjectural restoration of successive moments in travelling through the West Porch. Author with Justin Taylor.

Light reflecting from the walls and floor of the exterior court further brightens the ambiguously held space.

A spiralling path through the Corridor of the Procession and the Central Court leads to the Throne Room complex (see figs. 6.20 and 6.21), a lustral basin sanctuary[22] and the setting for dramatic enactments of kinetic epiphany. Here again, static and variable experience work in concert. A permeable polythyron (see fig. 6.22) leads west from the Central Court down four steps into the Throne Room anteroom. The anteroom focuses on an off-centred dithyron in the west wall (see fig. 6.23), containing operable wooden doors or screens that lead into the Throne Room.

The brightness of the Central Court, with the strong Cretan sunlight reflecting from the light surfaces of its limestone floor and the anteroom wall, gives way to cool half-shade inside the anteroom. The floor was originally covered in red stucco in the centre with white gypsum slabs around the perimeter, and a large, shallow gypsum basin found overturned in the corner was likely originally placed in the centre of the anteroom floor. Although most of the wall decorations were destroyed by fire,[23] a fresco fragment from the south wall suggests the presence of another bull fresco.

The relation between the bull fresco and the polythyron recalls the relation between the fresco and column of the West Porch. We obtain a fragmented and oblique view of the fresco from the Central Court, but we must pass through the polythyron, experiencing its depth closely on both sides, before viewing the fresco clearly. Even within the anteroom, facing the entrance to the Throne Room gives an oblique view of the fresco. If we turn to face the fresco, the goal of the Throne Room is momentarily denied.

As in the West Porch, all four walls of the anteroom have different degrees of solidity, forming an ambiguously bounded space that can be altered by opening and closing the polythyra. Changing sun angles at various times either light the anteroom fully and directly, send thin slivers of light obliquely through to the main sanctuary to illuminate the boundary of the basin, or light the space only indirectly.

After the semi-shade of the anteroom, the Throne Room is a darker space that could have been made darker still by closing the wooden doors in its entry wall. The Throne Room floor exhibits the same colour contrast between centre and periphery as the anteroom, indicating that everyday movement may have occurred around the periphery of the room,

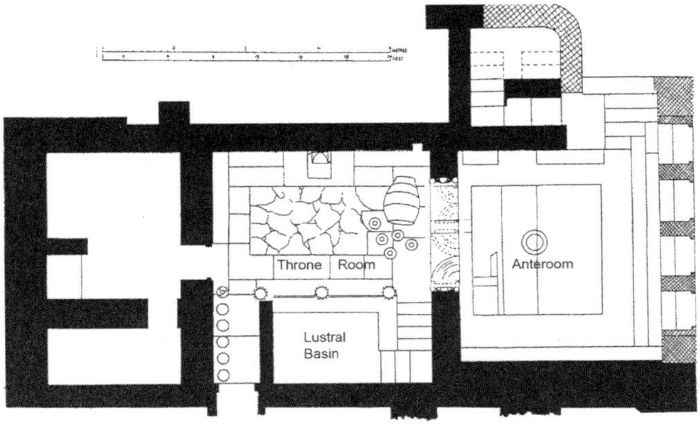

Fig. 6.20 Plan of Throne Room sanctuary and service areas. Author, after Evans.

Fig. 6.21 Perspective view of Throne Room, looking west. Evans, *Palace of Minos*.

reserving the centre as especially sacred space. The eastern dithyron creates a perceptual axis with a decorated doorway in the west wall through which a priestess entered the ritual space.[24] The room's north and west walls are lined with a stone bench, interrupted by a gypsum throne in the middle of the north wall. The throne faces a depressed lustral basin to the south (see fig. 6.21), creating a perceptual cross-axis.

The Throne Room basin (see fig. 6.24) is lined and paved with gypsum, reached by descending eight wide, shallow steps in an L-shaped stair. It is likely that a priestess descended into the basin to take on the persona of the goddess and then ascended to the main sanctuary to communicate

Fig. 6.22 Polythyron leading from Central Court to Throne Room anteroom. Evans restoration. Photograph by author.

Fig. 6.23 View of anteroom, looking west. Evans restoration. Photograph by author.

with her worshipers. The basin's walls are Venetian red with white and grey bands around the upper portion.[25] A low wall and bench run between sanctuary and basin, with Minoan columns rising from (or sunk into) the bench. The top of the wall would be just above eye level to a priestess in the basin. She would, however, be able to see the top area of the Throne Room frieze, the red walls and white bands so similar to those in the basin. The upper friezes unify the basin and the main sanctuary, while other architectural elements (such as the low wall, columns, and beam) separate them. The basin thus exists both as a part of the Throne Room and as a distinct sacred area. Some archaeologists, including Evans, postulate a clerestory above the basin, with a gallery above the Throne Room allowing views to the basin from an upper storey.[26] In addition to the gallery providing another layer of visual participation, a light well would greatly have increased the basin's manifestation of the *axis mundi*.

Fig. 6.24 View of basin from gallery above. Evans restoration. Photograph by author.

Fig. 6.25 View to basin from anteroom. Evans restoration. Photograph by author.

The Throne Room has several foci for ritual: the west door, the lustral basin, the central red square, and the throne. The basin itself, with its partial separation from the main room, the prescribed set of movements to enter and leave it, and its vertical associations with both the chthonic and the celestial realms, must have contributed to the crucial moment of taking on the goddess's identity. Afterward, the transformed priestess could have taken her place in the red centre to communicate with the occupant of the red gypsum throne or she could have occupied the throne.[27] A small group of people could witness the ceremony from the anteroom, screened by the polythyron (see fig. 6.25), and a larger group could participate less directly from the central court.

The interplay between the variable and the stable exhibited by the torsion and antithetical movement of Minoan art is embodied in the Throne Room sanctuary by the spiralling and antithetical movements of the priestess and other participants. Just as the space in Minoan art is activated by moving figures in a patterned, dynamic relationship, so the space of the Throne Room is activated by the movement of participants among the various foci of the sanctuary. The throne and the basin face each other across a void, charged centre through which a priestess moves. The centre is further activated by the attraction between the western door and the viewing frames of the dithyron. The priestess skirts the void centre in her spiralling movement from the western door down into the basin and, on re-emerging, moves into it to address or approach the throne. The priestess's clockwise spiral into the basin is mirrored in the larger counter-clockwise spiral of the celebrants who approach the Throne Room from the West Porch. The celebrants' path wraps around and contains the path of the priestess, combining to form opposing spirals wrapped around the basin. The layered and highly experiential architecture of the basin sanctuary sequence enables Minoan rituals to layer sacred time and space over the mortal realm through these interwoven movements.

CONCLUSION

In Minoan rituals and artefacts, visual and symbolic aspects are swallowed up in movement, and movement is also central to understanding Minoan architecture. The Palace of Minos's boundaries, a combination of solid walls, punched windows, polythyra, and columned parapets, are ambiguous and transformable, resulting in a spatial complexity impossible to clarify conceptually but richly understood through embodied experience. The temple's lack of frontality, its complex organization, and its subtle manipulations of light all invite participatory experience of the space.

To be understood, the Palace of Minos must be experienced not as an object presented to the gaze but, rather, through time, through the medium of movement. The approach to the Throne Room basin sanctuary juxtaposes oblique and frontal perception, offers changing relations among visual foci, and augments visual experience with corporeal presence. The permeable boundaries of the Throne Room sanctuary emphasize the interconnection of elements within a patterned whole. Its multiple foci, among which attention shifts during different stages of the ritual, downplay fixed hierarchy in favour of variable experience. The vertical relationships of the basin, along with its simultaneous separation from and containment within the main sanctuary, illuminate the layered complexity of Minoan religious experience.

Much has been written about the symbolic content of ancient architecture and about its material construction, but the embodied experience of the architecture – where mind and body intertwine – remains largely unexplored. Ancient cultures were immersed in the material and sensuous aspects of their surroundings, and were highly attuned to the dynamic processes and movements of those surroundings. Their architecture can be understood best through its interaction with the human body, materially and through movement. Thus, the way their architecture interacts with the human body materially and through movement is primary to understanding them. We need to understand the Palace of Minos in this layered way, taking into account the combined experience of moving, seeing – both directly and obliquely – and understanding symbolically, as cooperative participants in its perceptual unfolding.

NOTES

1 Elaine Scarry, *The Body in Pain: The Making and Unmaking of the World* (New York: Oxford University Press, 1985), "Introduction," esp. 3–4.

2 Martin C. Dillon, *Merleau-Ponty's Ontology* (Evanston, IL: Northwestern University Press, 1997), 12. Dillon draws attention to the difference between the quest for certainty, which has led us to reduce things to manipulable mental constructs, and a search for truth, which is "an attempt to pierce [but not eliminate] the opacity of the world" (10). He also gives a detailed explanation of why both empiricism and intellectualism, drawing as they do upon the dualistic ground of Cartesian thought, fail to solve the problem of gaining knowledge about the world.

3 It must be stressed that corporeal experience is not merely personal. As David Abram writes, "The phenomenal field [is not] the isolate haunt of a

solitary ego, but a collective landscape, constituted by other experiencing subjects as well as by oneself." See David Abram, *The Spell of the Sensuous: Perception and Language in a More-Than-Human World* (New York: Pantheon Books, 1996), 37. Corporeal experience is based in the body, which we share with all humanity, and is as universal as it is subjective. Symbolism, which has both commonalities and variations from culture to culture, is ultimately subjective as well. A full understanding of architecture must combine these two kinds of experience.

4 See Mircea Eliade, *The Sacred and the Profane: The Nature of Religion*, trans. Willard R. Trask (New York: Harcourt, Brace, and Company, 1959); Mircea Eliade, *The Myth of the Eternal Return*, trans. Willard R. Trask (Princeton: Princeton University Press, 1965); and Mircea Eliade, *Images and Symbols*, trans. Philip Mairet (Princeton: Princeton University Press, 1991). See Henri Frankfort, H.A. Groenewegen-Frankfort, John A. Wilson, and Thorkild Jacobsen, *Before Philosophy: The Intellectual Adventure of Ancient Man* (Harmondsworth, Middlesex: Penguin, 1949). For Minoan scholarship, see especially Sir Arthur J. Evans, *The Palace of Minos: A Comparative Account of the Successive Stages of the Early Cretan Civilization as Illustrated by the Discoveries at Knossos*, 4 vols. (London: Macmillan, 1900). See Nanno Marinatos, *Minoan Religion: Ritual, Image, and Symbol* (Columbia, SC: University of South Carolina Press, 1993). For a full bibliography, see Rachel McCann, "Corporeal Experience and Symbolic Communication in the Lustral Basins and the Temple at Knossos" (M.Phil. diss., University of Cambridge, 1998).

5 The storied universe that supported the rituals escapes us, but a culture without such stories is inconceivable. The tree that is being grasped or broken on several sealstones may be one example of such a story. Scholars interpret the tree as simply emblematic of an aspect of nature, but it may have figured in a narrative about the birth of the goddess or about one of her miracles. However, the Cretan tendency to depict isolated instances defies our attempts to piece together a coherent mythological narrative. We are forced back from a detached framework into the immediacy of frozen gesture.

6 H.A. Groenewegen-Frankfort, *Arrest and Movement: An Essay on Space and Time in the Representational Art of the Ancient Near East* (London: Faber and Faber, 1951), 191–2. In these ideas, Groenewegen-Frankfort follows the ideas of Friedrich Matz, *Die Frühkretischen Siegel* (Berlin: Walter de Gruyter, 1928). Matz calls the principle underlying the Cretans' multidi-

rectional patterns "unending rapport." This principle is readily observable in pottery, where diagonal designs emphasize the curvature of the vessel.

7 Groenewegen-Frankfort, *Arrest and Movement*, 199–200.

8 Gisela Walberg, *Tradition and Innovation: Essays in Minoan Art* (Mainz am Rhein: Verlag Philipp von Zabern, 1986), 10–11.

9 Therein lies the essential difference between pictorialized and pictorial motifs, as Walberg distinguishes them: pictorial motifs focus principally on their own representative content and are therefore relatively independent of the composition in which they occur and the surface they occupy; pictorialized motifs, by contrast, are formed in the first place by perceiving relationships and accentuating similarities. The relational tendencies of the latter are equal to their representational tendencies, leading them into close relationship with the overall composition and with the surface on which they appear (Walberg, *Tradition and Innovation*, 9).

10 Groenewegen-Frankfort, *Arrest and Movement*, 198.

11 Ibid., 196.

12 Ibid., 201.

13 John Dewey, *Experience and Nature* (New York: Dover, 1968), 27.

14 Ibid., 46.

15 Maurice Merleau-Ponty, *Phenomenology of Perception*, trans. Colin Smith (London: Routledge and Kegan Paul, 1962), 137.

16 These qualities led the Greeks to associate the Palace with the mythical labyrinth constructed by Daidalos to contain the Minotaur.

17 Although the archaeological remains at Knossos do not give us a clear picture of the temple façades, we have clues about their appearance from sealstones and fresco fragments that archaeologists believe represent "iconographical formulas" for temple facades. Fresco fragments found near the west façade of the Palace of Minos depict architectural elements thought to correspond to that façade. See Nanno Marinatos, "Divine Kingship in Minoan Crete," in *The Role of the Ruler in the Prehistoric Aegean*, Proceedings of a panel discussion presented at the Annual Meeting of the Archaeological Institute of America, New Orleans, Louisiana, 28 December 1992; with additions in *Aegaeum* 11: *Annales d'archéologie égéenne de l'Université de Liège et* UT-PASP, ed. Paul Rehak (Liège: Université de Liège, 1995), 44; and Kathleen Krattenmaker, "Palace, Peak and Sceptre: The Iconography of Legitimacy," in *Role of the Ruler*, 51. The fragments show multicolour tiles (or ashlar masonry) and large blocks of stone (or its

imitation) framed within wide, rectangular jambs, sills, and lintels, presumably on a lower storey. They also show pillars and a column with a capital that bears sculpted double axes. The pillars and column support elaborate entablatures made of stacked beams with carved or painted rosettes, which, in turn, support horns of consecration. The structural elements enframe the open space of balconies. These and other fragments show a complex interweaving of elements that includes level changes, a highly articulated rhythm of solid and void, a mix of colours, and a profusion of detail.

18 A.J. Evans, "Knossos: The Palace," in *The Annual of the British School at Athens*, 6th session, 1899–1900 (London: Macmillan, 1900), 12.

19 Its prominent placement here emphasizes its importance, while its fluting accentuates its height and verticality and manifests its relationship with the moving rays of the sun. Because of its orientation and its relationship to the palace mass, the column received direct sunlight only during the hours preceding sunset near the summer solstice. In addition to figural architectural placements, the column figures prominently on several sealstones and, perhaps most memorably, flanked heraldically by two lions in the Cretan-inspired Lion Gate at Mycenae. It is similar in form to the baetylic stone that figures so prominently in depictions of Minoan ritual, a stone associated with the goddess and often shown being embraced by worshipers.

20 The polythyron, the pier-and-door system typical in Minoan architecture, provides a permeable boundary between adjacent spaces that can be further manipulated by opening and closing sets of double doors. A dithyron is a polythyron with two openings.

21 The details of the south and west walls of the Corridor of the Procession are conjectural but based on other areas of the Palace. It is likely that at least the upper wall was punctuated by windows, if not opened up even further by a full clerestory.

22 The lustral basin sanctuary, associated with Minoan rituals of epiphany and initiation, typically consists of three intertwined spaces: an anteroom, a main sanctuary, and a depressed basin. The basin is contained within the main sanctuary, and all three spaces are separated either by column screens or by polythyron systems.

23 Evans, *Palace of Minos*, 4:935–6; and Evans, "Knossos," 36.

24 Griffins flank this doorway, suggesting a strong association with the goddess based on the many examples of Minoan art that show griffins flanking the goddess.

25 Evans, *Palace of Minos*, 4:907–8.

26 Ibid., 922. Clerestories are common in Minoan basins, and archaeological evidence suggests the presence of a gallery above the basin at Akrotiri. See Christos Doumas, *The Wall-Paintings of Thera*, trans. Alex Doumas (Athens: Thera Foundation, 1992), 130.

27 Before the arrival of the Mycenaeans, the priestess herself may have alternated positions between the throne and the red centre, or the throne's location may have held a cult figure or a shrine. After the Mycenaean occupation, it is likely that a king occupied the throne.

History as Storytelling in the Account of the Eleven Orders of Architecture According to Juan Caramuel de Lobkowitz

Maria Elisa Navarro Morales

MOST PEOPLE TODAY ASSOCIATE architectural treatises with the orders of classical columns; however, the term "order" appears relatively late in the history of architectural theory. Premodern writers thought about classical elements not as a canonic set of rules for proportioning but as a manifestation of symbolic meaning. It was not until Vignola published his *Regola delli cinque ordini d'architettura* in 1596 that the orders were conceived as pre-established rules to follow. Despite the acceptance and unprecedented translation and publication of Vignola's booklet, most writers continued to regard classical columns as a correspondence between part and whole that symbolized God's perfection through beauty. Vitruvius recognized only three types of columns: Doric, Ionic, and Corinthian. Renaissance authors later drew on Vitruvius's authority and added the Tuscan and the Composite, resulting in the set of five orders that architects recognize today.

In the sixteenth century, architectural discussion also included the Solomonic order as the archetypal order of the Temple of Solomon. A century later, Juan Caramuel de Lobkowitz introduced in his treatise *Architectura civil recta y obliqua* an original and perhaps unique account of the orders that increased their number to eleven. To the five traditional orders – Doric, Ionic, Corinthian, Tuscan, and Composite – Caramuel added six more: Syrian, Attic, Gothic, Mosaic, Atlantic, and Paranymphic. According to Caramuel, this number cannot be decreased or increased because each order is particular and is not a variation on another order.

Juan Caramuel de Lobkowitz was born in 1606 in Madrid, where he spent the first years of his life. Around 1631 he left Spain and never returned. Although he was a Cistercian monk, the influence of his early Jesuit education in Spain motivated him to participate in the most controversial debates of his time. Caramuel's erudition was evident in his mastery of twenty languages and the vast amount of work he produced, including two hundred manuscripts that have been kept in the city archive of Vigevano, Italy, and another seventy published volumes in libraries all over Europe. Caramuel dealt with various subjects, including theology, astronomy, mathematics, grammar, rhetoric, philosophy, steganography, Marian doctrine, and architecture; however, his moral theology, Probabilism, has been recognized as his major contribution. He corresponded with important figures such as Kircher, Mersenne, Gassendi, and Descartes. After leaving Spain, Caramuel travelled through the territories of the Empire in Bohemia, the Netherlands, and Central Europe, arriving in Italy in 1655 to join the papal court of his friend Fabio Chigi, Alexander VII. Two years later, due to the theological polemic raised by his Probabilism, he was sent as a bishop to Campana and Satriano, where he stayed until 1673. He was then appointed Bishop of Vigevano by intercession of the Spanish emperor, and it was in this Lombard city that he spent the last years of his life, dying in 1682 on the eve of the festival of the birth of the Virgin.[1]

Caramuel's architectural treatise, *Architectura civil recta y obliqua* (*Straight and Oblique Civil Architecture*), published in 1678, is a fascinating document in many ways. Behind its increase in the number of traditional orders is a concept of history as a series of stories. He understands antiquity and the more recent past not as precedents to be imitated but as precedents that help us understand the present and possibly act on the world. To do this in architecture, Caramuel not only incorporated traditions from Greco-Roman antiquity and from other places and times but also conceived the future of architecture as the leading edge of the past. Caramuel's discussion of the orders in *Architectura civil recta y obliqua* shows his understanding of the relationship between the ideal and the real as well as his recognition that humans cannot know absolute truth, which he did not regard as a limitation on action. The aim of this chapter is to unveil the various intentions behind the apparently whimsical description of the orders in his treatise. Caramuel's account presumes that history is genealogical: closer to storytelling than to modern historiography. This premise enabled history to legitimize the present, using a narrative style that helped convey moral lessons. The treatise *Architectura civil recta y obliqua* extended certain ideas presented in a previous work, *Mathesis biceps*,[2] that was published eight years earlier.

The dream of mathematics as an underlying universal language was a common thread in these two works. In the architectural treatise, mathematics, particularly geometry, played a reconciliatory role between architecture and theology. *Architectura civil recta y obliqua* was published as three large volumes. The first volume is divided into four chapters, preceded by a preliminary chapter on the Temple of Solomon. The first chapter explains the literary faculties that an architect needs, the second is dedicated to arithmetic, the third to logarithms, and the fourth to geometry. The second volume is divided into five chapters. The first one, chapter 5, is on "straight architecture," and it is in the second part of this chapter that the orders appear for the first time in the treatise. Chapter 6 explains his innovative principles on "oblique architecture"; chapter 7 is about the arts and sciences that accompany architecture; chapter 8 describes many buildings of the past; and the ninth and final chapter introduces the subject of the unpublished fourth volume on "natural architecture"[3] and provides a brief description of the plates in the next volume. The third volume of the treatise presents the 159 illustrations that accompany the text and, according to Caramuel, took thirty-five years to complete. The size of the treatise and its variety of topics may lead us to underestimate the importance of the orders in Caramuel's theory. Indeed, recent Caramuel scholars have commented on the surprising increase in the number of orders, from five to eleven, but few have paid attention to the section on "straight architecture."[4] A closer reading of the treatise reveals that every section of the book plays an important role in the elaboration of the theory and that the orders of the columns are the point of departure from which Caramuel built his innovative theory on "oblique architecture."

In Caramuel's understanding of progress, the past is important only as a stepping stone towards the present and the future. Despite his disbelief in dogmatic truths and his questioning of authority, he still recognizes earlier traditions. Contemporary analyses of Caramuel's text usually interpret his increased number of orders as radically anti-classical,[5] but his approach follows not only the Vitruvian and Renaissance traditions but also the Judeo-Christian interest in the Solomonic order.

Like almost every other architect of his time, Caramuel regarded Vitruvius as the point of departure for his argument, but he explains that Vitruvius mentioned only three types of columns – Doric, Ionic, and Corinthian – because they were the only ones he knew. He adds that if Vitruvius had known of other traditions, he would have included them in his treatise. Caramuel accepts the Vitruvian relationship between the columns and the stories of the people and places where they first appeared. He also accepts the classical relationship between the human body and the proportions of the orders, although his imagination runs free with a more detailed description in which the archetypal human body is replaced by the particular bodies of characters who speak about their own time and place. In Vitruvius, the Doric column exhibits the proportions, strength, and beauty of the body of a man; the Ionic symbolizes a woman; and the Corinthian symbolizes a maiden.[6] Caramuel starts with Vitruvius's general description of a Doric column but instead associates

Fig. 7.1 The five classical orders. From Caramuel de Lobkowitz, *Architectura civil recta y obliqua,* vol. 3, sec. 3, plate 19.

it more particularly with the body of a strong, gallant Greek soldier; the Ionic portrays the femininity of women; and the Corinthian presents not just a maiden but the very idea of virginity. In this series (see fig. 7.1) he also includes the Tuscan, which "must look like a rough man of huge strength ... a peasant or a worker,"[7] and the Composite, an order of columns that takes its ornaments from the others:

> In big cities there are always women who live licentiously and who constrain their feet in small shoes, making their feet stay small. Because of their freedom of occupation, they do not have a specific attire and instead take from the French, Italian, Tedesco, etc., what they find beautiful. It was necessary that there be columns in architecture that have a smaller base and are taller than the rest: columns that are licentiously adorned, stealing from the others their best qualities, and therefore are the most beautiful ones.[8]

The second influence on Caramuel's description of the types of columns is the Renaissance interest in the correct proportion of what are now called "orders." Caramuel alternates between "order" and "column," but he distinguishes carefully between them. For Caramuel, a column is a vertical element that supports a horizontal beam, whereas an order is "a combination of different parts that are proportioned and placed together like the parts of a whole body, with gracefulness and beauty that please the eye."[9] A column is a pragmatic support whereas an order is intended to be beautiful. It is important to remember that Renaissance architects before Serlio were not preoccupied with establishing the orders as a canonic set,[10] instead focusing their attention on proportion because beauty was identified with God. Caramuel's interest in correct proportions and proper ornaments is based on an intention to achieve beauty through human artefacts. This aligns with the tradition of his Renaissance predecessors. It may be surprising to a modern reader that Caramuel cites Alberti, Serlio, Palladio, and Vignola in only a secondary way. This is because he is more interested in the commentaries on Vitruvius by Henry Wotton, Philander, and Barbaro, which were included in the Latin edition of the *Ten Books* published by Johannes de Laet in 1649.[11]

For Caramuel, one of the ways to find truth – not only in architecture but in any science – is by following the opinions of the learned, although he would never consider authors without a critical examination and would not accept their principles if their proportions did not appear beautiful to the eye. As an example, we can consider how he determines the correct proportions of the classical orders. Caramuel assembles the opinions of various authors, compares their descriptions of each classical order, then presents a plate that compares the columns, drawn according to those individual opinions (see fig. 7.2).[12] With Caramuel, we can then choose the most perfect proportion for each type of column. Caramuel believed that reality is multifaceted and can include different opinions that may seem contradictory. Moreover, he believed that everything can be rearranged and reordered by human ingenuity. Caramuel was not satisfied with any of the arguments of the past. After assembling contradictory theories by different authors, he tried to prove that the correct proportion between the base and the shaft of the Tuscan order is 1 to 6, the Doric 1 to 7, the Ionic 1 to 8, the Corinthian 1 to 9, and the Composite 1 to 10. In trying to tame the apparently chaotic reality of the columns, the first principle he devises is an arithmetic series. By defining proportions in this way, he organizes the classical orders logically.

Caramuel's description of the Solomonic order at first seems to be a simple exegesis of the scriptures to explain contradictions among the various texts. Using the same method of comparison, he places the Old

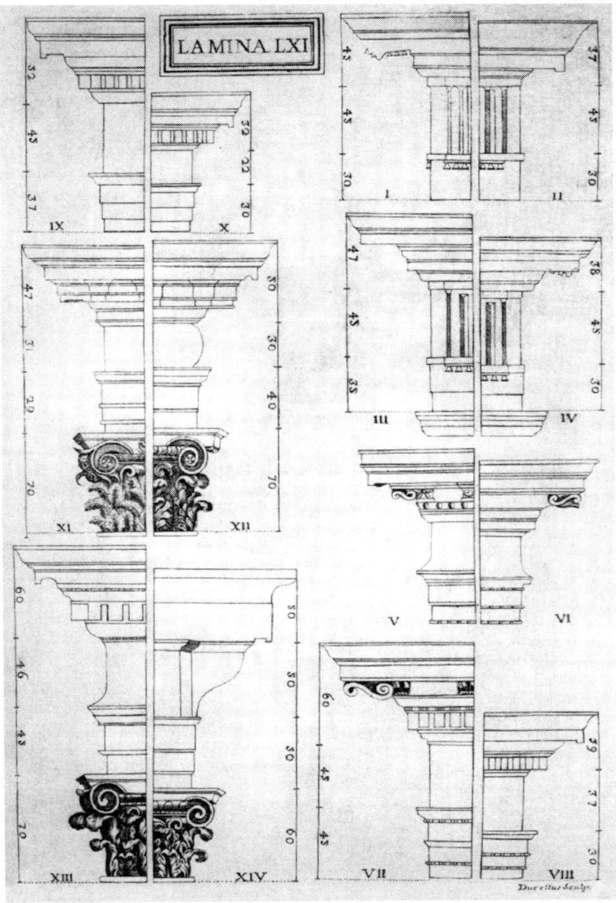

Fig. 7.2 Comparison of the classical orders. From Caramuel de Lobkowitz, *Architectura civil recta y obliqua*, vol. 3, sec. 3, plate 61.

Testament and the New Testament side by side with some Hebrew sources, including Maimonides and the reconstruction of Solomon's Temple by Jacob Judah Leon, to find the correct proportion and ornamentation for the columns of the Temple.[13] Caramuel was not the first writer to mention the columns of the Temple; the reconstruction by Juan Bautista Villalpando was an important precedent.[14] Nevertheless, Caramuel disagrees with Villalpando's description on two grounds. First, regarding proportion, Villalpando argues that the columns of the Temple had a proportion of 1 to 9 because they imitated the beauty of virgins, characteristic of the Corinthian or Composite order. Caramuel, on the other hand, believed that each type of column must have a different proportion, and after a long explanation he concluded that the columns of Solomon's Temple had a diameter of four cubits and a height of twenty.[15] Clearly, for Caramuel the proportion of this Syrian column had

Fig. 7.3 The Syrian order. From Caramuel de Lobkowitz, *Architectura civil recta y obliqua,* vol. 3, sec. 3, plate 17.

to be 1:5 so that it could be placed first in his arithmetic series, as the primordial order that God revealed to humanity as the basis for all good architecture. Caramuel also disagrees with Villalpando's reconstruction in its description of the ornaments of the columns of the Temple. In Villalpando's *In Ezechielem explanationes*,[16] the Solomonic order is described as a composite order in which ornaments combined from the other orders enabled it to be understood as the origin of architecture.[17] Caramuel, on the other hand, believed that proportion was the basis for understanding the columns of the Temple as the origin of architecture. He suggested that the columns Iachim and Booz at the entrance of the Temple were made of bronze rather than stone and that they had capitals adorned with flowers and pomegranates, very different from Greco-Roman columns (see fig. 7.3).

The next five orders that Caramuel includes in *Architectura civil recta y obliqua* do not belong to a traditional theory of the orders, so he needs to explain their principal characteristics. The Attic order had square columns on a square base (see fig. 7.4), and it is legitimized by references in Vitruvius's *Ten Books of Architecture*. Its ornaments and proportions can resemble those of the classical orders. This suggests the development of a different ordering principle, based on historical narrative rather than on the arithmetical series. The Gothic order has a shaft that consists of many slender columns. It does not have a capital but a cord that marks the joint between the column and the dome it supports. Nor do its columns have much ornament. To many contemporaries of Caramuel, it would have seemed scandalous to include an order that does not follow the canons of Roman or Greek architecture, but Caramuel's ambition to unify different historical ways of building could not disregard an architecture that was extremely beautiful and had been used frequently by the Roman Catholic Church in many places where he lived, including Spain and Bohemia. The Mosaic order is based on a Hebrew column with an undulating helical shaft (see fig. 7.5). It was known in Europe only after Tito brought back some pieces of it from Jerusalem, and it was interpreted as a modern continuation of the Solomonic order. Like the Attic order, it could adopt the proportion and ornaments of any classical order. The Atlantic order has a column shaft in the shape of a human figure that supports the load above. These figurative columns honoured important people whose memory was to be kept alive. Although the analogy between the body and the column was much more common in literary metaphors than in built examples in Italy or Greece, it seems that Asia Minor, Mesopotamia, and Egypt were more familiar with this type of column.[18] Caramuel may have included this order after discovering it in travel chronicles and recognizing several references to it in Vitruvius. Finally, the Paranymphic order is a modern descendant of the Atlantic order, in which the column is not a human body but a statue of a nymph – or one of the Graces, as he calls them. Interestingly, the plate that illustrates this order refers to military architecture, navigation, warfare, and agriculture as the graces praised in these columns (see figs. 7.6 and 7.7).

Caramuel believed that, in order to recognize rules or principles in any science, one needs to evaluate all available arguments – even if they seem contradictory – without privileging one over the others. This is evident in the genealogical, proto-historical description of the eleven orders that he attempts to integrate into a single, coherent discourse. To do so, he established a sacred origin from which architecture evolved.

Fig. 7.4 The Attic order. From Caramuel de Lobkowitz, *Architectura civil recta y obliqua,* vol. 3, sec. 3, plate 23.

The original moment occurred when God, the first architect, built the world as the first building, then revealed this divine architectural knowledge to humankind by communicating to Ezekiel the principles for the design of the Temple of Solomon. Caramuel relied on the authority of the Bible for a sacred origin that would legitimize his discourse on the orders. Based on the primordial order of the Temple of Solomon, he devised a simple arithmetic series of proportions to integrate the five classical orders as the first set of developments by humans. To these ancient orders Caramuel added two more – the Gothic and the Atlantic – that belong to traditions other than Greco-Roman, and through discourse he reconciled them with the previous ones. Finally, he characterized the three remaining

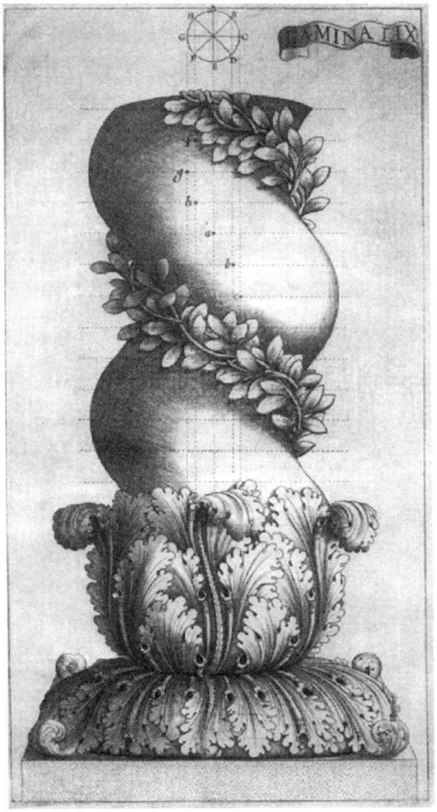

Fig. 7.5 Left: The Mosaic order. From Caramuel de Lobkowitz, *Architectura civil recta y obliqua,* vol. 3, sec. 3, plate 59.

Fig. 7.6 Right: The Atlantic order. From Caramuel de Lobkowitz, *Architectura civil recta y obliqua,* vol. 3, sec. 3, plate 62.

orders as modern continuations of the ones from antiquity. It was through historical narrative that Caramuel sought to integrate classical traditions, non-Christian civilizations, and Roman Catholicism into a unified story, using language to recognize order in a reality that otherwise seemed chaotic. According to Caramuel, stories use human imagination to show truth to unlearned people, just as biblical parables use analogy to convey important lessons and, ultimately, truth. Elsewhere in *Architectura civil recta y obliqua*, Caramuel incorporates pagan myths into the history of the church by explaining that their myths used the same type of storytelling as did the Bible and that Greek and Roman myths were based on Genesis. He even argued that Apollo was the same person as Moses.

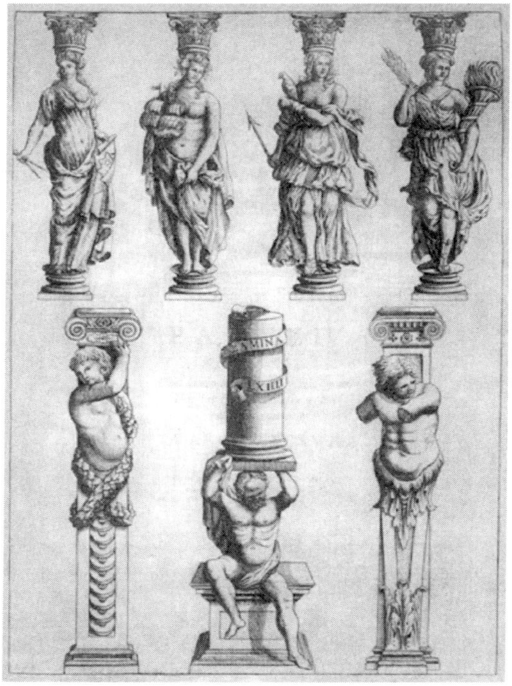

Fig. 7.7 The Paranymphic order. From Caramuel de Lobkowitz, *Architectura civil recta y obliqua*, vol. 3, sec. 3, plate 64.

Caramuel's narrative does not stop in the past; it also projects into the future. In the second part of his description of the Doric order, accompanied by plate 25 (see fig. 7.8), Caramuel proposes a new design that he thinks would be appropriate for Asia, where this order originated. Since they use elephants during both peace and war, there is nothing wrong with a column that has an elephant figure at the base and alternates elephant and deer heads as metopes.[19] The layout of the plate can also be understood as a historical narrative. At the centre is an interrupted column that divides the plate in two: at the bottom is the base; in the middle, the column shaft is replaced by a tool for lifting heavy stones; above, the column rises to meet the rest of the order. This column divides the order symmetrically. In the entablature the elephant and deer heads are not dead, as in the plates of the Renaissance, but alive. These animals have been chosen to represent both the power of the pope and the power of the prince. The prince of the church is placed at the centre, next to the prince of men, creating a perfectly balanced order. The middle part of the plate is also revealing, divided again by the broken column, with the lift-

Fig. 7.8 The Doric order. From Caramuel de Lobkowitz, *Architectura civil recta y obliqua*, vol. 3, sec. 3, plate 25.

ing tool constituting the second of three moments: to the left is the base of a column with references to classical antiquity, with a Latin inscription indicating that this is the stylobate of the Boarium Forum in Rome;[20] to the right is the aforementioned base with an elephant. This three-part layout suggests that our present practice links the past as a point of departure to the future, which is in our hands. Behind the extravagant style of Caramuel is an acute awareness of the power of human imagination to order the world through historical narrative. History helps humans not only to understand the world but also to reorder it. This early modern world is no longer simply a divine creation, and human acts are no longer predetermined by God's will. Free will presumes human responsibility for human actions but is also evidence of God's munificent creation.

The section on "straight architecture" follows the internal logic of its historical discourse but is also the basis for Caramuel's innovative principles of "oblique architecture." His political involvement in the Thirty Years' War and the conversion of the Protestants was very influential in shaping his ideas about knowledge in general, about the difference between law and absolute principles, and about the flexibility needed in particular situations. The violence he witnessed in the war made him question the premise of a dispassionate God whose law does not distinguish different degrees of human knowledge in different circumstances. To Caramuel it made no sense that a monk with a broad knowledge of the scriptures would be judged with the same rigour as a peasant or convert who had become acquainted with the commandments only recently. Caramuel believed that God is a compassionate being whose law has to be adapted to particular circumstances. In architecture he believed that principles of proportion in the orders should be modified to respond to particular situations. In politics Caramuel advocated not an ideal republic but a realist one in which peace and order would be preserved. He conceived order as an adaptation of ideal principles to real conditions. The section on "oblique architecture" presents Caramuel's proposal for architectural variations that respond to the imperfection of the world. The traditional architecture of the orders assumed ideal situations where the ground is perfectly horizontal but ignored situations where the ground is sloped or where the floor plan is round or elliptical. Caramuel responds

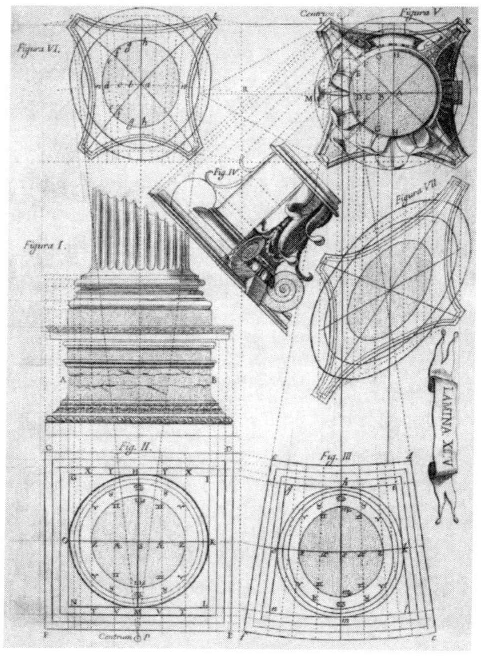

Fig. 7.9 Method to convert straight architecture into oblique architecture. From Caramuel de Lobkowitz, *Architectura civil recta y obliqua*, vol. 3, sec. 3, plate 45.

to such real site conditions by devising a geometric method that transforms "straight architecture" into "oblique architecture." The significance of his "straight architecture" is finally revealed not as an ideal but as a point of departure for his oblique method, enabling the orders to be inclined and transformed without losing their proportions (see fig. 7.9).

This previously overlooked account of the eleven orders in Caramuel's *Architectura civil recta y obliqua* plays an important role in his treatise. It also presents the mindset of an early modern world in which traditional knowledge had been shattered by scientific revolution, religious wars, and the conquest of the New World. Caramuel's intentions in his section on "straight architecture" offer us at least two lessons: (1) that historical narrative can reconcile a fragmented diversity into a more complex unity and (2) that humans can act responsibly in the world despite not having knowledge of absolute truth.

NOTES

1 Luigi Gambero, "The Authentic Marian Doctrine and Devotion of John Caramuel y Lobkowitz (1606–1682) in the Baroque Period," in *De cultu Mariano saeculis XVII–XVIII: Acta Congresus Mariologici-Mariani Internationalis in Republica Melitensi anno 1993 celebrati* (Rome: Pontificia Academia Mariana Internationalis, 1987), 4:457.

2 *Mathesis biceps, vetus, et nova in omnibus, et singulis Veterum, et Recentiorum Placita examinantur; interdum corriguntur, semper dilucidantur: et pleraque omnia Mathemata reducuntur speculative et practice ad facillimos, et expeditissimos Canones. Accedent alii tomi videlicet: Architectvra recta … Architectvra obliqva … Architectvra militaris … Mvsica … Astronomia physica*, 2 vols. (Campagna: Officina Episcopale, 1670).

3 This volume remained in manuscript form and only a few fragments of it are kept at the Archivio Storico Capitolare in Vigevano, Italy.

4 In the available literature on Caramuel's work in architecture, only Juan Antonio Ramírez devotes attention to the section on *architectura recta* and the orders. See Juan Antonio Ramírez, *Edificios y suenos: Ensayos sobre arquitectura y utopia* (Madrid: Universidades de Malaga y Salamanca, 1983), 179.

5 See Ibid., 175–82.

6 Vitruvius, *The Ten Books on Architecture*, trans. Morris Hicky Morgan (New York: Dover, 1960), 103.

7 Juan Caramuel de Lobkowitz, *Architectura civil recta y obliqua, considerada y dibuxada en el Templo de Jerusalem … promovida á suma perfeccion en el templo y palacio de S. Lorenço cerca del Escurial que inventó … el rey D. Philippe II*, 3 vols. (Vegeven: Camillo Corrado, 1678; reprint Madrid: Turner, 1984), 2:37.

8 Ibid., 2:39. My translation.

9 Ibid., vol. 2, pt. 2, art. 2, 33.

10 Joseph Rykwert, *The Dancing Column* (Cambridge and London: MIT Press, 1996), 4.

11 Juan de Laet, *M. Vitruvii Pollionis de architectvra libri decem* (Amsterdam: Apud Ludovicum Elzevirium, 1649).

12 Caramuel de Lobkowitz, *Architectura civil recta y obliqua*, 2:80–83.

13 Jacob Judah Leon, *Retrato del Templo de Selomo* (Middelburg: Moulert, 1642).

14 Juan Bautista Villalpando, *In Ezechielem explanationes et apparatus urbis ac templi hierosolymitani* (Rome: Typis Illefinsi Ciaccony, 1596–1604).

15 Caramuel de Lobkowitz, *Architectura civil recta y obliqua*, 2:53.

16 Juan Bautista Villalpando, *El Templo de Salomon*, ed. Juan Antonio Ramírez, 2 vols. (Madrid: Siruela, 1991), 1:350–1.

17 Alberto Pérez-Gómez, "Juan Bautista Villalpando's Divine Model in Architectural Theory," in *CHORA: Intervals in the Philosophy of Architecture*, vol. 3, ed. Alberto Pérez-Gómez and Stephen Parcell (Montreal and Kingston: McGill-Queen's University Press, 1999), 142.

18 Rykwert, *Dancing Column*, 138.

19 Caramuel de Lobkowitz, *Architectura civil recta y obliqua*, 2:61.

20 This is a curious inscription because the columns in the Forum Boarium were not Doric – at least not the ones that have survived – and because one of the two surviving temples has a round plan.

Prato della Valle, Reconsidered

Marc J. Neveu

THOUGH THE PRATO DELLA VALLE in Padua is one of the largest public squares in Europe, only a handful of articles regarding the piazza have been written in English.[1] Typically, authors have focused on the political manoeuvring to complete the work, the imaginative funding scheme devised by architect-politician Andrea Memmo, the physical nature of the site, or the nineteenth- and twentieth-century reception of the project. A continuous thread through existing scholarship is the belief that the work was influenced by the architectural theories of Carlo Lodoli relating to function, representation, and/or the truth of materials. I would agree that Lodoli's thinking influenced the work, but I do not believe that the significance of the project is based only on the issues noted above. This chapter shows that the Prato della Valle was also intended as a reconfigured Roman amphitheatre. Further, I propose that the Prato della Valle operates in an emblematic way as a guide to understanding the role of history in design.

Evidence indicates that the *prato* has been occupied in various ways since Roman times. Vincenzo Radicchio, an eighteenth-century writer, asserts that the open field was used as a circus, for mock battles, and even as a theatre that later provided the stone for constructing the Rialto Bridge in Venice.[2] The *prato* remained an open space outside the city walls until the fifteenth century, and for the next few hundred years it was used as a marketplace, a parade ground, and even as a place for manoeuvres by the cavalry. By the eighteenth century this marshy land was being used for fairs and for selling various wares. An etching by Canaletto shows opulent houses defining the irregular edge of the *prato*, connected by pathways worn into the field by use (see fig. 8.1). The *prato* was the focus of a massive urban renewal project by Andrea Memmo, the *Provveditore* (governor) of Padua, begun just after a major flood in 1772. The Prato della Valle, as the proposal became known, was one of a series of urban projects proposed by Memmo to make moral improvements to the city without straining the already tight economy. As a politician and architect, Memmo recognized its potential to boost tourism and the local economy as well as to improve the health and welfare of the citizens of Padua. To avoid the annual flood and the typically saturated soil condition, Memmo devised an elliptical canal to drain the land and divert the water into an existing canal. The project also proposed to transform the amorphous urban space into a site for large public gatherings such as annual fairs, firework displays, regattas, and horse races. Trees were to be planted

Fig. 8.1 *Il Prato della Valle*, an etching [probably by Antonio Visentini, 1770s] after a sketch by Canaletto.

to line the proposed elliptical island, and a scheme was devised to install eighty-eight statues of famous Paduans along the canal. Andrea Memmo enlisted Francesco Piranesi to make etchings and a textual description to persuade citizens to finance the project by purchasing subscriptions for the statues lining the canal.

Andrea Memmo (1729–93) was no ordinary Venetian.[3] He was groomed from birth for an important life in politics. Named after his uncle, the family patriarch and a well-respected statesman, the young Andrea followed his elder namesake into political life.[4] After a series of duties related to his standing as a patrician in Venice, he went to Padua in 1771 to become its governor. In 1777 he was appointed as the *Balio* (ambassador) to Constantinople, a position he held for five years. During his tenure there he made plans for reconstructing the ambassador's house. He was then appointed ambassador to Rome and arrived there in the spring of 1783. For this recently widowed father of two girls, Rome was full of empty excitement. The lack of influence wielded by the Venetian Republic was painfully clear to him, and he found himself amused but bored. He was elected as the *Procuratore di S Marco* in 1787 and two years later was narrowly defeated for the selection of doge by Ludovico Manin, the last doge of Venice. Memmo died in 1793 after a long bout of gangrene – one year before the Republic would do the same.

Eighteenth-century and current scholarship recognizes Andrea Memmo as Carlo Lodoli's most faithful student. Memmo presented Lodoli's theory of architecture in at least two texts. The first, *Elementi dell'architettura*

Lodoliana (1786), proposed new norms of architecture and critiqued almost everyone who had ever claimed to be an architect, especially Vitruvius.[5] The text also contains an outline for a treatise on architecture that Memmo claimed Lodoli gave him at the end of his life. An essential part of this outline is the metaphoric relation between function and representation. Thus, modern scholars often refer to Lodoli's anticipating the modern dictum "form follows function." The second text, *Apologhi immaginati* (1787), is a series of fifty-six fables that were presented during Lodoli's architectural lessons and written down after his death by Andrea Memmo.[6] Both texts by Memmo were written for students of architecture and explore the theme of *indole*, understood as "inherent nature."[7] Lodoli used the word to describe both the individual nature of students and the specific nature of materials.

SUBSTITUTIONS

Though Lodoli is often described as an architect, his architectural production was not vast. It consisted of a series of renovations to his living quarters at the San Francesco della Vigna in Venice. The most well-documented part of the renovations is a series of oddly shaped window frames (see fig. 8.2). Throughout Venice, Lodoli saw cracks in the centre of stone window sills. He believed this was due to a poor understanding of materials and a lack of foresight with respect to the weathering of buildings. To remedy this condition, builders typically would leave out a course of brick underneath the sill or would divide the sill into several pieces. Both solutions, as Lodoli observed, were still liable to fail under typical conditions. Lodoli believed that the downward force on the outer edges of the sill pushed the central portion of the sill upward and caused the stone to crack in the middle. To solve this problem, he reconstructed each window sill out of three pieces. The middle piece, wider in the centre and narrowed towards the outside edges, took the form of a catenary curve.[8] This middle piece was joined to the two side pieces with a mortise and tenon joint under the jamb (hidden under the plaster surface). Memmo claimed this was a completely new and totally Lodolian invention. He called Lodoli's solution a *sostituzione* (substitution) and said that it could be used by others but should be adjusted to suit each different situation.[9] According to Memmo: "Other

Fig. 8.2 Carlo Lodoli, Sill at S. Francesco della Vigna, Venice, Italy (1740s). Photo by author.

thresholds were made with circular segments, with catenaries, crushed stone, some with a menagerie of stone in the middle and sometimes without, depending on the various situations."[10] Following Lodoli's advice, Andrea Memmo designed very similar sills for his palazzo on the Grand Canal and for the Venetian Embassy in Constantinople.[11] According to Lodoli, each material has a specific nature (*indole*) that should be treated accordingly. Lodoli believed that the performance of stone must be understood in its particular situation and with common sense. In his sill it made sense for the stone to be thicker where the load is heaviest and where sills usually failed. Though none of Lodoli's writings on architecture have survived, Memmo describes a *Libro delle sostituzioni* (*Book of Substitutions*) in which Lodoli documents various architectural details he had construed.[12] For Lodoli there was never one typical solution; each substitution should be appropriate to the place and the nature of the material.

The same approach guided Lodoli's teaching. Rather than setting lessons or exercises for students to imitate or execute, Lodoli taught through apologues: the fables that Memmo recorded in the *Apologhi immaginati*. As with Lodoli's architectural substitutions, his teaching method depended on the nature of the student and the situation. The apologues were given orally, enabling Lodoli to adjust them each time. In the introduction of the *Apologhi*, Memmo notes that the apologues unfortunately had become fixed in written form and were unrelated to particular situations. Memmo explains Lodoli's intent:

> With this new method, while remaining free in the manner in which to espouse his Apologues, he was able to adapt each of the phrases to the various abilities of his listeners and their various interests. It was for this reason that the same Apologue told in a different situation would seem to be another. This change of style would make suspect anyone trying to make a faithful recording in writing of the Apologues.[13]

It was difficult for Memmo to transcribe Lodoli's apologues because it had been over twenty-five years since Lodoli's death and because all of his apologues had been presented in different versions for particular situations.

Lodoli used typical characters from fables – mules, flies, eagles, frogs, geese, and so on – but he also incorporated historical figures and various professions. Socrates might learn about patience from a snail, and an Athenian citizen might gain political insight from a more recent figure. In "The Dangerous Citizen," Lodoli describes the events surrounding the conspiracy involving the Roman politician Catiline, though in Lodoli's version a talking pomegranate provides the lesson about living peacefully within a society.[14] Clearly, Lodoli was aware of the tradition that preceded him. The introduction and first story in the *Apologhi* acknowledge previous introductions to fables with an appropriately named "Story of the Story."[15] Lodoli looked to historical precedent not simply to describe the past or to imitate it. His attitude towards historical precedent is shown in the story "The Young Nun and Her Mother,"[16] in which he describes a young nun who often made cakes for her family. Her mother was bored with having the same cakes all the time and asked her to make something else. The young nun made several attempts but eventually reverted to her old way of making cakes and had to turn to her mother for guidance. The mother then showed her daughter how to make new and more tasteful cakes. To break with her past, the nun relied on someone older, whom we might expect to be more traditional. Lodoli's lesson is to look to the past to find new meaning.

Memmo's first publication of his teacher's architectural theories, *Elementi dell'architettura,* is a rambling, point-by-point analysis of Vitruvius, the Greeks, the Romans, and, finally, the Moderns. Throughout its hundred and fifty pages, each of the Golden Ages prior to the eighteenth century is criticized for blindly following historical precedent rather than reason.[17] Vitruvius is criticized for being obscure and difficult and for giving impractical advice. This critique is based mainly on contradictions that Lodoli found in the translation of Vitruvius's work. However, like the young nun who returned to her mother, Lodoli repeatedly returns to Vitruvius throughout the *Elementi*. The Galiani edition of Vitruvius, to which Memmo refers, is a bilingual Italian/Latin edition that was considered the definitive Italian edition in the eighteenth century.[18] Lodoli did not simply cite Galiani's translation but made corrections to his Italian and used these more careful translations to develop his own theory. Memmo's architecture and political action were clearly influenced by Lodoli's thoughts on representation, materiality, and function, but the results were sometimes dubious. I would assert, however, that Memmo's historical awareness was developed from Lodoli's lessons and that his proposal for the Prato della Valle closely resembles Lodoli's tactics of substitution.

MEMMO'S *PRATO*

Memmo was more even-tempered than the acerbic Lodoli, and this advanced his political agenda. Whereas Lodoli's efforts were focused on the education of young patricians, Memmo used his position as a politician to seek social reform through architectural production. He believed that public works could enrich the lives of the citizens, boost the local economy, and increase tourism. He detailed his intentions in a small book: *Viste politiche sopra varie parti del Governo di Padova la maggior parte delle quail bisognose di lume, e di ben maturi esami.*[19] It outlines Memmo's vision for civic improvements such as installing street lighting, restoring facades, formalizing agricultural festivals, replacing wooden bridges with stone bridges, paving busier streets and squares, and organizing a fire brigade. He thought these improvements would make the city more attractive to foreigners. Memmo, the ever-conscious politician, kept a checklist to record work that had been completed. The Prato della Valle was clearly his most lasting project, and it included many of his ideas for improving the city.

We know of Memmo's thoughts for the *prato* from a strange book published in 1786. In the frontispiece of *Descrizione della general idea, ed in gran parte effettuata dall' eccellentissimo signore Andrea Memmo* (1786), Vincenzo Radicchio is named as Memmo's secretary.[20] There is no evidence that Vincenzo actually existed. It is more likely that this Signore Radicchio was a playful nom de plume for Andrea Memmo as well as a reference to the *prato*. "Vincenzo Radicchio" translates to "radicchio from the city of Vicenza." Radicchio is a bitter, leafy vegetable that is usually grown in late fall, when the ground is saturated and very moist, like the previous marshy condition of the *prato*. Domenico Cerato, the builder who carried out the work, was originally from Vicenza. Memmo, though clearly the author of the project, shied away from claiming this role, as is evident from correspondence between Memmo and Cerato.[21] Much of the text describes procedures for funding the project, difficulties in draining and grading the land, and thoughts about how pleasant the Prato della Valle would be for the citizens of Padua.

It is impressive that Memmo was able to fund and build one of the largest public spaces in Europe at a time when the Republic of Venice was almost bankrupt after many years of costly warfare.[22] Funding was obtained initially through a tax on goods and services sold at the annual fairs. This paid for canals to be dug and bridges and stairs to be constructed during the first four years.[23] When this funding proved insufficient to complete the project, Memmo changed tactics and began selling subscriptions for the individual statues that would line the canal. This ingenious plan enabled individuals to choose the subject for each statue they had funded. The cost of the statue depended on the wealth of the purchaser.

Memmo commissioned Giuseppe Subleyras to represent the project in a painting, from which Francesco Piranesi then made an etching. The top border on Subleyras's painting indicates the immense size of the proposal: 974,012 square feet (see fig. 8.3). Further, he explains that the proposed Prato della Valle will include a public garden on the newly formed island, an area for the annual agricultural fair, an amphitheatre, houses, permanent shops, a museum of statues, canals, paths for walking, a grove of trees, a lake, and fountains.[24] The painting shows details of each structure, including tiered seating beyond the outermost row of statues. Piranesi's etching is taken from roughly the same viewpoint (see fig. 8.4). The images are revealing in a number of ways. They clearly show a central axis leading to Memmo's residence at the Palazzo Angeli. The plan is not aligned to the cardinal points; instead, it follows previous paths that cut through the once-open space and led to the centre of the city. Both images also show a third ring of statues that was never built but would have lined the track for the *palio* (horse race) that Memmo proposed. There are a few differences between the two images. Piranesi's

Fig. 8.3 Top: Giuseppe Subleyras, *Generale idea per la definitive sistemazione del Prato* [Proposal for the final organization of the Prato] (1784–85). Biblioteca Civica, Padua.

Fig. 8.4 Bottom: Francesco Piranesi, *Generale idea per la definitive sistemazione del Prato* [Proposal for the final organization of the Prato] (1784–85). Biblioteca Civica, Padua.

version is more detailed and shows the city beyond but omits the details that frame Subleyras's version and removes the tiered seating, central pavilion, and differentiation between the second and third exterior rings.

Piranesi was originally asked to make a catalogue showing all of the statues, but at that time there were not enough subscribers to make it worthwhile. Therefore he represented another view from above, showing the entire proposal. The first statue to be placed was that of Cicero, though this was only a mock-up for others to imitate. This statue was destroyed, and a likeness of Cicero is not to be found in the Prato della Valle today. Memmo intended that the statues would represent illustrious men from any nation who had brought glory in some way to the City of Padua.[25] Though the subjects were to be noble, the statues remained somewhat ordinary. At least fifteen different sculptors carved the statues, but all appear to be by the same hand because they include similar features: all are made from similar stone, have the same scale, and are numbered and inscribed with the Latinized name of the subject.[26] Further, Memmo mandated that none of the subjects could be living.[27] Memmo funded the first statue: Antenor, the mythical founder of Padua, who occupies position number two. Four popes, five Memmos, and Paduans such as Galileo and Giovanni Poleni are represented.[28] The numbering begins on the right side of the path on the main axis leading from Memmo's house. The statue placed at position number one was originally Marc Antonio Memmo, but this was replaced by a statue of Antonio Diedo after the French destroyed the former. The numbering continues counter-clockwise along the outside of the canal until it reaches the left side of the path. It then continues, again counter-clockwise, on the inside of the canal.

AN AMPHITHEATRE, RECONSIDERED

Memmo's intention was that the public Prato della Valle would function in many ways: as a fairground, as an open theatre, and as a track for horse races. The canal was the setting for a regatta, and the interior quadrants could be used as a stage for hunting games and as a place to launch and view fireworks.[29] It was intended to accommodate a wide range of spectacles, and, indeed, Memmo refers to them as *spettacoli*.[30] In a recent article in *CHORA*, George L. Hersey describes the connection between the spectacle and the amphitheatre: "*Spectaculum* and *spectator* connote the act of seeing. Another name for the Coliseum does the same: amphitheatre. θεχτρσυ can mean 'the spectators,' 'those who are looking.'"[31] This clearly matches Memmo's intention for the project. Memmo/Radicchio is even more deliberate in the description of the form:

> He began to sketch designs, and in the somewhat triangular plan of the Prato he inscribed the most regular and pleasant form that he was able: the oval. And amongst all of the ovals, he chose the one that was most beloved by both the ancients and moderns alike, the Amphitheatre Flavius, also known as the Coliseum, a figure that had been altered only slightly since it was executed.[32]

The excavation for the canal revealed that the site was originally used by the Romans as a theatre. This serendipity notwithstanding, it is clear that Memmo looked back to the Romans for guidance in his proposal for the Prato della Valle. The elliptical plan is taken directly from a Roman amphitheatre. He knew and praised the Coliseum in Rome, as well as the one in Verona, just a short journey from Padua. Originally Memmo thought that an amphitheatre would be the ideal built form to house all of the public functions he was proposing. As the design developed, however, he decided that it was flawed in several ways. This partially explains the differences in the representations by Subleyras and Piranesi. The first problem was that the seating for an amphitheatre would block all of the houses around the *prato*. If he lowered the seating, this would give free views to those who live in the houses. Another problem was that the population of Padua was not large enough to fill all of the seats in an amphitheatre, so events would not be profitable. Although an exact replica of an ancient amphitheatre might not be appropriate, the public functioning of such an amphitheatre – as *spectaculum* – might be. I suspect it was at this point that Memmo substituted the Roman amphitheatre with the more appropriate public park that still functions today: the Prato della Valle. To develop this further requires speculation on Memmo's understanding of an ancient amphitheatre. For this, we need to look at the work of Scipione Maffei (1675–1755), the erudite author of theatrical and educational reform who was also an antiquarian, an Arcadian, and one of Lodoli's most important influences.

Memmo was not a particularly good scholar, but he knew where to look. His knowledge of amphitheatres was most likely derived from Scipione Maffei's massive study of the history of Verona, the *Verona illustrata* (1731).[33] Maffei even notes that Lodoli showed him a manuscript, now lost to history, describing the amphitheatres on the island of Candia. Giovanni Poleni, the doctor to the ailing dome of St Peter's, was also researching the form of the amphitheatre.[34] Alexander Gordon quickly translated the fourth volume of Maffei's study, on amphitheatres, into English.[35] In his introduction, Gordon states that Maffei's contribution was to distinguish between the theatre and the amphitheatre according to their respective events. Simply put, the theatre, a Greek invention, had no gladiators and was only for musical performances. Both Maffei and Poleni regarded the amphitheatre as a Roman invention that is not tied to the landscape, whereas a Greek theatre is situated on a hillside. Maffei further distinguished between them according to the height of the exterior wall and whether numbers were engraved on the arches of the openings. Maffei decided that the arena at Nîmes was not really an amphitheatre because it was only two stories tall, had no numbers engraved on the arches, and had no windows in the upper part of the building.[36] Another factor that distinguished the amphitheatre from the theatre was safety. Maffei explained that it was important to keep the animals in place and not to let them attack the spectators – surely a prudent decision that would encourage spectators to return. Though these two building forms are distinct, Maffei claimed that the form of the amphitheatre came from placing two circular theatres together, forming an ellipse.[37]

Much modern scholarship has attempted to determine whether the amphitheatre was indeed an ellipse or simply an oval. The confusion typically comes from inaccuracies that arise when replicating a drawing at a much larger scale on the ground. It is also difficult to make concentric curves truly parallel when constructing the seating and the exterior wall. Add to this the potential for a cosmic reading of the geometry and one can imagine the disputes over how amphitheatres were laid out. Mark Wilson Jones shows that the plan of the Coliseum was not simply a geometric or arithmetic construction but actually both.[38] The multiple reading is due to the differences between its ideal geometry and its material construction. A geometric trace was inscribed first and corrected later, when the exterior wall was built. Wilson Jones presents two very similar geometric constructions for the initial layout of the Coliseum (see fig. 8.5). They follow the same geometric steps but their initial triangles have different proportions.

Domenico Cerato (1715–92), the professor of *Practica architettura civile*, and his assistant Daniel Danieletti demonstrate the same geometry in a series of drawings from which the Prato della Valle was constructed (see fig. 8.6).[39] Cerato's plan is drawn to scale, the statues are numbered (though differently than as-built), a few statues – *Dose* (Doge), Antenor, and Azzo d'Este – are labelled, and the shops are outlined. As the exterior "wall" was a series of statues, the curves of the ellipses did not need to be parallel, and the difficult ellipse-versus-oval discussion is moot. The plan shows a geometric construction very similar to Maffei's drawing of the "subterranean" plan of an amphitheatre (see fig. 8.7) Both plans include light construction lines that help explain how they would be laid out. Both are constructed from a triangle whose base locates the two focal

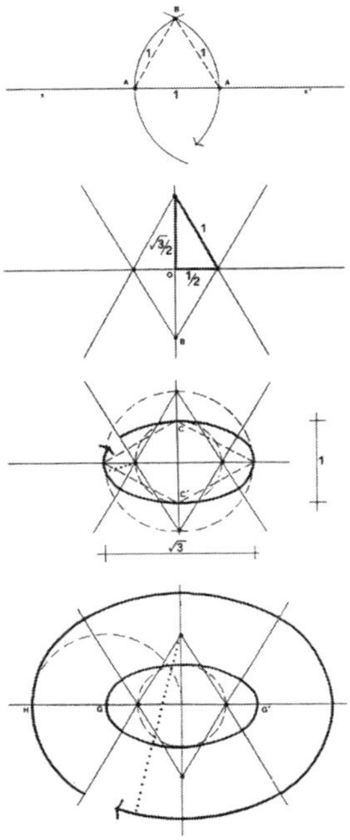

Fig. 8.5 Method for laying out monumental civic amphitheatres. From Mark Wilson Jones, *Principles of Roman Architecture* (New Haven: Yale University Press, 2000).

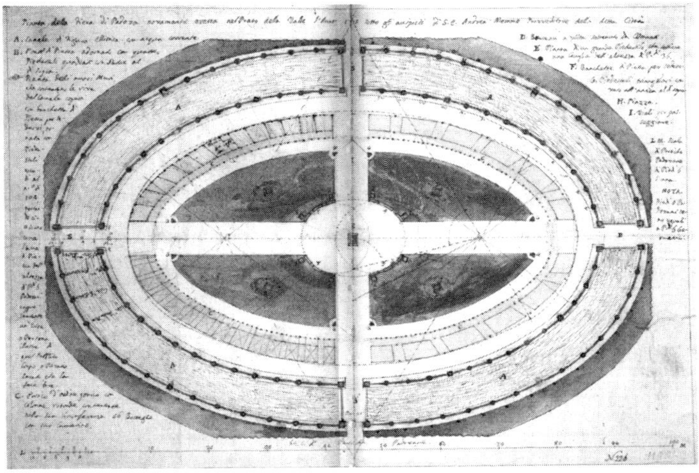

Fig. 8.6 Domenico Cerato, *Pianta della fiera di Padova nuovamente eretta nel Prato della Valle* [Plan of the recently built fairgrounds in the Prato della Valle] (1776). Biblioteca Civica, Padua.

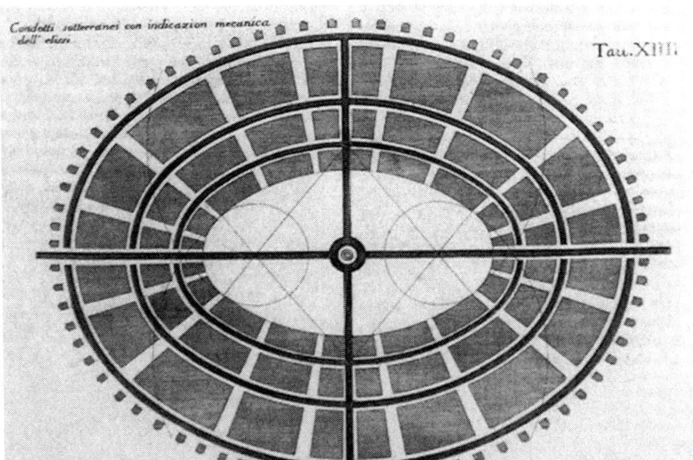

Fig. 8.7 Scipione Maffei, "Condotti sotterranei con indicazioni mecanica dell'elisso" [Underground conduits with description of the elliptical construction], *Verona illustrata*, vol. 4 (Verona: Per Jacopo Vallarsi, e Pierantonio Berno, 1731–32).

points; a circle is then inscribed around each focal point to help form the initial arc. There is a slight difference that can be explained by looking at Sebastiano Serlio's description of ovals, found in his *Tutte l'opera d'architettura* (1537–75) (see fig. 8.8). In the text, Serlio offers different methods of constructing ovals. The first begins with a pair of equilateral triangles, then extends four of the sides and uses radii to inscribe four arcs that form the shape. Ovals with different proportions can be constructed by varying the radii. The second method (*ovalo tondo*) also relies on a pair of equilateral triangles, though it begins with two circles and uses the two points of intersection to generate the arcs. These two ovals described by Serlio are the same as those described by Wilson Jones. Though he begins the second method with two arcs and not two circles, the result is the same: a Vesica Piscis (see fig. 8.9). Allow me to demonstrate: A point is made. A line is extended from that point. A circle is inscribed using the point as the centre and the line as the radius. Using the opposite end of the line as a centre point, a second circle is drawn. Connecting the endpoints of the line to one of the points where the circles intersect generates an equilateral triangle. This geometric proof is the basis of Euclidean geometry.

PRATO DELLA VALLE, RECONSIDERED

Andrea Memmo imaginatively substituted the public function of a Roman amphitheatre – as *spectaculum* – into an appropriate response for eighteenth-century Padua. The *prato* did not become an amphitheatre proper, but I would argue that it performed the same role in the public realm. Similar to Lodoli's substituting the characters and morals of ancient fables into specific responses for individual students, Memmo substituted the history of Padua into eighty-eight numbered statues. The references between old and new are obvious, though Memmo did not seem concerned that the urban form should be novel. Indeed, most references – the geometry, the numbering of openings and statues, the spectacles to be witnessed, and even the separation of animals into the four quarters of the plan – are quite direct. Memmo's references, however, are always adjusted to the new situation using common sense.

I would propose to read the geometry of the plan in a more emblematic way. The Vesica Piscis at the centre of Cerato's plan might also

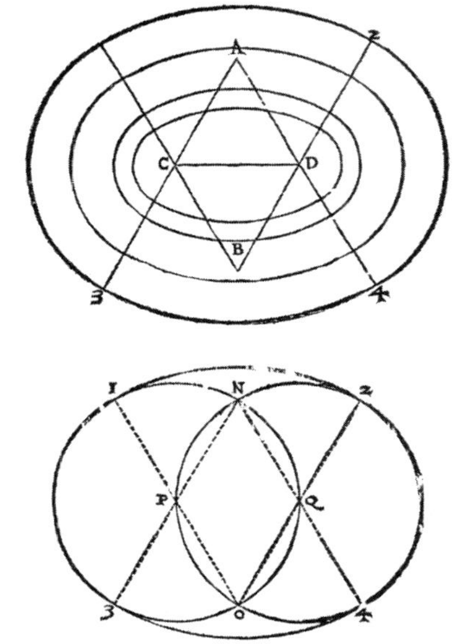

Fig. 8.8 Two methods for constructing an oval. From Sebastiano Serlio, *The Book of Architecture* (1611), translation of *Tutte l'opera d'architettura* (1537–75).

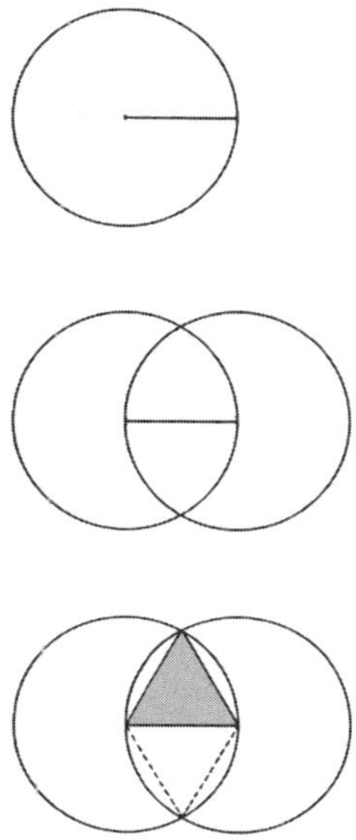

Fig. 8.9 Vesica Piscis. Drawing by author.

demonstrate an approach to history that, like the young nun returning to her mother, is productive rather than repetitive. I now very briefly explain how I understand this within the realm of architectural making. One forms a question within a given situation (a point is made and a circle is drawn). One then looks to others in history who have asked similar questions (a second circle is drawn). It is essential that the other work be viewed within its own world and not retrospectively. Through historical and philosophical dialogue the question is fleshed out and becomes specific. It is pursued through making and action, not through abstract thought (an equilateral triangle is constructed). Its fusion of horizons refigures new meaning and a work is created through historical dialogue. This is not historical kitsch, as the work generates meaning in this world and not solely by referring to another; nor is it simply historical inquiry or technical production alone. Its relation to history is metaphoric and it synthesizes heterogeneous elements into practical action. Judgment then may be based on the depth and rigour of research and not only on the manipulation of form, technical certainty, or ironic historical reference.

POSTSCRIPT

In the 1770s, Andrea Memmo discovered the ruins of a theatre on the site of the *prato*, a serendipity that foreshadowed the role of the project as a substituted amphitheatre. In researching this article I found my own happy coincidence. In his proposal for the 1985 Biennale di Venezia, Aldo Rossi uses the Prato della Valle as one of six sites for exploration. It is interesting that Rossi's own fascination with the form of ancient amphitheatres and his critique of naïve functionalism are based on the transcendence of form over use. In a perverse way, Memmo inverts Rossi's argument by referring back to the form of a ruin that was never there and by substituting its old use with a new use. It may not be coincidence, then, that another theatre appeared before Rossi discovered the Prato della Valle: in 1981 Rossi's *Teatro del mondo a Venezia* floated past the Grand Canal, into the lagoon, and then out to sea, where it became a ruin.

NOTES

1 See, for example, Joseph Rykwert, *The First Moderns* (Cambridge, MA: MIT Press, 1980), 317–23; and Rebecca Williamson, "Andrea Memmo's Prato della Valle," *Urban Design Studies* 6 (2000): 93–104. Manlio Brusatin, "Il Prato della Valle: Progetti, transformazioni, personaggi e spettacolo di un luogo urbano di Padova," *Lotus* 30 (1981): 47–56, was translated into English in the same issue. The standard reference in Italian is Lionello Puppi, ed., *Prato della Valle: Due millenni di storia di un'avventura urbana* (Padua: Signum, 1986).

2 See Vincenzo Radicchio, *Descrizione della general idea concepita in gran parte effettuata d'al eccellentissimo signore Andrea Memmo* (Rome: Antonio Fulgoni, 1786), 12–13.

3 See GianFranco Torcellan, *Una figura della Venezia settecentesca: Andrea Memmo* (Venice and Rome: Instituto per la collaborazione cultural, 1963) for the most informative biography of Memmo. His family, which included two doges, was considered to be one of the original twelve families

whose offspring formed the patrician class in Venice. The Memmo family line ended with Andrea's death in 1793.

4 The elder Andrea held many positions in the Venetian government, including Ambassador (*Balio*) to Constantinople, the city in which he was famously imprisoned and tortured. He ended his career as the *Procuratore di San Marco*, the highest position in Venice after the doge.

5 Andrea Memmo, *Elementi dell'architettura Lodoliana ossia, L'arte di fabbricare con solidità scientifica e con eleganza non capricciosa*, 2 vols. (Zara: Fratelli Battari, 1834) was first published in Rome in 1786. Memmo's daughter, Lucia Mocenigo, funded the publication of the second edition.

6 There are two editions of Andrea Memmo, *Apologhi immaginati, e sol estemporaneamente in voce esposti agli amici suoi / dal fu fra Carlo de' conti Lodoli* (Bassano: n.p., 1787). The first was published on the occasion of Memmo's being elected *Procuaratore di S Marco*. Gio Claudio Molini published another edition (Paris, 1800), with minor grammatical corrections and a smaller format.

7 See Marc J. Neveu, "Architectural Lessons of Carlo Lodoli (1690–1761): *Indole* of Material and of Self" (PhD diss., McGill University, 2006), in which both understandings of *indole* are developed more fully.

8 Memmo does not refer to Giovanni Poleni specifically, though he does describe the curve of the sill as a catenary – the same curve proposed by Poleni to cure the ailing dome at St Peter's in Rome. See Augusto Cavallari-Murat, "Giovanni Poleni e la costruzione architettonica," in *Giovanni Poleni (1683–1761) nel bicentario della morte* (Padua: Accademia patavina di scienze lettere ed arti, 1963), 55–94.

9 Lodoli proposed another such substitution for a door frame. It is not known if Lodoli did construct such a frame, but an example can be seen in the frontispiece of the Giovanni Ziborghi edition of Vignola. See Memmo, *Elementi dell'architettura Lodoliana,* 2:159. Memmo referred to Giovanni Ziborghi, *L'architettura di Jacopo Barozzi da Vignola: ridotta a facile metodo per mezzo di osservazioni a profitto de' studenti* (Bassano: Remmondi, 1748). Domenico Cerato, the professor of architecture, constructed a very similar frame in his renovation at La Specola.

10 "Altre soglie fece con segementi di circolo, con catenaries, di pietre cotte, con la serraglia di pietra viva nel mezzo ed anche senza, secondo le varie situazione." Memmo, *Elementi dell'architettura Lodoliana*, 2:159 (translation by author, emphasis added).

11 See Tommaso Bertele, *Il palazzo degli ambasciatori di Venezia a Constantinopolie le sue antiche memorie* (Bologna: Apollo, 1931). Though I have not seen the building, drawings can be found in the Bertele text and also in Manilo Brusatin, *Venezia nel settecento: stato, architettura, territorio* (Turin: Einaudi, 1980), images 107, 108. Both are reproductions of originals in the Archivo di Stato in Venice. Memmo's proposal was not completed. The Bertele text shows photos of the palazzo in 1931, without the "Lodolian" sills. I have no evidence of its current condition.

12 See Memmo, *Elementi dell'architettura Lodoliana,* 2:149. Memmo briefly describes the book.

13 "Con questo nuovo metodo, mentre tentavasi libero nella maniera di esporre i suoi Apologhi, onde meglio adattarne il frasario ancora alla diversa capacità degli ascoltatori, od alle varie loro inclinazioni, nasceva, che lo stessissimo Apologo, a chi in separatà societa l'aveva un'altra volta udito, paresse un altro. Un sì fatto cambiamento di stile potrebbe ancora far prendere in sospetto chi scrive per quanto fosse esatto, di non esserne fedel espositore." Memmo, *Apologhi immaginati,* 7 (translation by author).

14 Memmo, *Apologhi immaginati,* 69–73. Another example is Lodoli's retelling of the Platonic dialogue *Laches*, called "The Graceful Hunter" by Lodoli. In both, the main character possesses an unwieldy gun that is analogous to knowledge. The moral of the story is that knowledge without judgment is useless or, at best, misguided.

15 Giambattista Basile, Leon Battista Alberti, and Marsilio Ficino all introduce their collections with a "story of the story." See David Marsh's introduction to *Renaissance Fables: Aesopic Prose by Leon Battista Alberti, Bartolomeo Scala, Leonardo da Vinci, Berardino Baldi* (Tempe, AZ: Arizona Center for Medieval and Renaissance Studies, 2004).

16 Memmo, *Apologhi immaginati*, 18.

17 Memmo praises the Greeks for creating a Golden Age of architecture but criticizes them for blindly accepted the authority of those who came before them, as shown by their poor reasoning when they translated an architecture of wood into an architecture of stone. He praised the Romans more highly than the Greeks, though they made mistakes based on blind imitation and not clear reason. The same critique applies to the Moderns.

18 Berardo Galiani, *L'Architettura di M. Vitruvio Pollione colla traduzione Italiana e commento del Marchese Berardo Galiani* (Naples: Stamperia Simoniana, 1758). Memmo claimed that Lodoli had written on architecture and specifically on Vitruvius, though he did not refer to a particular source.

Lodoli's corrections are very specific and seem to have come from a textual source. It is difficult to imagine Memmo remembering corrections word-for-word after twenty years.

19 See Andrea Memmo, *Viste politiche,* ms. BP 2230/XL (1775?) in the Biblioteca Civica di Padova. See Williamson, "Andrea Memmo's Prato della Valle," 93–104, for a more complete description of the text.

20 The full title is *Descrizione della general idea concepita, ed in gran parte effettuata dall'eccellentissimo signore Andrea Memmo Cavaliere, e Procurator di S Marco, quando fu per la Serenissima Repubblica di Venezia nel MDCCLXXV, e Vi. Proveditor Straordinario della Città di Padova, sul materiale del Prato, che denominavasi della Valle. Onde renderlo utile anche per la potentissima via del diletto a quell popolo, ed a maggior decoro della stessa città, a maggior intelligenza delle due grandi incisioni, che stanno per uscire dalla calcografia Piranesi. Estesa da D. Vincenzo Radicchio Veneziano* (Rome: Antonio Fulgoni, 1786). Giuseppe Subleyras also made two etchings for marketing the Prato della Valle.

21 See Williamson, "Andrea Memmo's Prato della Valle," 100.

22 See James Davis, *The Decline of the Venetian Nobility as a Ruling Class* (Baltimore: Johns Hopkins Press, 1962).

23 See Radicchio, *Descrizione della general idea concepita,* 15–25, for a discussion of how the funding of the initial stages of the *prato* was handled and praised.

24 The full inscription reads: *Nuova piazza di Padova nel sito prima detto il Prato della Valle comprendente la riflessibile soma di piedi geometrici quadrati 974012 rialzato e livellato colla formazione dell'isola o publico giardino, e colla indicazione delle introdottesi mercantile fiere spettacoli, anfiteatro, case, e botteghe stabili, pinacoteca di statue, canale, passeggi, bosco, lago, tempio fontane, e dietro l'idea già concepita dal S.E.* [*sic*] *Andrea Memmo quando nel 1775 teneva il governo di quella città or nel 1784 in gran parte eseguitasi senza aggravio dell' e (eccelentissimo) senato della casa del pub. Padovano e senza alcuna imposizione sul popolo estraordinaria.*

25 It was only men. The sole female representation is that of the icon of Padua at the side of Andrea Memmo's likeness.

26 Pietro Danieletti of Padua made twelve (nos. 7, 10, 35, 36, 38, 39, 46, 47, 48, 51, 85, 86); Luigi Verona, also from Padua, made fourteen (nos. 8, 11, 13, 15, 24, 25, 27, 31, 43, 58, 62, 79, 81, 82); Giovanni Ferrari made nineteen (nos. 18, 19, 20, 21, 22, 23, 30, 59, 60, 64, 65, 66, 67, 71, 72, 73, 74,

75, 76); and Canova, the most prominent sculptor of the day, made only two: his own and Giovanni Poleni's (no. 52).

27 The only exception was Antonio Canova (1757–1822) (no. 68). He is represented sculpting the bust of Antonio Capello, *Procuratore di S Marco* (1523). In the sculpture, Canova is dressed in eighteenth-century costume, though covered by an ancient smock. A sculpture of Andrea Memmo was funded by Angelo Diedo and added in 1794, a year after his death.

28 The popes are: Pope Paul II (1418–71) (no. 22), paid for by Pope Pius VI in 1786; Pope Eugenio IV (1383–1447) (no. 23), donated by the Benedictine monks in 1782; Pope Alessandro VIII (Pietro Ottoboni) (1610–91) (no. 66), donated by the Duchess Ottoboni-Serbelloni in 1787; and Pope Clemente XIII (Carlo Rezzonico) (1693–1769) (no. 67), donated by two of the Rezzonico brothers in 1787. The Memmos are: Doge Marc Antonio Memmo, now destroyed (no. 1); Giovanni Maria Memmo (1509–79) (no. 30), paid for by Duke Peter of Curland in 1787; Maffeo Memmo (fourteenth century) (no. 42), paid for by Andrea Memmo in 1776; and Andrea Memmo (1729–93) (no. 44), paid for by Angelo Diedo in 1794. This last statue replaced Domenico Contarini and put Andrea's likeness at the entry to the main axis of the Prato della Valle. Prior to the move, Andrea Memmo occupied position number 33. For a description of each of the statues, see Puppi, *Prato della Valle*, 160–73.

29 See Radicchio, *Descrizione della general idea concepita,* 14–15. Radicchio/Memmo even discusses how the design for starting races around the oval would compensate for the length of the interior ring's being shorter than the length of the outer ring.

30 See Radicchio, *Descrizione della general idea concepita,* 54–61.

31 George L. Hersey, "The Colosseum: The Cosmic Geometry of a Spectaculum," in *CHORA: Intervals in the Philosophy of Architecture*, vol. 4, ed. Alberto Pérez-Gómez and Stephen Parcell (Montreal and Kingston: McGill-Queen's University Press, 2004), 122. I will not attempt to argue that the geometry of the Prato della Valle holds any cosmic implications.

32 "Cominciò a scarabocchiar disegni, e nella quasi triangular figura del Prato inscrisse la più regolata, e gradita che potè, qual'er l'ovale, e tra le ovali scelta quella, che tanto piacque all'universale antico, e moderno dell'Anfiteatro Flavio, o sia del Colosseo, figura che fu un poco alterata da chi poi ne ordino l'ececuzione, e che quando S. E. trovavasi fuor[i] di Città per veder gli esercizi dei Miliziotti, credendosi di fargli un piacere, fu collocata dirimpetto al suo Palazzo, ch'è ben contermine alla principale strada, che

dale piazze porta nel Prato, ma che non lasciava più che le Quattro strade ad angolo retti, che dovevano giustamente incontrar questa, e le altre tre strade venienti in Prato avess più luogo, come Egli disegnato." See Radicchio, *Descrizione della general idea concepita,* 8–9 (translation by author).

33 See Scipione Maffei, *Verona illustrata* (Verona: Per Jacopo Vallarsi, e Pierantonio Berno, 1731–32), 4:35, and its translation by Alexander Gordon, *A compleat history of the ancient amphitheatres. More peculiarly regarding the architecture of those buildings, and in particular that of Verona by the Marquis Scipio Maffei; made English from the Italian original* (London: W. Sare, 1735), 80.

34 See Giovanni Poleni, *Degli antichi teatri, e anfiteatri: lettere due critiche / l'una del signor marchese Giovanni Poleni ... l'altra del signor conte Giovanni Montenari* (1735) and Poleni's critical edition of Vitruvius, completed by his student Simon Stratico, *Architectura: textu ex recensione codicum emendato / cum exercitationibus notisque novissimis Joannis Poleni et commentariis variorum, additis nunc primum studiis Simonis Stratico* (1825–30). Though the work was completed later than Memmo's *Prato della Valle,* various pieces were available from Poleni as early as 1741.

35 Gordon, *Compleat history of the ancient amphitheatres.*

36 Based on these criteria, Maffei claimed that only three amphitheatres existed in the time of ancient Rome: the Coliseum in Rome, a second in Verona called the Arena, and a third in Capua. Maffei claimed that others at Nîmes in Languedouc, Pola in Istria, Syracuse in Sicily, and Puzzola near Naples were merely theatres and not amphitheatres. Maffei suspects the same of the arena in Pola, though he decided to reserve judgment until he has seen it. (It was only a theatre.)

37 Here, Maffei cites Pliny and Alberti. See Leon Battista Alberti, *On the Art of Building in Ten Books*, trans. Joseph Rykwert, Neil Leach, and Robert Tavernor (Cambridge, MA: MIT Press, 1988), 278.

38 See Mark Wilson Jones, *Principles of Roman Architecture* (New Haven: Yale University Press, 2000), 87–8.

39 Cerato, born in Mason, just outside Vicenza, began a school there but was forced to shut it down due to his "unnatural inclinations." These "inclinations" and other issues are discussed in Giambattista Fogaroli, *Notizie sulla vita dell'architetto abate Domenico Cerato, vicentino* (Padua: Prosperina, 1863). Ettore Motterle attributed his career path to his connections to wealthy Vicentines. See Ettore Motterle, "L'Abate D. Domenico Cerato, architetto e professore" (PhD diss., Università di Padova, 1959). See also

Giambattista Zanazzo, "L'Abate Architetto Domenico Cerato," *Odeo Olimpico* 4 (1943–63): 83–92. He travelled to Padua and began working with his friend Giuseppe Toaldo. His first project was La Specola, an observatory. Renovations to the building also included space for his new school of architecture. He assisted Memmo on other projects. For the curriculum of his school, see Domenico Cerato, *Nuovo metodo per disegnare li cinque ordini d'architettura civile conforme le regole di Palladio, e di Scamozzi, ed alcune regole di geometria pratica* (Padua: Penada, 1784).

Situating Pataphysical Machines: A History of Architectural Machinations

Peter Olshavsky

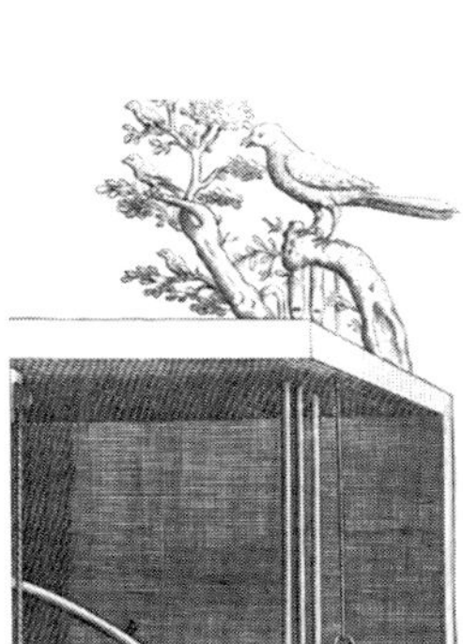

Chora

POPULATING THE MAJOR WORKS of Alfred Jarry (1873–1907) (see fig. 9.1) are mechanical contrivances in variegated garb. We may know them better by their Duchampian moniker "bachelor machines" (*les machines célibataires*), but "every bachelor machine," observes Michel Carrouges, "is first of all a pataphysical machine."[1] Jarry explains that pataphysics is a "science of these present and future beings and contrivances [*engins*] and the Power their Use confers."[2] This may seem like a normative statement on the agency and influence of technology, but appearances are not what they seem. As a result we must examine pataphysical machinations within a larger history of architectural machines.

To begin, the definition of "machine" is certainly not timeless and absolute. Due to its many historical alliances, it has acquired and shed various meanings and changed its status. Today, following the advent of modernity, the machine's association with mathematical thought has privileged its material and constructive properties. It is also associated with technology, as a possibility of the human will and the power to secure the future in advance. In such a world, Jarry's mechanisms may seem idiosyncratic, if not absurd.

During much of its history, the machine was associated neither with mathematical function nor with what can properly be called technology. In fact, the modern tendency to regard the premodern machine as a useless toy is undeniably a biased projection; instead, we must situate it properly within a larger history of the machine and consider what constitutes knowledge and wisdom in certain historical periods. To do this, we flush out the machine's relation to mathematics, metaphysics, and the human will. This provides a more meaningful context for interpreting Jarry's machines ontologically.

A HISTORY OF MACHINES

The fortunes of the architect have been tied to the machine for some time. It was Vitruvius who slid it firmly into the rear of our métier (see fig. 9.2). At that time, during the reign of Caesar Augustus, he defined the machine as "a continuous material system" and divided it into *machinae* and *organa*. This division already seems to imply the efficiency of instrumental technology, with Vitruvius carefully considering the number of workers needed to operate these machines.[3] While he focuses on the machine's

Fig. 9.1 Portrait of Alfred Jarry.

constructive properties and takes for granted the rituals that in*augur*ate a work, there is, in fact, more to the story. Traces of its fuller ontology become evident when he explains that machines are "moved by appropriate revolutions of circles, which by the Greeks is called *cyclice cinesis*."[4] The circles of the machine depend on the order disclosed in the "revolutions of the universe" as "all machinery is generated by Nature."[5] His statement assures us that machines are not merely a mechanical system; rather, the machine *allows* the regularity of the cosmos to resemble a labyrinth or a classical theatre.[6] The mimetic correspondence between the supralunar and sublunar worlds was brought forth and recognized through making. Still, this wilful undertaking was not intended to dominate nature because something at the very heart of the action remained unknowable. Aristotle explains: "Art dwells with the same objects as chance ... chance is beloved of art and art of chance."[7] Dalibor Vesely adds: "Because *tyche* [chance] is inscrutable to our intelligence, *mimesis* is equally so."[8]

The heavens were wedded to the earth in a mimetic manner that was associated with the enigma of fortune and was additionally found in the geometry of mechanics. In *The Mechanical Problems*, a pseudo-Aristotelian text, we are told that simple machines – the lever, wheel, inclined plane, wedge, and screw – are based on the properties of the circle. The circle is not a neutral geometric figure drawn in homogeneous space; rather, it is a paradoxical figure composed of a single line with no beginning and no end. Still, the circle is not infinite because it is generated by contraries. It is a line defined by one point that abides and another that moves. It is simultaneously convex and concave. When moving, it resolves two contrary motions, a geometric manifestation of *coincidentia oppositorum*. According to Marcel Detienne and Jean-Pierre Vernant, this Aristotelian text presents

> instruments which make possible a reversal of power such as that which is characteristic of *metis*, or – to use the author's own terms – which enable the smaller and weaker to dominate the bigger and stronger. He explains this amazing effect of the "machines" which human ingenuity uses, by the properties of the circle: … it [the circle] appears as the strangest, most baffling thing in the world, *thaumasiotaton*, possessing a power which is beyond ordinary logic.[9]

Fig. 9.2 Archimedean screw. From Vitruvius, *De architectura*, trans. Cesare Cesariano (Como: Gottardo da Ponte, 1521).

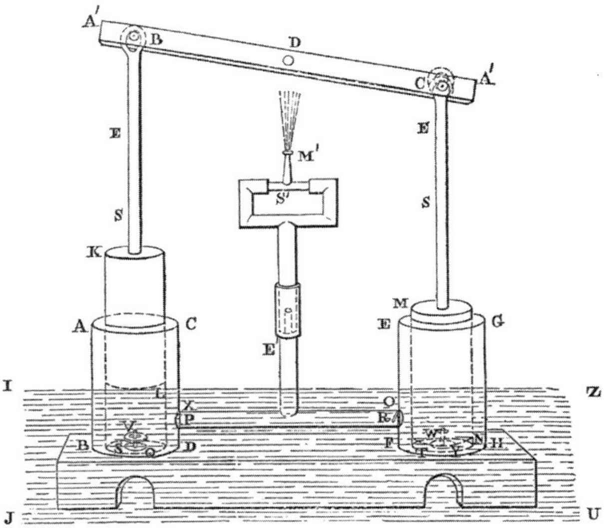

Fig. 9.3 Pump by Hero of Alexandria (first century CE), following Ctesibius. From *The Pneumatics of Hero of Alexandria, From the Original Greek*, ed. Bennet Woodcroft (London: Taylor, Walton and Maberly, 1851).

The Aristotelian author contends: "Artificers therefore perceiving this [admirable] nature of the circle have fabricated certain machines in which the circles that are the principles of the motions are latent, in order that what is wonderful in the mechanism may alone be apparent, but that the cause may be immanifest."[10] A similar bewilderment is expressed in the work of Hero of Alexandria. He understands mechanics as "shifts, devices, wiles" and as potentially "deceitful" because they produce appearances that do not match the *habits* of reality.[11] When a machine moves water upward, for instance, it overturns the natural order of things (see fig. 9.3). Hero, like the Aristotelian author, is fully aware of the contrivance, but he proposes to "hide" (*kryptô*) this mechanical cause and make it "invisible" (*aphanês*) to the audience in order to produce wonder. To Hero, wonder and utility are inseparable forms of knowledge, of which mechanics are an outward demonstration (*apodeixis*).[12] To Aristotle, on the other hand, knowledge (*epistēmē*) could surpass the initial state of wonder and lead one out of ignorance. Wonder sparks philosophizing. He offers several examples: a person being astonished by solstices, the incommensurability of a diagonal in a square and – most important for us – automatons with mechanical workings that one cannot readily grasp. Enigmatic machines, in both accounts, are associated with the "cunning intelligence" (*metis*) of Daidalos, "a propitiatory power or practical cleverness to overcome the obstacles that manifest a disorder of the world."[13]

Associated with knowledge and the growing capacity of the will, these machines anticipated modern technique.[14] They used local devices to try to understand the distant movements of the celestial sphere. Like mathematics (*mathēma*), this technical knowledge (*technē*) could be somewhat divorced from the particularities of a situation. Jean-François Lyotard describes this concept of the machine as a "trap ... to catch the forces of nature."[15] The machine was a "contrivance" that depended on natural forces but that was also freed from nature. It played a trick that enabled the wondrous to appear by making the weak become stronger. This notion, that the weak could overcome the strong, was also a common description of the sophists' *technē*. Like an ingenious machine, the sophists' equivocal argumentation could make the weaker seem stronger. Plato was troubled by them because they conflated being and non-being, employed both the good and the bad, and thus neglected ethical virtue.[16]

Seneca also writes scornfully about the servile arts and the labourer's contorted body. Certain mechanical inventions, he insists, are constructed with "an alert and sagacious intellect, but not an elevated and inspired one – as [is] anything else which has to be discovered by a bent back and a mind contemplating the ground."[17] Being upright, he argues, is an essential condition for philosophy and true wisdom because only in this position can one survey the heavens with "right reason" (*recta ratio*). According to Seneca, *machinatores* who devise stage scenery with bent backs belong to *artes ludicrae*, a lower category. Unlike the liberal arts, mechanical arts are not fit for a free person. Although not all are crude and unworthy, the more banausic or illiberal arts are regarded with disdain because they deteriorate the body and weaken the mind.[18] These arts, which bring humans into close proximity with physical matter and generate revenue, hold a lower status because they are only a means to an end, divorced from higher virtue and wisdom.[19]

In the ancient world, nonetheless, making was still steeped in ritual. Actions were not autonomous: one also had to curry the benevolence of the gods. Ancient machines belonged to a concept of nature (*physis*) as a living force with generative power. Consequently, ancient technique was not reducible to instrumental operations imposed on dead matter (i.e., technology). This would only come much later.

In the Middle Ages, the Aristotelian worldview was carried forward into new concepts of the machine, baptized in Christian waters. Saint Augustine asks the Divine: "By what means did you make heaven and

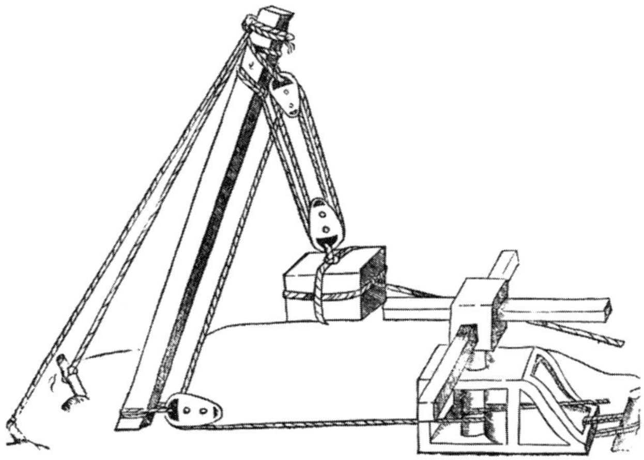

Fig. 9.4 Lifting tackle composed of post, lines, pulleys, and winch. From Leon Battista Alberti, *De re aedificatoria*, trans. Cosimo Bartoli (Florence: Lorenzo Torrentino, 1550).

earth?" and "What tool [*machina*] did you use for this vast work?" The cosmic machine (*machina universalis*), constructed on high, was the first contrivance built by God, the master builder (see fig. 9.4). Augustine likely imagined the divine *machina* as a crane or hoist-like device, derived etymologically from Latin and Doric Greek *makhana* (Attic Greek *mēkhanē*, from *mēkhos* "contrivance"), referring to a stratagem, expedient, and remedy. This meaning is evident in the contentious theatrical device *deus ex machina*, in which a crane lowers a god into a scene to resolve conflict. *Machina* was affiliated with building and could be any type of hoist or scaffolding. Isidore of Seville, similarly, understands it as a device that architects use to construct order. He derives the word *masiones* from *machina* because *architecti* (master builders) build on foundations and use these machines to construct walls and roofs.[20] In an analogous vein, Ignatius of Antioch's earlier "Letter to the Ephesians" interprets the cross as a machine.[21] Ignatius imagines a crane in which two upright posts form an upside-down V and are used in conjunction with a pulley, wheels, and rope to hoist materials for building. His analogy between the upright machine and the cross recognizes that both of these wooden contrivances lift and elevate to help build the church (*ecclesia*) and to undo the curse of Babel.

The mechanical analogy, borrowed from building practices, was equally applied to cognitive constructions. "The machine of the mind," said Gregory the Great, is "the energy of love" that lifts us upon high. Mary Carruthers argues that contemplation was an inventive construction, built from memory and not *ex nihilo*.[22] Memory devices can be found in many architectural mnemonics throughout the period. God gave

Fig. 9.5 Perpetual motion machine (thirteenth century). From Villard de Honnecourt, *The Sketchbook of Villard de Honnecourt*, ed. Theodore Robert Bowie (Bloomington, IN: Indiana University Press, 1959).

knowledge, and it was humankind's duty to disclose it through human works. The primary purpose of medieval machines was not to understand the cosmos as an objective entity but to demonstrate the wondrous workings of the Nature that God had created (see fig. 9.5).

Medieval philosophers regarded wonder as the appropriate response not only to the unfamiliar and the rare but also to a phenomenon of unknown cause that a machine might present. By emphasizing causal knowledge, they began to marginalize wonder. Augustine famously said that marvels are not "against nature" but "against what we know of nature."[23] Wonder was not rejected as false; rather, it was regarded as preternatural (*praeter naturam*), outside or beyond the habits of nature. It was defined in opposition to the ambiguous poles of the natural (which had a known cause) and the supernatural (which appeared by divine intervention). Wonder depended on the knowledge and experience of the observer: miracles were wondrous to all, but mechanical contrivances were wondrous only to the uninstructed. Despite this trend, the wonders of mechanical art still relied on natural forces to produce baffling effects. "Like natural wonders," observe Lorraine Daston and Katharine Park, "these heterogeneous creations were united by the psychology of wonder, drawing their emotional effects from their rarity and the mysteriousness of the forces and mechanisms that made them work."[24]

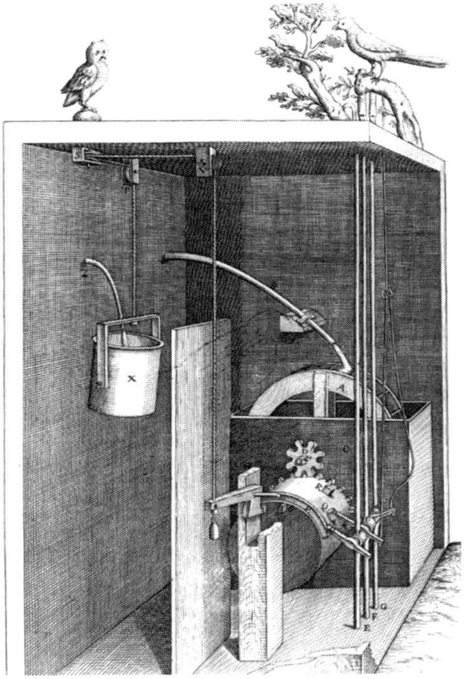

Fig. 9.6 Automaton after Hero. From Salomon de Caus, *Les raisons des forces mouvants avec diverses machines* (Frankfurt: Jan Norton, 1615).

Mechanical art was able to seduce observers with artefacts that were too ingenious to be apprehended causally. In medieval epistemology the mechanical and the machine alluded positively to Daidalos and Aristotelian wonder but were simultaneously suspect. Hugh of St Victor traces the word "mechanical" to *moechus*, "adulterer."[25] Hugh borrows his etymology from the Carolingian Martin of Laon, who argues that "*moechus* means adulterer, a man who secretly pollutes the marriage bed of another. From *moechus* we call 'mechanical art' any object which is clever and most delicate and which, in its making or operation, is beyond detection, so that beholders find their power of vision stolen from them when they cannot penetrate the ingenuity of the thing" (see fig. 9.6).[26] Frequently cited to illustrate the lower status of the mechanical arts, the adulterer is not so much an impudent soul as a trickster who can fool sight and induce wonder. These various connotations show that mechanics evoked a range of passions, from condemnation to praise. Still, the growing use of physical mathematics in certain mechanical arts could elevate their standing.

The status and use of machines began to change in the sixteenth century. Here we find machines for various purposes: from daily tasks such as milling flour (see fig. 9.7) to more refined activities such as reading (see fig. 9.8). Mathematics had been an ontologically distinct realm, but with the proliferation of machines and mechanics, it was extended and applied in many different situations. This expansion accompanied the growth of human dignity and demonstrated the human ability to transcend one's immediate circumstances. As scholars have observed, this is evident in the work of Leonardo da Vinci. The famous résumé he sent to the Duke of Milan, Ludovico Sforza, shows that he was a well-versed machinator: "I shall contrive catapults, mangonels, trabocchi, and other engines of wonderful efficacy."[27] His subsequent drawings show profound ingenuity and a remarkable ability to delineate the nuances of innovative machines. Although Leonardo's brilliant work seems prophetic, his numerous fragments, vague apprehensions, inconsistencies, and speculations thwart all attempts to read his work systematically as modern science or engineering. E.J. Dijksterhuis explains: "One can realize no more clearly how difficult it was to pass from peripatetic to classical science than by seeing a man of his genius, diligence, interest, and high technical ability wrestling with the essential obscurities shrouding the foundations of mechanics" (see fig. 9.9).[28] This shows the difficulty of projecting mechanics systematically and rationally into the thickness of the lived world in the sixteenth century. This world still had a profound *depth* that resisted total instrumentality. "Mechanics," Leonardo argues, "are the Paradise of mathematical science, because here we come to the fruits of mathematics." Mathematics in the Renaissance still symbolized the greater order of the cosmos. Leonardo's machines recall Daniel Barbaro's commentary on Vitruvius, who "sees the force that makes a machine moving, analogous to imagination (*fantasia*), the force that moves the human mind."[29] *Fantasia*, Marco Frascari elaborates, was used to probe reality and "expand the potentialities of new knowledge."[30] In Leonardo's well-known words: "Wisdom is the daughter of experience." He struggled with the fact that his work was rooted in the probable and situational. It was bound up with the task of the artisan and its many contingent difficulties.

The notion of a machine began to shift rather drastically with Galileo Galilei, who declared that the essential structure of our world is mathematical: "It [the universe] is written in the language of mathematics, and its characters are triangles, circles, and other geometric figures, without which it is humanly impossible to understand a single word of it; without these, one wanders about in a dark labyrinth."[31] This radically questions the earlier ontological distinction between the realms of metaphysics and

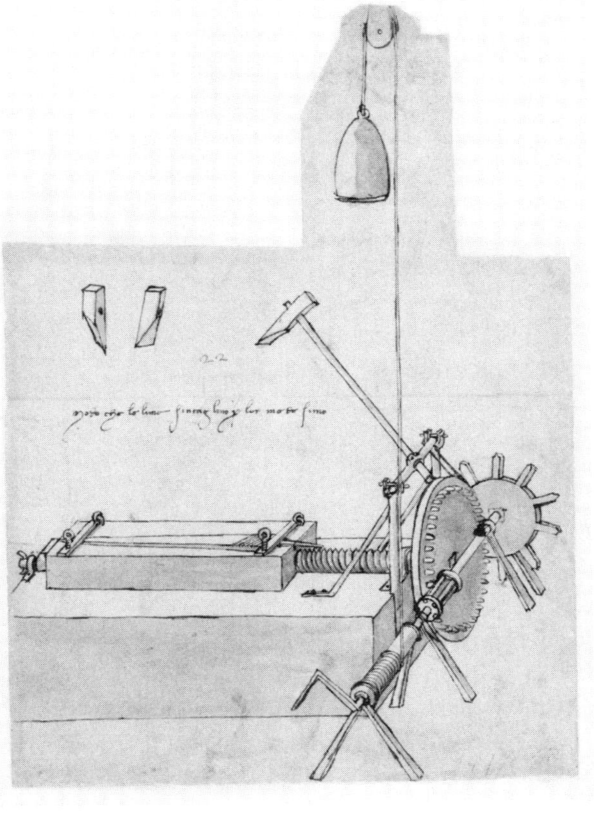

Clockwise from top left:

Fig. 9.7 Flour mill and water wheel. From Vitruvius, *De architectura*, trans. Cesare Cesariano.

Fig. 9.8 Reading machine. From Agostino Ramelli, *Le diverse et artificiose machine* (Paris: the author, 1588).

Fig. 9.9 Leonardo da Vinci, Machine to manufacture files (1505). Codex Atlanticus f. 24r. Biblioteca Ambrosiana, Milan (F158/10).

physics. Although Galileo's wager retains a degree of idealism and abstraction, the earthly realm with which Leonardo grappled could now support mathematical experimentation. Natural phenomena could be reduced drastically to convey the clarity of a model. As he puts it: "It is necessary to abstract from them."[32]

The form of a machine and the extension of its logic into a building no longer followed a divine "idea" but were governed by the mathematical behaviour of materials (see fig. 9.10). Galileo argues: "For every machine and structure, whether artificial or natural, there is set a necessary limit beyond which neither art nor nature can pass."[33] Liane Lefaivre and Alexander Tzonis suggest that Galileo's notion of "limit" presupposes "efficiency."[34] At the same time, with Galileo's condemnation of concepts of motion that are "against nature," for the Enlightenment, earlier notions of wondrous mechanisms and the passions surrounding them would become abject: "Wonder and wonders became simply vulgar, the very antithesis of what it meant to be an *homme de lumières*, or for that matter a member of any elite."[35] With this rather modern concept, the machine slid closer to the domain of engineering: "Only Galileo formulated clearly the problem of statics and strength of materials as part of the geometrization of human space: to determine, by means of a geometrical hypothesis, the dimensions of structural elements in relation to the weights they had to carry and the quantitative properties of the building materials."[36] Nevertheless, his concept of the universe remained tied to the past. To him it was still bound, and it retained Aristotle's innate inclination of objects towards the centre of the earth.

According to E.J. Dijksterhuis, "Not everyone was as ready ... to substitute the noetic simplicity of rational mechanics for the empirical complications of the world of observed physical phenomena."[37] Regardless, ramifications appeared clearly in the "middle sciences" (*scientiae mediae*), including astronomy, optics, and mechanics. These sciences contributed to an "indirect mathematization of reality" because they were situated between metaphysics (theology) and physics.[38] The mechanical arts developed into practical mathematics but still remained separate from natural philosophy. The machines indeed played an important role in shaping and understanding the world. Unlike the autonomous abstractions of modern machinery, seventeenth-century machines were embedded in a rich cultural sphere and were developed with a speculative thrust that was more metaphysical than technical. The function of a machine was

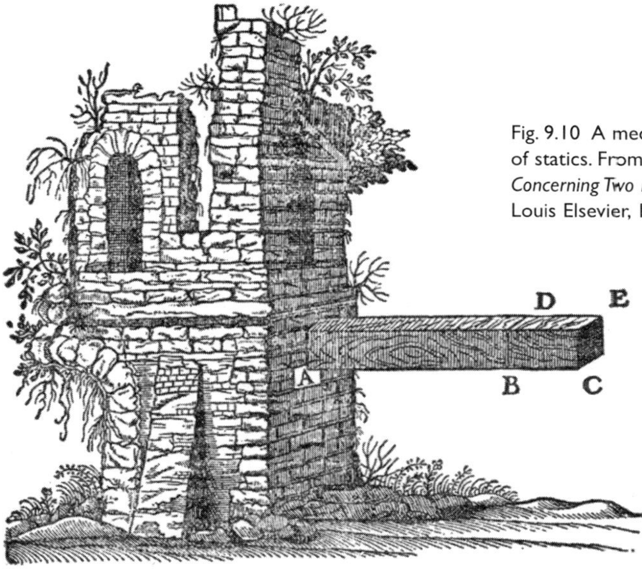

Fig. 9.10 A mechanical demonstration of statics. From Galileo Galilei, *Dialogues Concerning Two New Sciences* (Leiden: Louis Elsevier, 1638).

secondary to its significance as a metaphysical "understanding and representation of movement in the created world."[39] The scope of the mechanical arts encroached on the natural world and began to be applied convincingly. In the preface of *Micrographia*, Robert Hooke (1635–1703) contends that, with mechanical knowledge, "we may perhaps be inabled to discern all the secret workings of Nature, almost in the same manner as we do those that are the productions of Art, and are manag'd by Wheels, and Engines, and Springs, that were devised by human Wit" (see fig. 9.11).[40] Nature was placed increasingly under mechanical laws or, at least, was restrained by mechanical metaphors.

The metaphysics of René Descartes soon applied the machine metaphor to the body. It departed from the late medieval trope in which the human body was a *machina rerum*, a microcosmic analogy to the *machina aetherea* of the cosmos. The Galilean conquests caused such analogies to wane, but Descartes' concept of the body as a machine was unprecedented and literal. Although its divine *inventor* was still implied, the Cartesian body operated silently according to mechanical laws. The *res extensa* included the body (in which an "I" resided) and everything else with extension and motion. The body was ruled entirely by number. Shape, size, quantity, and motion were the only properties needed to describe or explain it. States of consciousness were excluded from the conversation as merely secondary qualities, with no bearing on truth. This conception was radicalized by Julien Offray de La Mettrie, who posited not only that the human body is a watch-like "machine" that functions

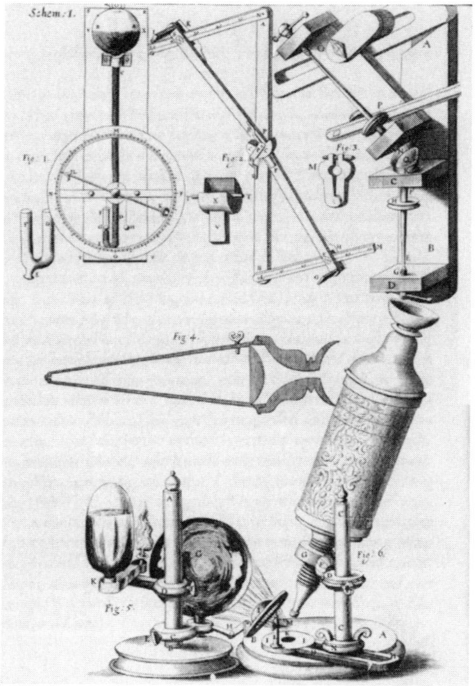

Fig. 9.11 Microscope. From Robert Hooke, *Micrographia, or Some Physiological Descriptions of Minute Bodies Made by Magnifying Glasses, with Observations and Inquiries Thereupon* (London: Royal Society, 1665).

with "the living image of perpetual movement" but also that the soul (*esprit*) is part of the very same machine.[41] This is a step that Descartes did not or was unable to take. As the machine became *the* exemplar, the older notion of a supersensible "idea" withered away. With the body and soul understood as mechanisms, this notion could be extended with ingenious inventions in other situations.

Although this development was assumed to be divinely sanctioned, it required tremendous faith in the human ability to step into divine shoes. Despite occasional failures, humankind was able to understand, command, and utilize *res extensa with greater authority*, culminating in the natural (i.e., mechanistic) philosophy of Isaac Newton. His work explains the actions of the physical world in mechanical terms, replacing speculative metaphysics with "induction and experimentation."[42] Through observation, he discovered mathematical principles in worldly situations, stripped of symbolic significance and their individual nature. They operated in an infinite and abstract void of homogeneous space and time, defined entirely by number. Edmund Halley's "Ode to Newton" declares that "mathematics drives away the clouds."[43] Beyond these metaphoric clouds, one could discern the "first cause," the transcendental "always and everywhere" at the very source of Newtonian space and time.

With the spread of Newtonian and Enlightenment ideals, the mechanical arts were elevated in status. They were promoted, in particular, by Denis Diderot in the *Encyclopédie* (see fig. 9.12). The society of the past, he argues, had suffered from the "disdain [of] useful men."[44] Even during the Ancien Régime, practitioners of the *arts et métiers* were placed at a middle level in the social hierarchy because their works involved both the hand and the mind (*esprit*). Bodily labour was still considered base, prompting some workers to stress their art (i.e., intellectual virtue) over the labour of other workers.[45] In response, Diderot sought to "pull the mechanical arts up from the debasement where prejudice has held them for so long" so that their technical knowledge could advance society.

Like other Enlightenment thinkers, Diderot believed that human beings belong to the natural order. Noting that the mechanical arts engage nature directly, he also believed that they occupy a more privileged position than the liberal arts. Empirical observations of wondrous nature

Fig. 9.12 Mineralogy machine. From *Encyclopédie, ou Dictionnaire raisonné des sciences, des arts et des métiers*, ed. Denis Diderot and Jean le Rond d'Alembert. Planches, vol. 5 (Paris: Briasson, David, Le Breton, 1768).

would lead to a proliferation of the arts, accelerated by "a detailed examination of the different aspects under which the same production can be considered."[46] In his essay "Art," he argues that "every art has its speculative and its practical aspect: the former consists in knowing the principles of an art, without their being applied; the latter in their habitual and unthinking application."[47] The artisan's habitual practice was still questionable and must conform to the natural laws discovered by human reason.

In this period there remained a separation between representation and realization. Diderot quips: "How many bad machines are suggested every day by men who imagine that levers, wheels, pulleys, and cables perform in a machine as they do on paper!" In *Géométrie descriptive* (1795), Gaspard Monge (1746–1818) establishes the first method for mapping the lived space of the world systematically onto a set of two-dimensional planes. Monge's rigorous rules for recording geometric figures became the basis of "mechanical drawing." According to Pérez-Gómez, "The invention ... was a crucial step in achieving a systematic mathematization of praxis."[48] Many considered Monge's method to be "indispensable" for the Architect.

Monge's method was adopted by Jean Nicolas Pierre Hachette (1769–1834), who was given the task of designing a curriculum on machines at the École Polytechnique after Monge was called away to Egypt to serve Napoleon. The course's text, *Traité élémentaire des machines*, was published in 1811 and became highly influential because its machines "ma[d]e the least skilled worker more skilled."[49] The text classifies machines on purely functional and geometric criteria, according to their conversion of one motion to another (e.g., circular to linear) (see fig. 9.13). The Englishman Robert Willis (1800–75), best known for his writings on the architecture of Cambridge, attempted to limit the problem of machines to "the domain of the mathematician." He argues: "For every machine will be found to consist of a train of pieces connected together in various ways, so that if one be made to move they all receive a motion, the relation of which to that of the first is governed by the nature of the connexion."[50] He also attempted to simplify the numerous combinations into a single system of "mere motion."

As a new possibility of the human will sought to secure the temporal world for future consumption, the machine became fully technological,

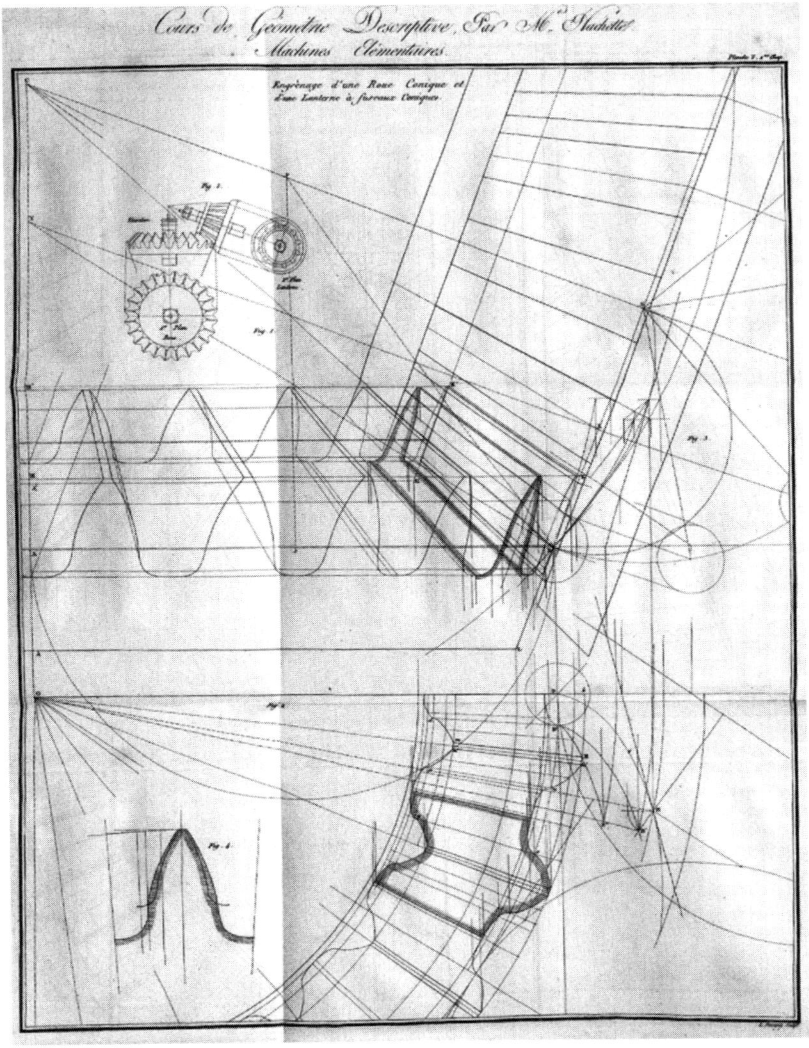

Fig. 9.13 Conical wheel gears and a lantern with conical spindles. From Jean Nicolas Pierre Hachette, *Traité élémentaire des machines* (Paris: Klostermann, 1811).

shedding its association with the elbow grease of the mechanical arts.[51] The autonomy and power of technology proper was indeed startling. In the nineteenth century, constructed and instrumental systems could be mapped onto entire areas of reality. Railroads, for instance, offered "emancipation from nature" and a "destruction of space and time" that required the synchronization of local and national time.[52] But we must remember that technology is *not* what is most visible (such as machines or engines), nor is it simply a tool that one has on hand. It is the knowledge that pre-exists the arrival of something and the means with which it is manifested. "The project at work in Technology," philosopher Michel Haar explains, "is a metaphysical project because it concerns all domains of reality and not only machines. It marks beings in their totality."[53]

PATAPHYSICAL MACHINES

In early modern French literature, before 1850, the machine was merely a marginal theme, often representing utility or inhumanity. It moved into the foreground with the utopian concerns of the Saint-Simoniens in the 1830s and 1840s, paralleled by the growing regard for the mechanical arts and, as Jarry puts it, "a universal substitution of Science for Art." The aesthetic of the machine in literature has been described as being "discovered" during the second half of the 1800s.[54] This interpretation is problematic because it presumes a re-presentation of the world that divides the machine into functional and aesthetic properties, as two sides of the same reductive Cartesian *phynance*. The functional interpretation, wedded to progress, moves teleologically towards the rapture of mathematical certainty, yielding ever more effective and efficient ejaculates. The aesthetic interpretation derived from eighteenth-century aesthetics, which sought to be the science of "things perceived," as logic was the science of "things known."

The history of the machine shows that these developments are very recent and not satisfactory. To redress this deficient dichotomy of function and aesthetics, I consider Jarry's literary machines by examining what Gianni Vattimo describes as their "ontological bearing" and their ability to found a world. Jarry, in short, takes a critical stance against these reductions and attempts to concoct a "science" that is otherwise.

Etymologically derived from epi (μετα τα φυσικα), pataphysics investigates "that which is superinduced upon metaphysics, whether within or beyond the latter's limitations, extending as far beyond metaphysics as the latter extends beyond physics." In *Gestes et opinions du Docteur Faustroll, pataphysicien* (1911), Jarry explains that a pataphysician studies *epiphenomena*: "An epiphenomenon being often accidental, pataphysics will be, above all, the science of the particular, despite common opinion that the only science is that of the general." This counters the claim that there is no *episteme* (knowledge or science) of the accidental since all *epistēmē* is lasting or at least occurs regularly.[55] Therefore, Jarry's "science" "will examine the laws governing exceptions." Obviously, he is giving the *digitus medius* to the scientific project that discredits what does not fit neatly into its apodictic framework. Modern physics is based on the world of appearances and quantifiable phenomena, while metaphysics is lost in abstractions that neglect the concrete and historical. Pataphysics targets precisely where we live. This includes dreams, hallucinations, and other outpourings of the imagination that modern science does not regard as "real."

"Hornstrumpot!" declares Jarry rather succinctly through the jaw of Père Ubu, "We shall not have succeeded in demolishing everything, unless we demolish the ruins as well. But the only way I can see of doing that is to use them to put up a lot of fine, well-ordered buildings."[56] For better or worse he admits, we find ourselves inheritors of these ruins and have little recourse except for a positive "architecturing." With its "ethernal" wager of world building, Jarry's "science" recognizes our singular, embodied position, with the earth underfoot and the sky above.[57] In doing so, it offers a philosophic orientation that "used science as a weapon against science."[58]

To plumb this realm, he invents a series of machines. With no apparent function, Carrouges argues, these "improbable" contrivances are governed neither by mere mechanics nor by conventional utility. It also makes little difference whether they are materially feasible. By suspending the functional aim of mechanics, these contentious pataphysical machines may seem "useless," but instead they present "the semblance of machinery, of the kind seen in dreams, at the theater, at the cinema."[59] This allies them more closely to their earlier architectural heritage of wondrous and imaginative contrivances in search of meaning.

In the modern age of rampant instrumentality, Jarry construes pataphysical machines against instrumental contrivances. He works pataphysically by adopting rational, deductive, and constructive facets of science and technology, then troping them, often ironically. Particularly "useful" for Jarry were the works of Lord Kevin, C.V. Boys, and William Crookes. His playful twisting of their technologies has further implications for temporality, the will, and, ultimately, the pursuit of signficance.

"Although technology is future-oriented," explains philosopher Lorenzo C. Simpson, "it is so in a way that seeks to annihilate the future *qua* future, that is as free possibility, so that the future remains open, but open for increased control."[60] Is Jarry's Père Ubu *not* a patent symbol of the failures of such wilful domination? The answer is, perhaps too obviously, yes. In theory, Ubu originates "nowhere" and is precisely he "who wants to erect his Will as sovereign law." As Gilles Deleuze argues: "It is Ubu who represents the fat being, the outcome of metaphysics as planetary technology and a completely mechanized science, the science of machines in all its sinister frenzy."[61] In Jarry's terms, Ubu is all things "grotesque" (see fig. 9.14). It is due to his ironic existence that our task of reading this "science ... for which a great need has been widely felt" is not obviated.[62] The playfulness and widespread irony of Ubu and his promotion of technology enable us to see the intentionality in full gear.

Pataphysics, Jarry reveals, "is the science of imaginary solutions, which symbolically attributes the properties of objects, described by their virtuality, to their lineaments."[63] These solutions hinge on certain definitions that are allied deeply to the real practice of the architect. The workings of pataphysical machines are precisely a ludic technology: a technology not of precision, but of suggestion. As Frascari observes, Pataphysical technology "enriches the perception of reality by making room for the play between objects and the parts of construction, rather than limiting the design by defining tolerances among its parts."[64] Play is not devoid of intention: it incorporates rationality and the ability to "outplay this capacity for purposeful rationality," just as a child sets limits to its games and pushes them without becoming a "spoil-sport": "In this fashion we actually intend something with effort, ambition, and profound commitment."[65] The crux of play is self-representation: it is "*intended as something*, even if it is not something conceptual, useful, or purposive, but only the pure autonomous regulation of movement."[66] According to Paul Valéry, "No skepticism is possible where the rules of a game are concerned, for the principle underlying them is an unshakeable truth."

By "defining tolerances" with increasing exactitude in mechanistic representations (e.g., realism or naturalism) or specifications, technology attempts to secure control here and now, negating the future as future. Pataphysical machines operate in ways that counter this egocentric demand. The aim of Jarry's machinations, like his writing, is to "suggest

Fig. 9.14 *Véritable portrait de Monsieur Ubu*. From Alfred Jarry, *Ubu Roi* (Paris: Edition du Mercure de France, 1896).

rather than to state,"[67] to dis*play* what is essentially singular and to reveal "laws governing exceptions." Pataphysical machines work *through* the appropriation (plagiarism?) and playful repositioning of technological doings, while embodying its cognitive endeavour. Jarry says that "the Machine is born in the ashes of the slave" and is made to "serve the lowly intelligence." The "improbable" workings of pataphysical machines are of a variant order. The "Power their Use confers" is the discovery of similarities (metaphor, metonymy, and other alignments of lineaments) that would be barred by the technological criteria for assessing the truth of a non-rational proposal. This discovery of similarities is a temporal event that finds unpredictable arrangements but does not preclude rigour and "symbolic accuracy," as in Dr Faustroll's polyvalent vessel (*un as*), a bed, boat, and sieve used for his journey "From Paris to Paris by Sea" (see fig. 9.15).

To manifest "accuracy," pataphysical machines rely on a form of mimesis. Jarry's essay, "Du mimétisme inverse chez les personnages de Henri de Régnier," describes his notion of mimesis (*mimétisme inverse*) and differentiates it from the camouflage of mere imitation. It is associated with the process of "exomosis": a form of play in which spaces swell in the presence of a work or a character, and they "congeal [*figent*] their

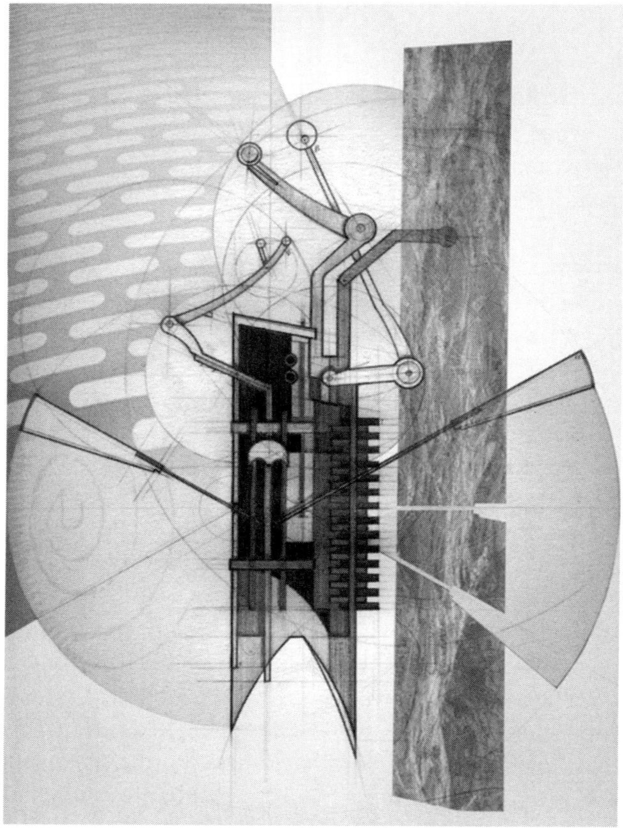

Fig. 9.15 Docteur Faustroll's *skiff*. Mixed media drawing by author.

surroundings into their own image and erect palaces of space around themselves."[68] Faustroll's voyage and the transformation of Paris into a "hyper-artistic environment"[69] are precisely this. Looking closer at Jarry's definition, the idea of congealing, or thickening, in the process of edification is opposed to Romanticism's creation *ex nihilo*: "We cannot create something out of nothing," avers Jarry, "but we can create out of chaos."[70] Etymologically, chaos is both a space and a substance, akin to the alchemical *prima materia* (or Platonic *chora*).[71] It is the erotic space/place that may be grasped only by "spurious reasoning," as Plato reminds us.

Pataphysics is perhaps such a reasoning that discloses a deeper commonality within the mute horizon of the world prior to division. This anterior *chaos* certainly counters the reductive and mechanistic premises of the Newtonian void. Since the self-same mechanisms "by which we only meant at first to explain our conduct will end by also controlling it ... we shall witness permanent associations being formed," Henri Bergson argues, "and little by little ... automatism will cover our freedom."[72]

Creation then springs from our embodied experience of the world and the pre-categorical phenomena that are assimilated by Jarry's biking at rapid speed (see fig. 9.16). Following Deleuze, pataphysics is "inseparable from a phenomenology" or a new – and by "new" we mean older – comprehension of phenomena. Jarry notes that most people assume that a phenomenon will always show itself in exactly the same manner, as if it were a perpetual machine. "This is true," he says, "only in a majority of cases, [though it] depends on the point of view." He suggests that custom is involved in all forms of *measure* and is not neutral. Bergson, who was Jarry's professor at Lycée Henri IV, later wrote "that an element of convention enters into any measurement."[73] Jarry argues that this "universal assent" is "codified only for convenience," often under the pretext of utility.[74] The target of his rebuke shows that the well-worn distinction between the liberal arts and the mechanical arts is still prevalent, although modernity leans heavily towards the mechanical arts due to their utility and capacity to manifest predictable results.

The exceptional nature of phenomena suggests that neither we nor our machines are solely responsible for a phenomenon coming into being. While technology expects total foresight and consistency to harness things in a productive manner, the pataphysician's world embraces opacity and contingent accidents.[75] Hannah Arendt maintains that the contingent is "an act that by definition can also be left undone" and, consequentially, is attached to the free will.[76] "Implicit in the faculty of the Will," she argues, is the "notion of human freedom." Freedom of choice and the desire for something new and unpredictable have often been defeated by divine providence or mechanistic laws of causality. Therefore, it is no surprise that pataphysics "will examine the laws governing exceptions" since "free acts are exceptional," according to Henri Bergson.[77] The pataphysical embrace of radical contingency and chance is double-edged: if all is indeed accidental, the totalizing technological will is castrated and the

Fig. 9.16 Alfred Jarry on "that which rolls" (1898). Roger-Viollet/Topfoto.

future cannot be secured completely – a circumcision of fore ... sight. Still, the pataphysician does not repudiate the will, for without it nothing happens. Jarry espouses the free act but limits the will, breaking from positivism and the technological ideal.

Opposing the Ubu-esque desire to dominate and possess, his Docteur Faustroll imaginatively works *through* the technological towards participation, eros, and death – themes explored by almost all of Jarry's machines. He also avoids falling into personal expressions of sentimentality and emotion, as he is much too detached and "scientific" for such trite things. He ultimately seeks a unique world with a "science" that "will explain the universe supplementary to this one; or, less ambitiously, will describe a universe which can be – and perhaps should be – envisaged in the place of the traditional one, since the laws that are supposed to have been discovered in the traditional universe are also correlations of exceptions."[78] More radically than most, he did his damnedest to live this world. It likely cost him his life. Yet, his was ultimately an ethical stance, Octavio Paz argues, based on "the subversion of self."[79]

Pataphysics and its machines are undeniably controversial in an age when machines and their rationale are assumed to have a direct line to reality. Jarry's machinations, if appropriately translated, offer a positive alternative – analogous to the play of the work of art – that speaks to the pataphysician-cum-architect's "ethernal" and "improbable" wager of world building. But, as Jarry notes at the conclusion of his book, one must "acquire enough experience to savour all its beauties in full."[80]

NOTES

1 Michel Carrouges, "Directions for Use," in *The Bachelor Machines* [*Le machine celibi*], ed. Harald Szeemann (New York: Rizzoli, 1975), 44. In the following, Jarry's machines are not described along Duchampian lines, as this tends to obscure certain features.

2 Alfred Jarry, *Oeuvres complètes*, 3 vols., ed. Michel Arrivé, Henri Bordillon, Patrick Besnier, and Bernard Le Doze (Paris: Gallimard, Bibliothèque de la Pléiade, 1972–88), 1:341. All translations of Alfred Jarry are mine unless otherwise noted.

3 Indra Kagis McEwen, "Instrumentality and the Organic Assistance of Looms," in CHORA*: Intervals in the Philosophy of Architecture*, vol. 1, ed. Alberto Pérez-Gómez and Stephen Parcell (Montreal and Kingston: McGill-Queen's University Press, 1994), 125.

4 Vitruvius, *On Architecture*, trans. Frank Granger (Cambridge, MA: Harvard University Press, 1970), 2:275.

5 Ibid., 2:277.

6 McEwen, "Instrumentality and the Organic Assistance of Looms," 129.

7 Aristotle, *Nichomachean Ethics*, trans. Rev. P. Wicksteed and F.M. Cornford (Cambridge, MA: Harvard University Press, 1937), 199a7.

8 Dalibor Vesely, "Architecture and the Question of Technology," in *Architecture, Ethics, and Technology*, ed. Louise Pelletier and Alberto Pérez-Gómez (Montreal and Kingston: McGill-Queen's University Press, 1994), 33.

9 Marcel Detienne and Jean-Pierre Vernant, *Cunning Intelligence in Greek Culture and Society*, trans. Janet Lloyd (Atlantic Highlands, NJ: Humanities Press, 1978), 46.

10 *The Mechanical Problems* [attributed to Aristotle], in *The Works of Aris-*

totle, vol. 23, trans. Thomas Taylor (Somerset: Prometheus Trust, 2003), 497.

11 The term "habit" is used here to suggest that nature (*physis*) was not understood as having immutable laws until perhaps the eighteenth century.

12 Karin Tybjerg, "Wonder-Making and Philosophical Wonder in Hero of Alexandria," *Studies in History and Philosophy of Science* 34 (2003): 443–66.

13 Alberto Pérez-Gómez, "The Architect's Métier," *section A*, 2, 5/6 (1985): 12.

14 "Only in the work of the Alexandrian engineers, especially Heron, is there any evidence of interest in the instruments and machines as such, and only here was their construction undertaken with an attitude that we can describe as truly technical" (Detienne and Vernant, *Cunning Intelligence*, 295).

15 Jean-François Lyotard, "Considerations on Certain Partition-Walls as the Pontentially Bachelor Elements of a Few Simple Machines," in *The Bachelor Machines* [*Le machine celibi*], ed. Harald Szeemann (New York: Rizzoli, 1975), 98.

16 Plato, *The Sophist*, trans. Harold North Fowler (Cambridge, MA: Harvard University Press, 1986), 455–9. Sophistry differs from the mechanical in that it operates not on the world but on people.

17 Seneca, *17 Letters*, trans. C.D.N. Costa (Warminster: Aris and Phillips, 1988), 91.

18 Aristotle, *Politics*, trans. H. Rackham (London: Heinemann, 1932), 638–9.

19 Elspeth Whitney, "Paradise Restored: The Mechanical Arts from Antiquity through the Thirteenth Century," *Transactions of the American Philosophical Society* 80, 1 (1990): 32.

20 Isidore of Seville, *The Etymologies of Isidore of Seville*, ed. and trans. Stephen A. Barney, W.J. Lewis, J.A. Beach, and Oliver Berghof (New York: Cambridge University Press, 2006), 377.

21 Ignatius of Antioch, "Letter to the Ephesians," in *The Epistles of St Clement of Rome and St Ignatius of Antioch*, trans. James A. Kleist (Mahwah, NJ: Paulist Press, 1978), 63–4.

22 Mary Carruthers, *The Craft of Thought* (Cambridge: Cambridge University Press, 1998), 23.

23 Augustine, *The City of God*, trans. Rev. Marcus Dods, in *The Works of Aurelius Augustine, Bishop of Hippo* (Edinburgh: T. & T. Clark, 1871), 2:417–32.

24 Lorraine Daston and Katharine Park, *Wonders and the Order of Nature, 1150–1750* (New York: Zone Books, 1998), 90.

25 Hugh of St Victor, *The Didascalicon of Hugh of St Victor: A Medieval Guide to the Arts*, trans. Jerome Taylor (New York: Columbia University Press, 1961), 191.
26 See Martin of Laon, *Scholica graecarum glossarum*, ed. M.L.W. Laistner, in "Notes on Greek from the Lectures of a Ninth Century Monastery Teacher," *Bulletin of the John Rylands Library* 7 (1922–23): 439.
27 Leonardo da Vinci, *Notebooks*, ed. Thereza Wells (London: Oxford University Press, 2008), 276.
28 E.J. Dijksterhuis, *The Mechanization of the World Picture* (London: Oxford University Press, 1961), 255.
29 Marco Frascari, *Monsters of Architecture: Anthropomorphism in Architectural Theory* (Savage, MD: Rowman and Littlefield, 1991), 24.
30 Ibid., 46.
31 Galileo Galilei, "The Assayer," in *Discoveries and Opinions of Galileo*, trans. Stillman Drake (New York: Doubleday, 1957), 237.
32 Galileo Galilei, *Dialogues Concerning the Two Chief World Systems*, trans. Stillman Drake (Los Angeles: University of California Press, 1967), 232.
33 Galileo Galilei, *Dialogues Concerning Two New Sciences*, trans. Henry Crew and Alfonso de Salvio (New York: Macmillan, 1914), 3.
34 Liane Lefaivre and Alexander Tzonis, "The Machine in Architectural Thinking," *Daidalos* 18 (1985): 16–26.
35 Daston and Park, *Wonders and the Order of Nature*, 19.
36 Alberto Pérez-Gómez, *Architecture and the Crisis of Modern Science* (Cambridge, MA: MIT Press, 1985), 238-9.
37 Dijksterhuis, *Mechanization of the World Picture*, 363.
38 Dalibor Vesely, *Architecture in the Age of Divided Representation* (Cambridge, MA: MIT Press, 2004), 295–6.
39 Ibid., 296.
40 Robert Hooke, *Micrographia, or some Physiological Descriptions of Minute Bodies Made by Magnifying Glasses, with Observations and Inquiries Thereupon* (New York: Dover, 1961), iv.
41 Julien Offray de La Mettrie, *Man a Machine* (Chicago: Open Court, 1912), 41.
42 Pérez-Gómez, *Architecture and the Crisis of Modern Science*, 77.
43 Edmund Halley, "Ode to Newton," in Isaac Newton, *The Principia: Mathematical Principles of Natural Philosophy*, trans. I. Bernard Cohen and Anne Whitman (Berkeley and Los Angeles: University of California Press, 1999), 379–80.

44 Denis Diderot and Jean le Rond d'Alembert, *Encyclopédie, ou Dictionnaire raisonné des sciences, des arts et des metiers* (Stuttgart-Bad Cannstatt: Frommann, 1966), 1:714.
45 William H. Sewell, *Work and Revolution in France: The Language of Labor from the Old Regime to 1848* (New York: Cambridge University Press, 1980), 24.
46 Ibid., 67.
47 Diderot and d'Alembert, *Encyclopédie*, 1:714 (my translation).
48 Pérez-Gómez, *Architecture and the Crisis of Modern Science*, 281.
49 Pierre Hachette, *Traité élémentaire des machines* (Paris: Klostermann, 1811), vii (my translation).
50 Robert Willis, *Principles of Mechanisms* (London: Cambridge University Press, 1871), iv.
51 "The will to will forces the calculation and arrangement of everything for itself as the basic forms of appearance, only, however, for the unconditionally protractible guarantee of itself. The basic form of appearance in which the will to will arranges and calculates itself in the unhistorical element of the world of completed metaphysics can be stringently called 'technology.'" See Martin Heidegger, *The End of Philosophy*, trans. Joan Stambaugh (Chicago: University of Chicago Press, 2003), 93.
52 Gerhard Dohrn-van Rossum, *History of the Hour: Clocks and Modern Temporal Orders*, trans. Thomas Dunlap (Chicago: University of Chicago Press, 1996), 337–9.
53 Michel Haar, *The Song of the Earth: Heidegger and the Grounds of the History of Being*, trans. Reginald Lilly (Bloomington, IN: Indiana University Press, 1993), 80.
54 Jacques Noiray, *Le Romancier et la machine: L'image de la machine dans le roman français (1850–1900)*, vol. 2: *Jules Verne et Villiers de L'Isle-Adam* (Paris: José Corti, 1982), 7–28; Herbert L. Sussman, *Victorians and the Machine: The Literary Response to Technology* (Cambridge, MA: Harvard University Press, 1968), 1–12.
55 Aristotle, *Metaphysics*, trans. Hugh Tredennick (Cambridge, MA: Harvard University Press, 1979), 1027a.
56 Jarry, *Oeuvres complètes*, 1:427.
57 Alberto Pérez-Gómez and Louise Pelletier, *Architectural Representation and the Perspective Hinge* (Cambridge, MA: MIT Press, 2000), 296–7.
58 Octavio Paz, *Marcel Duchamp: Appearance Stripped Bare*, trans. Rachel Phillips and Donald Gardner (New York: Seaver Books, 1981), 136.

59 Carrouges, "Directions for Use," 21.

60 Lorenzo C. Simpson, *Technology, Time and the Conversations of Modernity* (London: Routledge, 1995), 54.

61 Gilles Deleuze, *Essays Critical and Clinical*, trans. Daniel W. Smith and Michael A. Greco (Minneapolis: University of Minnesota Press, 1997), 92–3.

62 Jarry, *Oeuvres complètes*, 1:497.

63 Ibid., 1:722.

64 Frascari, *Monsters of Architecture*, 61.

65 Hans-Georg Gadamer, *The Relevance of the Beautiful and Other Essays*, ed. Robert Bernasconi (New York: Cambridge University Press, 1989), 23.

66 Ibid.

67 Jarry, *Oeuvres complètes*, 1:171. Here Jarry is following a well-known statement by Stéphane Mallarmé: "*To name* an object is to suppress three-quarters of the enjoyment of the poem, which derives from the pleasure of step-by-step discovery; to *suggest*, that is the dream. It is the perfect use of this mystery that constitutes the symbol: to evoke an object little by little, so as to bring to light a state of the soul or, inversely, to choose an object and bring out of it a state of the soul through a series of unravelings." See Henri Dorra, *Symbolist Art Theories: A Critical Anthology* (Berkeley: University of California Press, 1995), 139–42.

68 Jarry, *Oeuvres complètes*, 2:415. Alfred Jarry, *Selected Works of Alfred Jarry*, trans. Simon Watson Taylor (New York: Grove Press, 1965), 91.

69 Ben Fisher, *The Pataphysician's Library* (Liverpool: Liverpool University Press, 2000), 203.

70 Jarry, *Oeuvres complètes*, 1:770.

71 "Linked etymologically to the Indo-European *chasho*, chaos maintains its connotations as a primordial gap, opening, or abyss, as well as a primordial substance." See Alberto Pérez-Gómez, "Chora: The Space of Architectural Representation," in CHORA: *Intervals in the Philosophy of Architecture*, vol. 1 (Montreal and Kingston: McGill-Queen's University Press, 1994), 9.

72 Henri Bergson, *Time and Free Will: An Essay on the Immediate Data of Consciousness*, trans. F.L. Pogson (London: George Allen and Unwin, 1950), 237.

73 Henri Bergson, *The Creative Mind: An Introduction to Metaphysics* (New York: Philosophical Library, 1946), 12.

74 Jarry, *Oeuvres complètes*, 1:669; Jarry, *Selected Works*, 193.

75 See Bergson, *Time and Free Will*, 73. Against the causal relation of events and asserting the exceptional nature of free acts, Bergson argues that phenomena are ordered retroactively.

76 Hannah Arendt, *The Life of the Mind*, vol. 2: *Willing* (New York: Harcourt Brace Jovanovich, 1978), 29.

77 Bergson, *Time and Free Will*, 167.

78 Jarry, *Oeuvres complètes*, 1:668; Jarry, *Selected Works*, 192–93.

79 Paz, *Marcel Duchamp*, 136.

80 Jarry, *Oeuvres complètes*, 1:1237–8.

The Tree, the Cross, and the Umbrella: Architecture and the Poetics of Sacrifice

Santiago de Orduña

Chora

The city opens like a heart
like a fig the flower that is a fruit
more desire than incarnation
the incarnation of desire
Something is about to happen
the poet said

– Octavio Paz[1]

ACCORDING TO AZTEC MYTHOLOGY, the world fell into darkness with the end of the Fourth Sun. The gods gathered at Teotihuacan to discuss who would be sacrificed to put the universe into motion again (see fig. 10.1). Tecciztecatl ("the old man-on-the-moon") came forward and offered himself for immolation. The gods made a fire at the centre of a square platform, a *momoxtli,* but when Tecciztecatl was about to jump into the fire, he stepped back. Nanahuatzin ("the blistered one") immediately threw himself into the fire instead. The other gods then gathered on the platform to look towards the place on the horizon where the new sun, a transformation of this god, was expected to appear. It rose in the east. Contemplating this heavenly sphere shining in all its magnificence, the other gods felt ashamed. Wanting to share the glory of being part of the universe, they too cast themselves into the fire, thus forming the moon and the stars.[2]

The gods felt *ashamed*, and it was shame rather than guilt that characterized the ethos of the people who inhabited Mesoamerica before the Europeans arrived. To them, the living world gave itself as heat, air, water, and food for every living being. At birth, all creatures inherited this original debt, which could be paid in full only with one's death.

What we call "ritual sacrifice" was referred to by the Nahua as *(i)xtlahua*,[3] which means "payment of debt." The related word *(i)xtlahui* refers to the satisfaction that is experienced by both debtor and creditor when the final payment is made. Through sacrifice, the cosmic order was re-established and both gods and humans found relief.

Performing sacrificial acts enabled the Nahuas to live in harmony among beasts and others, under the sky. Sacrifice was a response to a world of natural forces that were personified by their gods. To ask favours from the gods, the Nahuas had to offer blood.[4]

The *momoxtli* was the paradigmatic place of sacrifice. In ritual compounds it was usually located at the centre of a courtyard, where it rep-

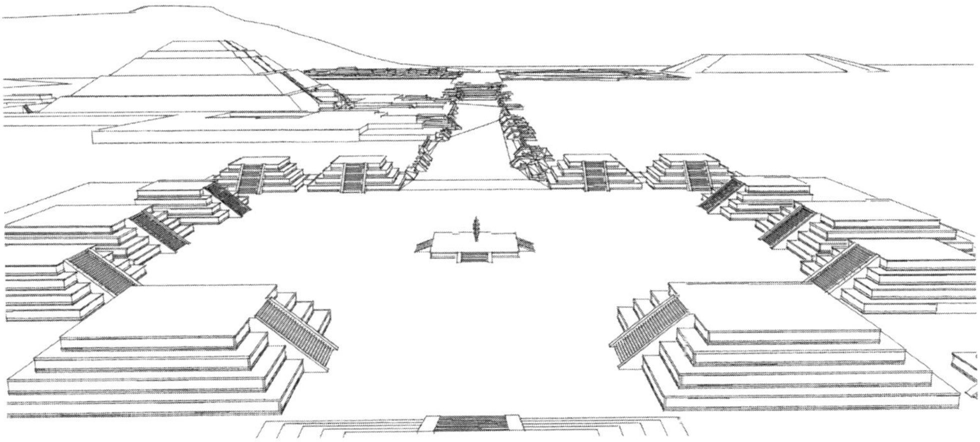

Fig. 10.1 View of Teotihuacan from the Pyramid of the Moon. Digital image by author.

resented the *Cemanahuac yollotli* ("the heart of the universe"). As shown in the map of the *Primeros Memoriales* (see fig. 10.2), daily offerings of *copal* incense were made to the four cardinal directions from the top of a *momoxtli*. This primordial ritual oriented the world and reinforced the bond between the world and humans. With pristine clarity, its simple geometry marked a centre, an above, a below, and the world's four cardinal directions. A *momoxtli* was more than just a representation of the cosmos: it was its *teixiptla*, its incarnation, and it had a cosmic magnetism that maintained an energetic bond with the world.[5] Anything that occurred on the *momoxtli* had cosmic resonance. Like the gods who inhabited the living mountains, whoever stood on a *momoxtli* acquired a god-like perspective. This was where humans and gods became *coates* (twins).[6] The *momoxtli* was a place of mediation between humans and the forces of nature, a stage for the drama of life and death. It was a place for both existential orientation and cosmic battle. This battle was not between antithetical forces (such as good and evil) but between symmetrical forces. Both sacrificer and sacrificed personified the gods and opposed one another as mirrored images. One's opponent was not "the other" but an image of oneself.[7] Attired with ornaments of the gods, the sacrificer and the sacrificed were a single manifestation of a dual god immolating himself.

Sacrificial death collapsed the distance between gods and humans, and between self and other. At the moment of sacrifice the two became one, like the monstrous face of Coatlicue, in which two serpent heads emerge from a decapitated body and attack one another, as if reflected in a mirror (see fig. 10.3). Attacking one's image symbolized the tense symmetry between life and death.

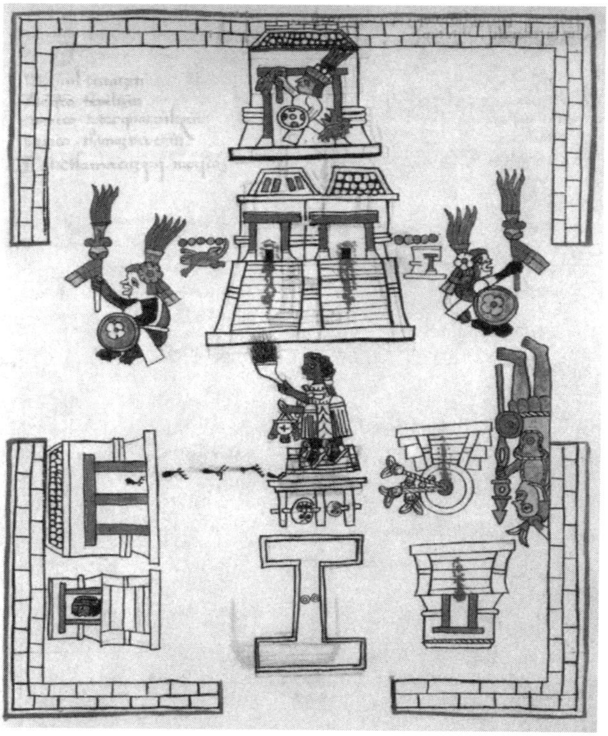

Fig. 10.2 Ritual precinct of Tepeapulco. Bernardino de Sahagún, *Primeros Memoriales* (early Colonial, 1559–61), from *Códices Matritenses,* fol. 269r.

Fig. 10.3 Coatlicue (fifteenth century). National Museum of Anthropology, Mexico City.

This pairing of elements resembled the way for creating new words in the Nahuatl language by pairing existing words. This hierarchic layering, known as *difrasismo*, gave the Nahuatl language a poetic character and reflected how these people of Mesoamerica interpreted the world as a dualistic ritual: life fed death and death fed life. Sacrificial death promoted life through an interchange of cosmic energies. The alternative of a single universe, in which either life or death prevails, would be unbalanced and would end catastrophically.

The *momoxtli* was a condensed, irreducible representation of the universe. It was conceived as a floating mountain, the *Cemanahuac*,[8] emerging from the polished surfaces of the courtyards, just as the primordial mountain had emerged from the original waters. In Mesoamerican architecture almost every building was raised above ground level on an altar-platform. The *teocallis* (temples, pyramids; from *teo* [god] and *calli* [house]) were *momoxtlis* of different sizes, layered vertically, with the shrines of the gods on the uppermost platform.

The Nahuas understood the *momoxtli* in several dualistic ways: it was simultaneously a *tepetl* (mountain) and a *xico* (navel); a phallus and a vagina; a sacrificial stone and a spring of water; a battlefield and a cornfield. It was where the gods of life (Ometeotl and Ometecihuatl) and the gods of death (Mictlantecutli and Mictlantecíhuatl) met to immolate themselves and regenerate. In the space between the *momoxtli* and the walls of the temple precinct, audiences gathered to witness and contemplate this cosmic battle. It was often enacted in a "gladiatorial sacrifice," in which a captive warrior was tied by the foot to a round stone placed on a *momoxtli* and, armed with only a wooden club, engaged in mortal combat against a fully armed warrior.

Dramatic enactments at the *momoxtli* enabled the universal scale to be represented at a human scale. The corners of the universe were reachable because they were also the corners of the courtyard. In Mesoamerican thought, everything existed "within the circuit."[9] All architectural forms were conceived as units within other, analogous units. Households (*calli*), districts (*calpulli*), ritual compounds (*calpolco*), and towns (*altepetl*) were a nested series of units, all with centres and limits, with the cosmos as their ultimate model.

Architectural elements in the ritual compounds were aligned to indicate solstices and equinoxes and to mark where planets and constellations appear on the horizon. The shadow of a gnomon signalled the exact moment of sacrifice. During some ceremonies a *cuahuxicalli* vessel,[10] containing the hearts of sacrificed victims, was placed at the centre of the *momoxtli*, the point of connection between north and south, east and west, upper world and underworld, life and death. During the ceremonies dedicated to Tlaloc, the god of rain, an *ahuehuete* tree called Tota ("our father") was planted at the central *momoxtli*. Four other trees representing the corners of the universe were placed around it. Thick ropes connected the central tree to the four others, forming a spatial quincunx. The metaphor of the tree shows how sacrificial death enabled life to drive its roots into the underworld, elevate its branches into the sky, and define the four directions of the world (see fig. 10.4).[11]

At the beginning of the Colonial period (1521–1821), the Nahua *momoxtli* was used by missionaries for Christian rituals and theatrical performances. Later, in the monasteries built by the mendicant orders, these rituals were performed in an "open chapel" in the monastery courtyards. The place of sacrifice – now the sacrifice of Christ – was moved

Fig. 10.4 Tota ("our father"). A tree at the centre of the courtyard in front of Tlaloc's temple on the feast of Huey Tozoztli is tied to four other trees, actualizing the cosmos as a quincunx. Fray Diego Durán, *The Book of the Gods and Rites and the Ancient Calendar* (Norman, OK: University of Oklahoma Press, 1971).

from the centre to the side of the precinct. This displacement marginalized the audience and dissociated them, to some degree, from the ritual. The ritual *enactment* of the Nahua sacrifice was replaced by Christian *acting*.

It has been argued that the model to build the Franciscan monasteries was the Tabernacle in the Desert.[12] The model to build the Tabernacle was presented to Moses by God, and, in that sense, it represented an external ideal reality to the world. Rather than *being* the cosmos, the "open chapel" and monastery represented an "otherworldly" reality.

At the centre of the monastery courtyard the missionaries planted wooden crosses that evidently were understood by the natives as surrogates of the "cosmic tree" (see fig. 10.5).[13] The skull of Adam (believed to be buried in the Golgotha Mount just behind Christ's crucifix)[14] was represented at the bottom of these crosses, closely resembling the arboreal "death-is-life" metaphor of the Mesoamerican natives, represented in the

Codex Vindobonensis Mexicanus.[15] In time, these wooden crosses were replaced by stone versions that still conflate the figure of Christ with the wooden cross: the tree of life and death (see fig. 10.6).

Although the Christian symbolism was easily accepted by the Nahua because of its apparent similarities with their own, there were important differences. Christian sacrifice was not meant to promote cosmic balance but to cleanse human sin. Nahua ritual cannibalism and Christian communion were strikingly similar, but they were also very different: the Nahuas consumed the flesh of a sacrificial victim to establish a vital communion with cosmic energies, whereas Christians consumed the holy host to reinforce their communion with a transcendent entity that cleansed them of sin and liberated them from worldliness. Nahua sacrifice emphasized the present through ritual death and the re-establishment of cosmic order, whereas Christian communion promoted an incarnated ideal order in a messianic future.[16] According to Jaime Lara, the so-called fortress-monasteries of sixteenth-century New Spain were representations of heav-

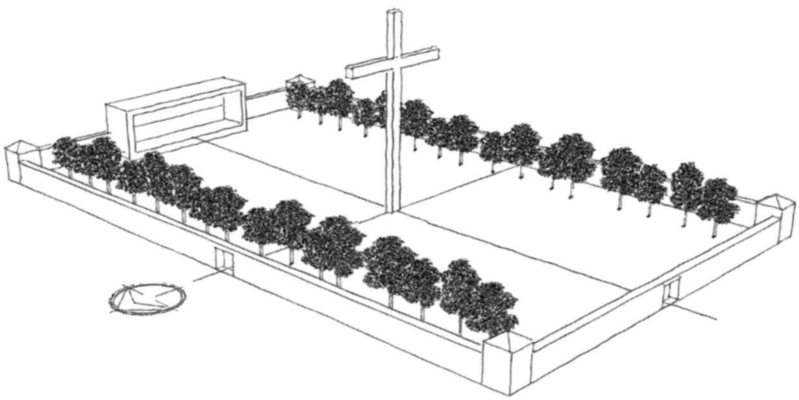

Fig. 10.5 San Jose de los Naturales, the first fortress-monastery in New Spain (sixteenth century). Drawing by Eduardo Mijangos, based on an image in Jaime Lara, *City, Temple, Stage: Eschatological Architecture and Liturgical Theatrics in New Spain* (Notre Dame, IN: University of Notre Dame Press, 2004).

Fig. 10.6 The Tree of Apoala is immolated by two gods giving birth to the first human couple. *Codex Vindobonensis* (pre-Hispanic, Mixtec). *Codex Vindobonensis Mexicanus* (Graz, Austria: Akademische Druck-u. Verlagsanstalt, 1974), fol. 37.

enly Jerusalem, a transcendent idea that yearned for the end of time. This would have been difficult for the Nahuas to grasp as their rituals engaged the phenomenal world in the present. The Christians believed that humans were not intrinsically bound to the fate of the universe and that the Christian persona[17] was bound not to the world but to a "totally other" absolute entity. In other words, Christians felt exiled on earth, while Mesoamericans felt at home. This illustrates the profound difference between these two cultures and how they inhabited the world.

Sacrifice was a natural way to promote good crops. On the *momoxtli*, life was sacrificed so that it could return as corn and beans. Modern technology has abandoned this reciprocity in favour of a unilateral relationship. It no longer imagines nature as a living entity that must be engaged but, rather, as an inert substance that must be transformed into something else according to an ideal model.

Western civilization regards the eradication of human sacrifice as a major moral victory;[18] however, we have also abandoned a sense of responsibility towards the living world. Whereas indigenous peoples tried to maintain a balanced cosmos and to avoid or postpone the end

Fig. 10.7 Mexico City. Photograph by author.

of the Fifth Sun, Christian missionaries sought to hasten the end of time by constructing an ideal model on earth that would prepare humankind for the second coming of Christ. By regarding the earth as a resource to be transformed or as a transitory purgatory from which to escape, the Christian vision disrupted the natural balance between the earth and its living creatures.

In Mexico, as in other modern nations, abstract isotropic space has neutralized the older magnetic centres and has blurred the limits of the cosmos that were once represented by the *momoxtli*, the walls in the ritual compounds, and even the colonial monastery courtyards. Limitless space has become the site for limitless human action. Mexico City has extended beyond all recognizable proportions. The mountainous boundaries of ancient Tenochtitlan are now blurred by residual substances and advertisements. The lake that was once the paradigmatic limit of the Aztec universe is now covered with asphalt. The profound relation that once existed between the inhabitants and their surroundings has been systematically debased. The character of the Mexican landscape has been forgotten. Except on an occasional clear day, the two great volcanoes, Popocatepetl and Ixtlacihuatl, are no longer visible from the city (see fig. 10.7).

But native legacies are still evident. Indigenous undercurrents continue to be potent forces that combine with modern intentions to shape Mexican reality. This *mestizo* fusion of heterogeneous elements cannot be analyzed under the singular light of rational thought: it can be apprehended only through poetic imagination.[19]

Death still retains a dual cultural meaning. Rather than being solely tragic, it usually has an ironic or even comical aspect. The Day of the Dead is perhaps the most festive time of year, when family altars are adorned with bright orange *cenpaxuchitl* flowers. Sugar skulls, with the names of deceased family members on their forehead, are placed in colourful altars, along with food for those who have departed: sweet potatoes, candies, alcoholic beverages, and *pan de muerto* (bread of the dead).

The *momoxtli* as a cosmic drama may have survived in the popular *Lucha Libre*: wrestling matches in which the contenders wear masks and ornaments, as if they were modern gods. These masked wrestlers perform as saints and demons, heroes and villains. All of them belong to one of the two major groups in Mexican *Lucha Libre*: the *técnicos* (fair players) and the *rudos* (rudes, bullies), both with a similar number of followers. Since the late 1950s, popular movies have portrayed them as national icons. After defeating the toughest enemies in the ring, Santo, Blue Demon, and Mil Máscaras had to fight zombies, vampire women, Aztec mummies, and various alien creatures to keep the world in order. In these movies, action in the gladiatorial arena was followed naturally by action in everyday life. In *Lucha Libre*, wrestlers are not really fighting for a title or for supremacy; rather, they are embodying conflicts between social and cosmic energies. The arena is a modern *momoxtli*, a framed universe in which the daily struggle for existence is dramatized by these masked saints and demons. The spectators are not merely watching them but fighting alongside them in struggles that are analogous to their own daily existence.

An architectural example of Mexican *mestizaje* (mixture) is the National Museum of Anthropology in Mexico City. Its architect, Pedro Ramírez Vázquez, intended to make a modern museum that would not be alien to the Mexican pre-Hispanic tradition. This intention would seem paradoxical if one regarded modernity simply as a denial of traditional models. Ramírez Vázquez, however, did not see modernity and tradition as contradictory. He assembled heterogeneous elements in a metaphoric process that was uncannily similar to the structure of the Nahuatl language,

Fig. 10.8 Central "umbrella-fountain" at the National Museum of Anthropology, Mexico City (1963). Photograph by author.

resulting in a hybrid that can be understood as both modern and traditional: a *mestizo* building.

While this combination of pre-Hispanic and modern architectures was part of the museum's program, it is both revealing and ironic that certain elements from the Mesoamerican tradition were not evident to Ramírez Vázquez himself. The best example is the central "umbrella" in the courtyard of the museum. When I asked him about its significance, he stated emphatically that it has no symbolic meaning but is solely a practical element that protects visitors from rain and sun, and allows them to move freely from hall to hall (see fig. 10.8).[20]

Despite his denial, the umbrella resonates strikingly with the Mesoamerican tradition. It recalls the *ahuehuete* tree that was planted at the *momoxtli* during the celebrations for the god of rain. This "umbrella" protects people from rain, but it also functions as a fountain that *makes* rain and provides a joyful microclimate in the courtyard. This converts an otherwise practical intention into a metaphoric and poetic event. In a revealing moment during my interview with Ramírez Vázquez, he pointed

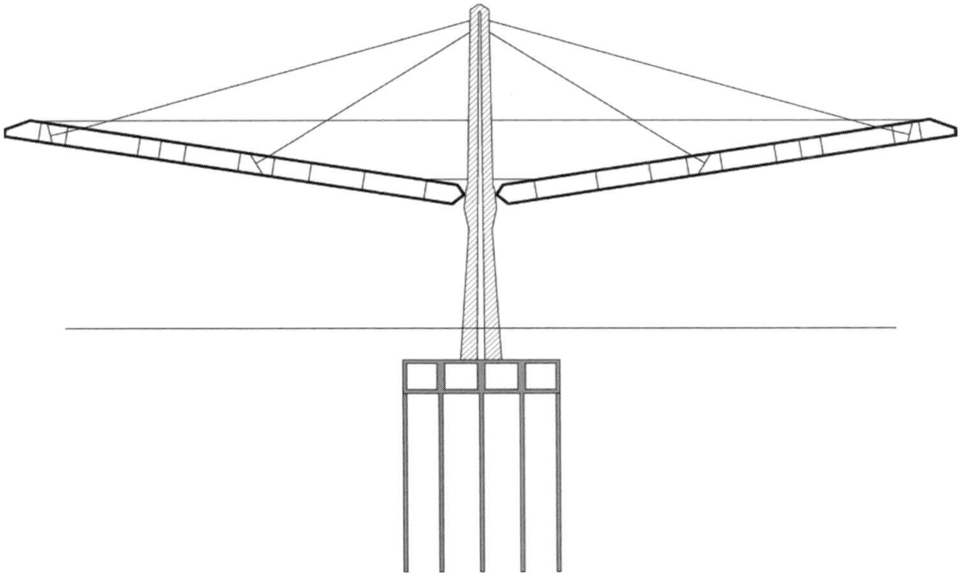

Fig. 10.9 Cross-section of the "tree-umbrella" at the National Museum of Anthropology, Mexico City (1963). Digital image by author.

to a section drawing of the umbrella and remarked, "Look, it is a tree" (see fig. 10.9). This cross-section shows how the structure hangs from the central post, recalling the Nahua rituals that actualized the limits of the cosmos by tying thick ropes from the central tree to four others (see fig. 10.4). The foundations of the "umbrella" appear as roots: the underworld counterpart of the upper structure, completing the dual meaning of the cosmic tree as both a tree of life and a tree of death. The umbrella also represents a bold inversion of the pyramidal mountain/altar, a *momoxtli* reflected by a mirror into the sky, where its true symbolic nature is revealed.

This historic metaphor is invoked by the *Papantla* fliers in the entrance esplanade of the museum. The fliers recreate an ancient ritual in which four people hang from a thirty-metre post and gradually descend, rotating to form a quincunx. At the top, a fifth participant dances and plays a flute and a tambourine (see fig. 10.10). This ritual re-enacts the old metaphor of the cosmic tree. It also resembles the umbrella at the centre of the courtyard, with its structure hanging from the central post.

Fig. 10.10 Voladores de Papantla at the exterior esplanade of the National Museum of Anthropology, Mexico City. Photograph by author.

Just as the wooden crosses in the sixteenth-century monastery courtyards were interpreted by the natives as surrogates of the cosmic tree, the umbrella in the twentieth-century museum suggests similar metaphorical meanings. These three central architectonic elements – the tree, the cross, and the umbrella – are connected through their function as devices for existential, ethical, and cosmic orientation.

NOTES

1 Octavio Paz, "Sleepless Night," *The Collected Poems of Octavio Paz, 1957–1987*, trans. Eliot Weinberger (New York: New Directions, 1991), 95.
2 Natives informed the Dominican missionary Diego Durán of the origin of the different orientations of the gods' temples:

The four main temples had entrances facing the directions I have mentioned and the four gods standing in them also face the same directions. Even though the reason given for this [plan] is fictitious, I shall not refrain from narrating it so that this arrangement is comprehensible.

The ancients believed that before the sun rose or had been created, the gods discussed lengthily among themselves, each insisting stubbornly on the direction he thought appropriate for the rising of the sun, which had to be determined before its creation. One, desirous of having his own way, said it was necessary that the sun rise in the north; another contradicted him, saying the south was better; another said no, that it should appear in the west; still another said that the east was most convenient for its rising. The last had his way. He turned his face [toward the direction] in which he wanted the sun to appear, and the rest turned their faces toward the directions they had chosen.

See Diego Durán, *Book of the Gods and Rites and the Ancient Calendar*, 1st ed., trans. and ed. Fernando Horcasitas and Doris Heyden (Norman, OK: University of Oklahoma Press, 1971), 78.

3 The Nahua were the various groups who spoke the Nahuatl language. They included the Mexicas, or Aztecs.

4 To the Nahuas there was no essential difference between humans and animals. The human soul was not conceived as a substance per se but as cosmic energy. See Arild Hvidtfeldt, *Teotl and Ixiptlatli: Some Central Conceptions in Ancient Mexican Religion* (Copenhagen: Munksgaard, 1958), 11–64.

5 Arild Hvidtfeldt associates the term *teotl* (god, sacred) with the Polynesian notion of *mana* (a natural force invested in an object or being). See the introductory note on myth in Hvidtfeldt, *Teotl and Ixiptlatli*, 11–64.

6 In Nahua architectural iconography the twin serpents represent connectors, thresholds, limits, and paths. See "Coatenamitl, the Serpent-Wall," in Santiago de Orduña, "Coatepec: The Great Temple of Tenochtitlan: Recreating a Metaphoric State of Dwelling" (PhD diss., McGill University, 2008), 60–4, available at http://digitool.library.mcgill.ca:8881/R/?func=dbin-jump-full&object_id=19261.

7 This conflict is represented paradigmatically by two battling children of Coatlicue: Coyolxauhqui, a lunar goddess, and her brother Huitzilopochtli, a solar god.

8 *Cemanahuac yollotli* (*centro del universo* [the heart of the universe]), as

defined by Fray Alonso de Molina, *Dictionary of Spanish and Nahuatl* (1555). The universe is described as *nelhuayotl* (*enraizado* [to be rooted]), meaning that it is rooted at the navel and provides sustenance for everything. The root *nel* is present in the compound *neltiliztli* (*verdad* [truth]). *Yotl* or *yollotl* (heart) is also synonymous with movement, implying that she/he is the source of all life and movement. See Miguel León Portilla, *Aztec Thought and Culture: A Study of the Ancient Nahuatl Mind*, 1st ed., trans. Jack Emory Davis (Norman, OK: University of Oklahoma Press, 1963), 92–6.

9 The primordial double force of the universe was personified by Ometeotl ("God-Two"), who informed all that existed. Several sources called Ometeotl *tloque-nahuaque*, from *tloc* (near; what is near) and *nahuac* (in the circuit of; in the ring). The personal possessive suffix "*-e*" is appended twice (*tloqu-e* and *nahuaqu-e*), indicating that "being near" and the "circuit" or "ring" are "of him." This has been translated in various ways: "It applies to him who is the very being of all things, preserving them and sustaining them" (Fray Alonso de Molina); "he who has everything in himself" (Francisco Javier Clavijero); "the lord of what is near and of what is in the ring or circuit" (León Portilla); and "the one who is near to everything and to whom everything is near" (Angel Maria Garibay). See León Portilla, *Aztec Thought and Culture*, 92.

10 From *cuah* (eagle), *xi* (*co*) (in the navel), and *calli* (house).

11 See Durán, *Book of the Gods and Rites*, 336. The *ahuehuete* (old water tree), known also as Moctezuma cypress, is a large tree that grows on the shores of lakes and rivers in the high plateaus of Mesoamerica. It can live for more than two thousand years and, like the *Árbol del Tule* in the State of Oaxaca, can reach a girth of fifty metres. The *ahuehuete* is associated symbolically with the ancient god Huehueteotl, another manifestation of the primordial dual god Ometeotl ("God-Two"), whose four sons, the Tezcaltlipocas, reigned at the four cardinal directions of the cosmos. See also John Bierhost, *History and Mythology of the Aztecs: The Codex Chimalpopoca* (Tucson: University of Arizona Press, 1992).

12 For more about this, see "Fray Diego Valadés: The Mestizo Paradox," in Orduña, "Coatepec," 133–62.

13 The tree planted during the festivities to Tlaloc, god of rain, was called *Tota*, *Topitzin*, and *Yollotl* by the Nahua. It was defined by the Dominican friar Diego Durán as the Father, the Son, and the Heart that unites them.

See Durán, *Book of the Gods and Rites*, 161. This is strikingly similar to the Christian Trinity and is probably a Christian reinterpretation of the Nahua ritual.

14 "Then delivered he Him therefore unto them to be crucified. And they took Jesus, and led Him away. And He, bearing His Cross, went forth into a place called the place of a skull ... where they crucified Him." See John 19:16–18 (New Advent Bible). From this passage came the idea that Adam was buried where Christ was crucified: "And He came to the place of a skull. Some say that Adam died there, and there lies; and that Jesus in this place where death had reigned, there also set up the trophy. For He went forth bearing the Cross as a trophy over the tyranny of death: and as conquerors do, so He bare upon His shoulders the symbol of victory." See Homily 85 on the Gospel of John, *New Advent Catholic Encyclopedia*, available at http://www.newadvent.org/fathers/240185.htm. It was then easy to see the cross as the tree of paradise and the victory of life over death: "Hidden in a cave under the earth is 'the skull of Adam.' We are thus reminded that Adam our forefather lost Paradise through the tree from which he wrongly partook; Christ is the new Adam, bringing us Salvation and Paradise through the tree of the Cross." See *Living Orthodoxy* 4, 3 (1982): n.p.

15 *Codex Vindobonensis Mexicanus I*, ed. Otto Adelhofer (Graz, Austria: Akademische Druck-u. Verlagsanstalt, 1974), fol. 37.

16 According to Jaime Lara, the recovery of Jerusalem from Muslim hands was a precondition for the second coming of Christ and the beginning of the thousand plentiful years announced in Revelation 20, when Christ would reign until the last judgment at the end of time. In Tlaxcala this was exemplified in the theatrical representation of the conquest of Jerusalem by Emperor Charles, in which the Tlaxcalans fought side by side with the Christians against the infidel Muslims. It seems reasonable that the natives believed this battle was not a theatrical representation but an authentic ritual.

17 *Naturae rationalis individua substantia* (an individual substance of a rational nature); first Christian definition by Boetius of Dacia (thirteenth century) in "De persona et duabus naturis," c. ii. *New Advent Catholic Encyclopedia*, available at http://www.newadvent.org/cathen/11726a.htm. The Nahua understanding of the human soul is quite different. The Nahua words for "soul" (*anima* or *alma* in Spanish) are *tetonalli* and *elhuayotl*, as defined by Fray Alonso de Molina (1555). *Tetonalli* comes from *teo* (sacred, god) and *tonalli* (the sun's warmth that permeates the universe and

makes it move). *Elhuayotl* comes from *yollot* (heart) and is associated with *nelhuayotl* (*raíz* [root]; and *fundamento* [foundation]). The two words that describe the Nahua understanding of the soul thus bring together the sun, the heart, and the condition of being rooted. This suggests a strong but distant relationship between two living forces of nature: one anchored centrally in the ground, the other situated at the limits of the cosmos. The metaphor of the universe as a living cosmic tree was prevalent in Mesoamerica. The afterlife was understood as a parallel and symmetrical world, as the roots of the cosmic tree that nourishes the living world above.

18 See Walter Burkert, *Homo Necans: The Anthropology of Ancient Greek Sacrificial Ritual and Myth*, trans. Peter Bing (Berkeley: University of California Press, 1983).

19 The *Zocalo*, the central square of Mexico City, took its name from the basement in which the national flag used to stand, a clear reminiscence of the ancient *momoxtli*. See Jaime Lara, *City, Temple, Stage: Eschatological Architecture and Liturgical Theatrics in New Spain* (Notre Dame, IN: University of Notre Dame Press, 2004), 177.

20 Ramírez Vázquez was educated in the functionalist school of José Villagrán García, which stressed the social role of architecture and regarded other aspects as secondary. His reluctance to admit any symbolic connotations in his own architecture may be due to this background.

Utopian Knowledge: Eidetics, Education, and the Machine

Jonathan Powers

UTOPIAS AS *EIDE*

SINCE THE APPEARANCE of *Utopia* in 1516, readers have speculated on what Thomas More might have meant in composing and publishing it. Is it a scathing social and political satire, a radical proposal for new laws and social forms, or a trap designed to embarrass those who accept its "suggestions"? More feints in each of these directions but never fully commits to any of them. The delicious and irrefragable polyvalence of *Utopia* proves that More cultivated an intense authorial self-consciousness as he wrote the work; it has also so charmed and fascinated readers that we have come to think of utopia as something foggy and ill-defined in itself.[1]

Due largely to this unjustified conflation of authorial ambiguity with conceptual ambiguity, contemporary commentators treat utopia only rarely as a self-contained cultural idea, replete with its own genealogy and implications. J. Max Patrick and G.R. Negley's definition is representative of the current state of commentary:

> There are three characteristics which distinguish the utopia from other forms of literature or speculation:
> (1) It is fictional.
> (2) It describes a particular state or community.
> (3) Its theme is the political structure of that fictional state or community.[2]

Patrick and Negley offer an analytic – as opposed to essential – definition. As it stands, it is difficult to see how their definition can do more than serve as the foundation for an endless, fatuous argument about whether this or that literary work "really is" a utopia, without any reference at all to literary works that are only somewhat utopian or to the utopian dimension of non-literary works. Their definition astutely identifies utopia's characteristic fusion of speculation and description in the treatment of politics, but it treats these elements as literary conventions. We recognize utopias as utopias, according to Patrick and Negley, because they are *not* romances, mysteries, or westerns; for them, utopias have their identity in their constellation of literary tropes. Ultimately, Patrick and Negley presuppose utopia's identity as a literary genre, even though the obvious inadequacy of their own definition suggests that it is no such thing.

Fig. 11.1 Crispin de Pas, frontispiece to *Didactica Opera Omnia* by John Amos Comenius (Amsterdam, 1627–57), reprinted in *John Amos Comenius (1592–1670): Selections*, trans. M.W. Keatinge and Iris Unwin (Paris: UNESCO, 1957).

A brief re-examination of More's *Utopia* – both progenitor and paragon of the genre – may help explode utopia's false identity as a literary genre. *Utopia* comprises two principal parts: (1) a brief episode that sets up a meeting of Raphael Hythlodae, a traveller, and two well-educated contemporaries (one of whom is a fictionalized version of More himself), followed by (2) the traveller's dispassionate and disinterested description of Utopian society. The plot in More's work restricts itself to the meeting of Hythlodae and his listeners and to Hythlodae's brief historical sketch (really a speculative mythological history) of the founding of Utopia as a nation. Readers learn about Utopia through Hythlodae's positivistic account and armchair interpretation of the Utopians' laws, customs, and professions of belief. No thinking, feeling Utopians are introduced or interviewed, and Hythlodae never relates any stories of rebellion, transgression, or dissent.

Utopia's enduring fame thus rests on More's success in using Hythlodae to construct a credible *eidos* – a *concept-image* – of an entire polity's way of life.[3] As Miriam Eliav-Feldon observes in her comprehensive survey and analysis of Renaissance utopias, "the unique trait of utopias as documents of social theory is that in them the concrete explains the abstract, the vivid picture lends attraction to the theory."[4] Utopias derive their persuasive power and moral authority not from rational argument but from the rhetorical plausibility of the concept-images they sketch.[5]

Despite the granularity and thinness of Hythlodae's account, More obviously intends that readers should grasp the Utopian polity as an integrated whole. By providing a mere skeleton of society, as it were, More invites readers to imagine the flesh by interpolating their own social experience and assumptions into Hythlodae's schema. Eliav-Feldon (citing Lewis Mumford) suggests that the essential innovation of utopia as an imaginative technique lies in precisely this gestalt: its representation of an entire city or society as an integrated system of discrete parts.[6] Patrick and Negley thus confuse things. Literary utopias do not "describe a particular state or community" in such a way as to take "the political structure of that ... state or community" as a theme; rather, utopias describe the political structure of a *schematic* state or community. Whatever innovations and additions the authors of subsequent utopias introduce into More's formula, they tacitly accept his premise that the analytic schema sketched in *Utopia* constitutes the essence of sociopolitical life. Indeed, it is precisely this "sketching" of a polity, this giving of eidetic content to the word "polity" (and "city"), that makes it possible for us to think of polities as configurable systems of analyzable parts.

CAMPANELLA: UTOPIAN EDUCATION, UNIVERSAL KNOWLEDGE

Every literary utopia in its essence constitutes an idealizing image that establishes the limits and meaning of politics. In addition to its status as a concept-image, the well-known *City of the Sun* (1623) by Tommaso Campanella (1568–1639) deploys images within the framework of the fiction for more narrowly conceived pedagogical purposes. The city, as Campanella succinctly describes it, "is divided into seven rings or huge circles named from [*sic*] the seven planets, and the way from one to the other of these is by four streets and through four gates, that look towards the four points of the compass."[7] At the very centre of the city's concentrically circular walls and radial street pattern sits the Solarian temple: the sun at the centre of a city that models the Copernican solar system.[8]

> The temple is built in the form of a circle; it is not girt with walls, but stands upon thick columns, beautifully grouped. A very large dome, built with great care in the centre or pole, contains another small vault as it were rising out of it, and this is a spiracle, which is right over the altar. There is but one altar in the middle of the temple … Nothing is seen over the altar but a large globe, upon which the heavenly bodies are painted, and another globe upon which there is a representation of the earth. Furthermore, in the vault of the dome there can be discerned representations of all the stars of heaven … with their proper names and power to influence terrestrial things marked in three little verses for each. There are the poles and greater and lesser circles according to the right latitude of the place, but these are not perfect because there is no wall below. They seem, too, to be made in their relation to the globes on the altar.[9]

Although cities have often been organized in imitation of a cosmological or mythical order, Campanella adds a detail that opens up an entirely new dimension: the use of paintings that do not merely adorn the interior or depict important personages or things but that also transform the entire interior of the temple into a coherent representation of the cosmos. Although the temple's architectural design interprets the cosmos's structure schematically, the temple's interior design, with its "representations of all the stars of heaven," attempts to interpret the cosmos's structure hypothetically. Stars and lines of latitude are represented as both real and unreal. Campanella's admission that the lines of latitude "are not perfect" confirms that the ultimate intention of the interior is to provide a perfect image of the cosmos, yet the size of the dome and the intrusion of architectural elements such as the altar render the model an inexact replica. In its overall form, the temple is an idealizing image that symbolizes the cosmos but patently does not depict it exhaustively. The interior murals, though, enable the temple to teach the structure of the cosmos to visitors.

The Solarians use similar murals to depict scientific knowledge in general. Their knowledge – which, thanks to their globetrotting emissaries, amounts to the aggregated knowledge of all humanity – has been incised into and painted onto the very walls of the city. Images, always accompanied by pithy labels, cover every upright exterior surface.[10] Solarian teachers actively use these murals to teach young Solarians everything from astrology to languages, but Campanella suggests that the mere presence of the murals influences the children's intellectual development. While Campanella's utopia is often singled out for its use of pedagogical murals, Frank and Fritzie Manuel point out that Campanella's belief in the pedagogical power of images is shared by his contemporaries.[11] In line with Eliav-Feldon's observation above, Campanella's innovation lies not in the specific notion of using images to teach but, rather, in his comprehensive vision for integrating that notion into a whole sociopolitical organism.[12] Envisioning an entire city as the concrete image of a compendium of human knowledge, Campanella assumes that the totality of human knowledge can be represented eidetically and that such representations can be fully integrated into a city, socially as well as architecturally.

CAMPANELLA: SOCIETY IN THE IMAGE OF SCIENTIFIC KNOWLEDGE

Solarian society organizes itself according to the structure of the knowledge it depicts in the city's murals. As their hierarch the Solarians appoint the one among them who is most learned and has mastered every field of scientific knowledge. The hierarch receives the name "Metaphysic." Beneath Metaphysic, the Solarian bureaucracy first is divided into three categories of social experience – Power, Wisdom, and Love are the titles of Metaphysic's chief lieutenants – and then into academic subdivisions of knowledge within each division.[13] When a person is recognized for having mastered a certain body of knowledge, that person is authorized to administer those activities on which his knowledge bears. Solarian society organizes itself according to what it knows, and though it has pretensions to know everything known by humans, it ultimately recognizes as knowledge only what it can sketch and label. Conversely, every visible thing – by which I mean not merely those things that fall within someone's field of vision but also those things that can be pointed out to others as identifiable, nameable, or indictable – corresponds to some part of the social hierarchy in Solarian society, but only and precisely insofar as social structure itself admits of eidetic representation.

As a utopia, *City of the Sun* teaches its readers the meaning of politics through the simple eidetic technique of sketching a schematic concept-image and calling it a city or a society. Campanella deploys an analogous pedagogical program in the fiction of his utopia. Solarian murals depict reality as the Solarians know it (in the strict sense). They present images of things to young viewers, and the corresponding labels name the images and transform them into *eide*, into idealizing images. Every image must be grasped not in the particularity of its style or material but in its generality. Solarian murals do not depict particular oak trees, for example; rather, they depict the general concept of an oak tree. The project at the heart of Solarian society, which organizes both their architecture and their social structure, boils down to establishing and enforcing an isomorphism between knowledge and society by means of images. Images thus act as the common currency in one of the great equivalences of our culture: we can make our societies "scientific" partly because both social structure and scientific knowledge are eidetically fungible.

Although Campanella describes Solarian pedagogy as a tour of the city to look at the walls and to listen to further explanations from teachers, it is interesting – and perhaps ironic – that his book contains no images or pictures of any kind.[14] Given the great attention to eidetic techniques during the Renaissance – especially in his native Italy – Campanella surely imagined particular images communicating particular facts or bits of knowledge.[15] It would fall to one of Campanella's intellectual heirs, however, to produce exemplars of such images. The results would form the kernel of the theory that would reform education throughout Europe.

COMENIUS: EIDETIC PEDAGOGY

The Manuels trace the line of intellectual heredity from Campanella through Johann Valentin Andreae (1586–1642), who wrote *Christianopolis* (1619), to John Amos Comenius (1592–1670) of Moravia (now part of the Czech Republic). Comenius, the man hailed as the "Copernicus of education," and who emerged as one of Campanella's intellectual progeny, prefaced his lifework in pedagogy with a curious pseudo-utopia written early in his career. Comenius's pedagogical oeuvre either foreshadows or simply lays out many of the educational theories, practices, and conceits that our culture now holds most dear. Among his most important contributions were a call for truly universal education (irrespective of gender, class, or age), an insistence that curricular content be connected to the pupil's life experience, and a universal method based on graduated complexity and empirical contact between the student and the subject of learning.

Comenius sees the world and human knowledge as isomorphic. For students to learn about the world, all they need is direct contact with it:

> Those things ... that are placed before the intelligence of the young, must be real things and not the shadows of things. I repeat, they must be things; and by the term I mean determinate, real, and useful things that can make an impression on the senses and on the imagination.[16]

Comenius almost immediately qualifies this condition: "If the objects themselves cannot be procured, representations of them may be used."[17] Visual representations adequately substitute for real objects in Comenius's pedagogy – notwithstanding his earlier insistence on direct contact – because the eye and the mind share an analogous structure:

> Science, or the knowledge of nature, consists of an internal perception, and needs the same accessories as the external perception of the eye, namely an object to observe, and light by which to observe it. If these are given, perception will follow. The eye of the inner perception is the mind or the understanding, the object is all that lies within or without our apprehension, while the light is the necessary attention.[18]

The visible world is not a *source* of knowledge: attention to the visible world *is* knowledge. To perceive the world with the mind's eye is to have knowledge of it; or, put otherwise, those things that we image to ourselves, we know. Comenius thereby replaces the living world – animated by mysterious forces and symbolizing an uncanny order that surpasses human understanding – with the clear and distinct world available to the inner eye.

On the basis of his epistemology, Comenius drafted his watershed *Orbis Pictus*, our culture's first educational picture book, which organizes the entire world into a series of images that strikingly resemble Campanella's description of Solarian murals.[19] A typical woodcut, such as *Ferae*

Pécudes "Wilde Cattel" (number 28) in Hoole's 1659 Latin-English translation of the original 1658 Latin-German version (see fig. 11.2), depicts several animals that are numerically indexed to their Latin and English names.

Once we have a Solarian image in front of us – and the woodcuts in *Orbis Pictus* are Solarian in all but name – we see clearly that the connection between retinal percept and mental concept is nomenclature. Comenius's woodcuts do not depict particular harts or hares but the general concepts *hart* and *hare*. The essence of nature is its look, its *eidos*, but our inner perception parses nature by how we name it as much as by how we see it. Images – even retinal images – become meaningful only through relation to a larger reality. By adding the name "hart," a mere squib of ink becomes the token of a type defined by an *eidos*. In indexing the images to names, Comenius populates his book with herds of concepts. Knowledge, for Comenius as for Campanella's Solarians, consists essentially of named images.

In his preface to a modern selection of some of Comenius's pedagogical writings, Jean Piaget explains that Comenius's eidetic pedagogy extends Campanella's equivalence between knowledge and society to include nature: "The central idea [of Comenius's pedagogy] is probably that of nature as a creator of forms, which, being reflected in the human mind, thanks to the parallelism between man and nature, makes the ordering of the educative process automatic."[20] For Campanella, knowledge and society are fungible because they are equally susceptible to eidetic representation. Comenius's pedagogy appends the natural world to Campanella's equation because the natural world, too, is eidetically fungible.

In Comenius's thought, however, the world is not only phenomenal reality; rather, it includes anything that can be brought as an image before the inner eye. The full title of Comenius's picture book, *Orbis sensualium pictus: hoc est Omnium principalium in mundo rerum, et in vita actionum, pictura et nomenclatura*, might suggest that the work merely catalogues sensible phenomena. In fact, the book attempts to make all knowledge available to the eyes in the form of indexed images.[21] The first lesson presents the Latin alphabet as a correspondence of written letters, images, and natural sounds, united by a short descriptive sentence and an onomatopoeic representation of the sound made by the subject of the image (see fig. 11.3).

The Elephant, 6.	*Elephas*, (Berus) 6.
draweth his meat to him	pabulum adtrahit
with his Trunk, 7.	*Proboſcide*, 7.
He hath two Teeth, 8.	*Dentes* duos, 8.
ſtanding out,	habet prominentes,
and is able to carry	& portare poteſt
full thirty men.	etiam triginta viros.

Wild Cattel. XXIX. *Feræ Pecudes.*

The Buff, 1.	*Urus*, 1.
and the Buffal, 2.	& *Bubalus*, 2.
are wild Bulls.	ſunt feri Boves.
The Elke, 3.	*Alces*, 3.
being bigger than an Horſe	major equo
(*whoſe back is impenetrable*)	(cujus tergus eſt impenetrabi-
hath knaggy Horns;	lis) habet ramoſa cornua;
as alſo the Hart, 4,	ut & *Cervus*, 4.
But the Roe, 5.	Sed *Caprea*, 5.
and the Hind-calf, *almoſt none.*	cum *Hinnulo*, ferè nulla.
The Stone-back, 6.	*Capricornus*, 6.
huge great ones;	prægrandia;
The Wild-goat, 7.	*Rupicapra*, 7.
hath very little ones,	minuta,
by which ſhe hangeth	quibus ſe ad rupem
her ſelf on a Rock.	ſuſpendit;

Fig. 11.2 John Amos Comenius, "Wild Cattel" (*Feræ Pecudes*), in *Orbis sensualium pictus: hoc est Omnium principalium in mundo rerum, & in vita actionum, pictura & nomenclatura*, trans. Charles Hoole (London: J. Sprint, 1705), 35.

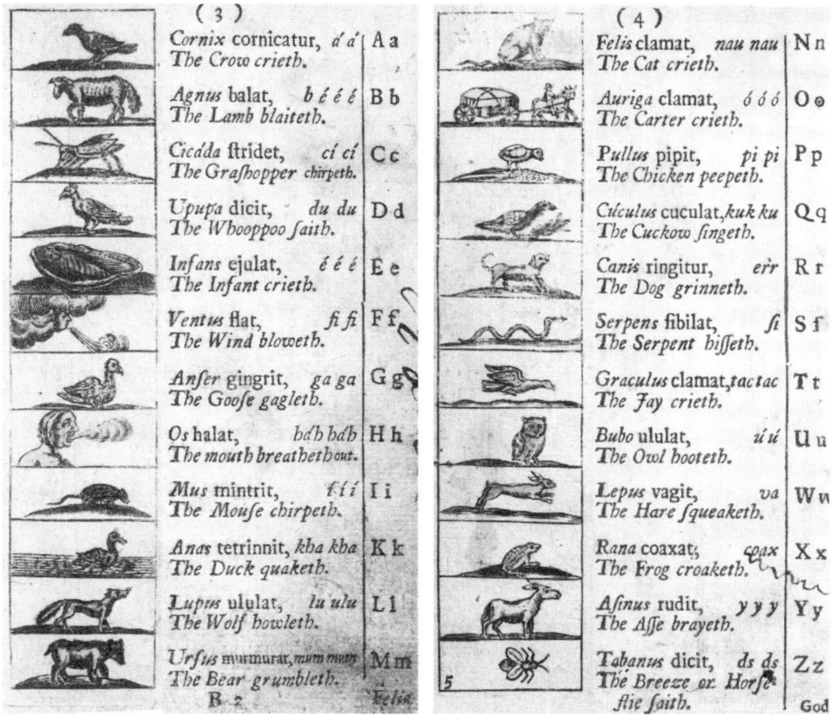
(3)
Cornix cornicatur, á á Aa
The Crow crieth.
Agnus balat, b é é é Bb
The Lamb blaiteth.
Cicáda ſtridet, cí cí Cc
The Graſhopper chirpeth.
Upupa dicit, du du Dd
The Whooppoo ſaith.
Infans ejulat, é é é Ee
The Infant crieth.
Ventus flat, fi fi Ff
The Wind bloweth.
Anſer gingrit, ga ga Gg
The Gooſe gagleth.
Os halat, háh háh Hh
The mouth breatheth out.
Mus mintrit, í í í Ii
The Mouſe chirpeth.
Anas tetrinnit, kha kha Kk
The Duck quaketh.
Lupus ululat, lu ulu Ll
The Wolf howleth.
Urſus murmurat, mum mum Mm
The Bear grumbleth.
B 2 Felis

(4)
Felis clamat, nau nau Nn
The Cat crieth.
Auriga clamat, ó ó ó Oo
The Carter crieth.
Pullus pipit, pi pi Pp
The Chicken peepeth.
Cúculus cuculat, kuk ku Qq
The Cuckow ſingeth.
Canis ringitur, err Rr
The Dog grinneth.
Serpens fibilat, ſi Sſ
The Serpent hiſſeth.
Graculus clamat, tac tac Tt
The Jay crieth.
Bubo ululat, ú ú Uu
The Owl hooteth.
Lepus vagit, va Ww
The Hare ſqueaketh.
Rana coaxat, coax Xx
The Frog croaketh.
Aſinus rudit, y y y Yy
The Aſſe brayeth.
Tabanus dicit, ds ds Zz
The Breeze or Horſe
flie ſaith.
5 God

Fig. 11.3 John Amos Comenius, the Latin alphabet, in *Orbis sensualium pictus*, 3–4.

While Comenius obviously intends his images to serve as mnemonics for learning the alphabet, he also regards the body's eyes as plenipotentiaries of the mind's eye. Pupils will know the letters – and sounds – of the alphabet because they have seen them.

Even the foundational, primordial ur-reality of God himself can be reduced to a picture-book concept. Though Comenius diagrams rather than pictures the divine, and undoubtedly would qualify the representational power of his diagram (see fig. 11.4), the very fact that he includes God in his book testifies to his enormous confidence in the power of images to capture and communicate the real nature of things.

For Comenius, knowledge is what can be imagined. Therefore, if students are to know the authentic world and not merely the image of the world, their eyes must be presented with not an image *of* the world but the world *as* image. The "true character" of the world, in Comenius's locution, relies on clear images. He elaborates in his *Great Didactic*:

We must look straight at objects and not squint, for in that case the eyes do not see that at which they look, but rather distort and confuse it. Objects should be placed before the eyes of the student in their true character, and not shrouded in words, metaphors, or hyperboles.[22]

In placing vision at the centre of his pedagogy, and in conflating bodily vision and mental understanding, Comenius effectively transforms the world into an image. While Comenius never quite admits that the world is only what we see, he nevertheless insists that what we see adequately represents the world:

If any be uncertain if all things can be placed before the senses in this way, even things spiritual and things absent (things in heaven, or in hell, or beyond the sea), let him remember that all things have been harmoniously arranged by God in such a manner that the higher in the scale of existence can be represented by the lower, the absent by the present, and the invisible by the visible.[23]

We cannot know what we cannot put into images because what we cannot put into images cannot exist. Invisibility cannot be essential to a thing. If a thing cannot be "placed before the senses," it does not exist.

COMENIUS: ACHIEVING UTOPIA

Comenius's oeuvre offers more than pedagogical technique; it also posits a teleology. Seeing that Comenius's pedagogy differs little from modern educational theory and practice, the fact that he proclaims the realization of utopia on earth as the goal of his educational system should give us some pause. The Manuels argue that, in Comenius's view,

man was created all potential. Education had to fashion him so that he became as perfect a being as possible. His formation, however, was not to be limited to the development of skills and the acquisition of factual knowledge about the external world, significant as these might be. The main concern was always moral and religious perfectibility, else the accumulation of mere sensate knowledge would sow chaos ... If the educational ideal is realized, the world will become utopia, "full of order, light, and peace."[24]

Education, for Comenius, does not entail simply the transference of knowledge but also the perfection of human nature through visible

(5)

God. II. Deus.

GOD is of himſelf from everlaſting to everlaſting. | Deus eſt ex ſeipſo, ab æterno in æternum.
A moſt perfect and a moſt bleſſed Being. | Ens perfectiſſimum & beatiſſimum.
In his Eſſence Spiritual, and One. | Eſſentiâ Spiritualis, & unus.
In his Perſonality, Three. | Hypoſtaſi Trinus.
In his Will, Holy, Juſt, Merciful and True. | Voluntate, Sanctus, Juſtus, Clemens, Verax.
In his Power, very great. | Potentiâ maximus.
In his Goodneſs, very ciful and good. | Bonitate optimus.
In his Wiſdom, unmeaſurable. | Sapientiâ immenſus.
A Light inacceſſible; and yet all in all. | Lux inacceſſa; & tamen omnia in omnibus.
Every where, and no where. | Ubique & nullibi.

B 3 The

Fig. 11.4 John Amos Comenius, "God" (*Deus*), in *Orbis sensualium pictus*, 5.

knowledge. Students learn about the world in order to shape themselves within its totality, which is perfectly ordered and "harmoniously arranged by God."

Commentator Jacques Prévot characterizes Comenius's ultimate aim as the conflation of the natural world, including human fallibility, into the divine order. For Comenius, he argues,

> no distinction is any longer possible between the natural order and the divine order. The sensible world of physical phenomena is as clearly ordered and as veridical as the bible; it presents to man, imposes on the teacher, and proposes to the student the same divine teaching, the same unavoidable sum of truths, even as it determines just as surely one's path toward knowledge.[25]

In Comenius's view, we need not fear that, in passing over the invisible, we miss anything important because the visible has been "harmoniously arranged by God" to represent the invisible perfectly. The visible world is co-extensive with (and therefore, in a way, constitutive of) religious truth as well as scientific truth. The eyes of Comenius's students consume the world and leave nothing behind because the invisible – mystery itself – no longer differs in any significant way from the visible. To them, clear internal perception of the world leads to perfect knowledge, and perfect knowledge leads to utopia – the entire chain made possible by eidetic reductions and equations.

COMENIUS: UTOPIA'S MACHINE HEART

Until Comenius's practical pedagogy aimed to realize utopia in fact, all utopian schemes retained a degree of innocence, as purposes without processes. But Comenius's project is neither literary nor aesthetic: his pedagogy is both practical and technically detailed. Its operation does not depend on its creator's intention, will, or energy. Like our culture's many literary utopias, the full meaning of Comenius's project enjoys considerable independence from its author's intentions, but his project differs from, say, More's in being not only rhetorical but also practicable. To grasp the full implications of Comenius's pedagogy, we must turn to one of his early works, the closest thing to a utopian fiction that he ever wrote.

Published in 1623, Comenius's *The Labyrinth of the World and the Paradise of the Heart* portrays the world as a city organized according to one's trajectory from birth, through livelihood, to death. In the text, the reader accompanies a pilgrim on his survey of potential occupations that a human may take up during his life. Bookended by allegorical depictions of birth and death, the journey enables the pilgrim to tally the accomplishments of each occupation, to witness how variously employed people amuse themselves, to evaluate the personal tastes and habits they acquire, and in general to become familiar with the circumstances that frame their lives. On his journey, the pilgrim enjoys the (unpleasant) company and (useless) counsel of two guides, Ubiquitous and Delusion.

The pilgrim begins his journey with a bird's-eye view of the world. From this great distance, the world appears as a tranquil and orderly city. Shaped like a circle, with six large paths or streets joining the easternmost point to the westernmost, Comenius's world city (see fig. 11.5) strongly resembles Campanella's City of the Sun, with its concentric walls. Ironically, this similarity is misleading since Comenius's world city quickly reveals its real nature as a seething bedlam of confusion and fakery.

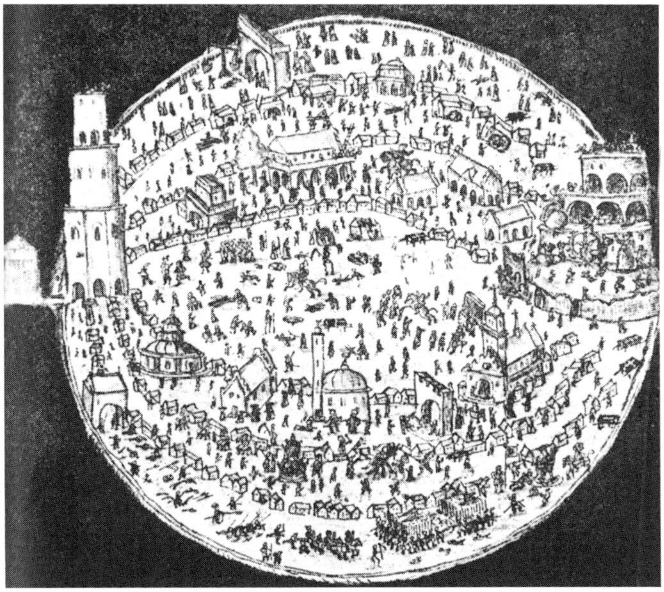

Fig. 11.5 John Amos Comenius, sketch of the world city, as found in the original manuscript of *The Labyrinth of the World and the Paradise of the Heart* (Brandýs nad Orlicí, 1623), reprinted in *John Amos Comenius (1592–1670)*.

Describing the pilgrim's first closer look, Comenius introduces a mild contempt for the superficial harmony and, with a sense of foreboding, suggests a more fundamental disorder:

It displeased me that these streets intersected and ran into each other at various points. This seemed to be an indication of confusion and a cause of straying. Moreover, when I looked at the round shape of the world, I clearly felt that it turned and moved in a circle, so that I feared dizziness. For wherever I cast my eyes, I saw that everything down to smallest items swarmed about. When I listened, everything was filled with beating, rustling, whispering, and shouting.[26]

Comenius deliberately casts his world city as a deceitful anti-utopia, preparing his reader for the moment when he rejects it in favour of a utopian vision.

After a series of lavishly imagined adventures that demonstrate the wretched, miserable, and hopeless state of the world, an inner voice prompts the pilgrim to return to his heart. There he finds consolation in Christ, who offers an effulgent vision of the world, clearly intended to stand in complete contrast to the anti-utopian world city:

Before me, I saw the world as a great clocklike machine, composed of visible and invisible parts. Transparent and fragile, it was fashioned completely from glass. It had thousands, nay, thousands and thousands of larger and smaller shafts, wheels, hooks, teeth, and notches that all moved and hummed together. Some moved quietly; others whirred or rattled. In the middle of everything was the largest and principal wheel, which was invisible, and from which the motion of all the others proceeded in some unfathomable manner. For the spirit of that wheel was diffused through them all and directed everything. Although it seemed to be impossible for me to comprehend fully, nevertheless I observed it clearly and distinctly.[27]

The machine becomes an anti-anti-utopia – the secret dream of utopia. Comenius thus proposes in his writings a *telos*, a method, and an aesthetic. From almost the very beginning of his career as a practical pedagogue and reformer, the image of the machine serves as the keystone in Comenius's conception of a perfected, well-ordered world.[28]

The importance of Comenius's vision of the machine as the utopian antidote to the depraved world lies not in the specifics of the machine's mechanism but, rather, in its character as an *eidos*. As a post-Renaissance phenomenon, the machine is entirely a function of teleology. The essential meaning of modern machines lies not in their specific operations or mechanisms but in the fact that they carry out their purposes independently of human agents – that they act automatically. The essence of a modern machine therefore falls somewhere near "automaticity." Modern machines exist as purposes that have been squeezed off, so to speak, from the intentional life of their makers. Modern machines can accomplish those purposes for which they were designed, but they cannot change their purposes on their own account. The mechanical is not something that acts without purpose but something whose purpose can be forgotten.

For Comenius, the invisible heart of the well-ordered world – the invisible wheel at the centre of the world machine – is obviously God. Comenius's metaphorical clockwork can never act entirely automatically since God provides both its power and its purpose. Like Campanella's pedagogy, Comenius's pedagogy relies on an automatic eidetic equivalence that passes over the unfathomable gaps between seeing, saying, and knowing without acknowledging them. Comenius imagined only the world as a machine, but after him the entire process of education became automatable, mechanical. The whole aesthetic of his oeuvre suggests a shaping of young humans into "perfect cogs for the perfect social machine."[29] With Comenius's automatable pedagogy, it becomes possible to set aside utopia's contemplative function as a hypostatic *eidos* that opens up a speculative horizon. After Comenius it becomes possible for utopia to function as a hypostatic *eidos* that acts as a normative ideal for an automated social process. In other words, Comenius makes it possible to think of societies as machines – ethical processes (read: pedagogy) given a self-referential purpose (read: social stability) and cut free from the intentions of their planners, governors, and inhabitants. Only after Comenius can we think of utopias as either "blueprints" or "engines" of social change.

THE HABIT OF UTOPIA

By reducing the world, human knowledge, and human society to an economy of images, Comenius unleashes the power of an automated social process onto European societies and everything they touch. Because he viewed God's purpose as the only truly independent purpose, Comenius remained largely unconcerned about the potential ramifications of his pedagogical processes. He could construct a pedagogical machine to teach children to view polities – as well as everything else – as *eide* (as opposed to full-blown, radically embodied phenomena), to accept as knowledge only what can be placed before the mind's eye, and to grasp even the world itself as a great, named picture for the simple reason that he saw in each of these images a mirror in which the divine finds itself reflected.

Comenius's great machine, like all machines, continues to accomplish its purpose, despite the fact that its maker has died, that no one can remember why the machine exists, and that the cultural framework that made it possible to imagine and desire the machine in the first place has evolved. Perhaps something else now occupies the spot reserved for Comenius's invisible wheel; perhaps Comenius never knew what was there – perhaps, but it does not much matter. The problem with machines is precisely their great advantage: they keep plugging away until they run down or someone stops them.

With its capacity for independent function and purpose, the machine uncannily resembles the basic human capacity for habituation – that is, the capacity to develop a reflex, reaction, or attitude that forgets its original purpose. The integrated whole of a person's habits is one's character.

All machines possess astounding ethical power because they represent purposes to which we can become habituated and, thereby, forget. Machines do not merely serve as metaphors for habits; in truth, they externalize and instantiate habits. Although we often speak of machines as performing work for us, it is more accurate to say that machines perform work *as* us. In doing the work of our bodies – and increasingly nowadays the work of our minds – machines insinuate themselves into our souls. Machines change us because they become us.

Ours is a culture habituated to the social machine that is utopia. We intend utopia constantly, mechanically, having lost the awareness that we are doing so. The phantom possibility of actually achieving utopia haunts our every endeavour, sneaks into every hope and dream. We practise utopia constantly in our positivistic science, our technocratic social structures, our banal nomenclature, our over-familiar contempt for the visible world, and, above all, our pedagogy. At every step, we prepare our world and our lives for the arrival of utopia – any day now, surely – by liquidating our world, our knowledge, our society, and our minds into the currency of images.

NOTES

1 In *More's Utopia: The Biography of an Idea* (New York: Princeton University Press, 1952), Jack H. Hexter convincingly demonstrates that *Utopia*'s reputation as an ambiguous book is an intellectual artefact of recent origin.

2 J. Max Patrick and G.R. Negley, "A Definition of 'Utopia,'" in *Twentieth-Century Interpretations of Utopia: A Collection of Critical Essays*, ed. William Nelson (Englewood Cliffs, NJ: Prentice-Hall, 1968), 109.

3 By defining *eidos* as "concept-image," I mean specifically to emphasize the thoroughgoing unity of images and words in human thought: we can see – in both the mental sense and the perceptual sense – only what we can say, and we can say only what we can see.

4 Miriam Eliav-Feldon, *Realistic Utopias: The Ideal Imaginary Societies of the Renaissance, 1516–1630* (Oxford: Clarendon Press, 1982), 2.

5 See, for example, Elisabeth Hansot, *Perfection and Progress: Two Modes of Utopian Thought* (Cambridge, MA: MIT Press, 1974), 4–5.

6 Eliav-Feldon, *Realistic Utopias*, 133.

7 Tommaso Campanella, *City of the Sun*, in *Famous Utopias of the Renaissance*, trans. T.W. Halliday, ed. Frederic R. White (New York: Packard and

Co., 1946 [Frankfurt: Tobias Adami, 1623]; reprint, Putnam, VT: Hendricks House, 1981), 158–9.

8 I am hardly the first to notice the Copernican form of Campanella's Solarian city plan. See, for example, S. Lang, "The Ideal City: From Plato to Howard," *Architectural Review* 112, 668 (1952): 90–101.

9 Campanella, *City of the Sun*, 160–1.

10 In addition to their knowledge-pictures on the walls, the Solarians possess a universal compendium of knowledge: "They have but one book, which they call Wisdom, and in it all the sciences are written with conciseness and marvelous fluency of expression" (Campanella, *City of the Sun*, 162).

11 See Frank Edward Manuel and Fritzie Prigohzy Manuel, *Utopian Thought in the Western World* (Cambridge, MA: Belknap Press, 1979), 208.

12 Eliav-Feldon, *Realistic Utopias*, 2.

13 See, for example, Campanella, *City of the Sun*, 162.

14 While I would hardly describe my search as exhaustive, I have made a serious inquiry into the question of whether woodcuts, engravings, paintings, or indeed pictures of any kind were ever prepared as an accompaniment to Campanella's text for *City of the Sun*. Given Campanella's excellent reputation in Italy, I thought it likely that at least one sympathetic reader would have attempted to draw either the City of the Sun itself or the murals for which it is now so famous. None has turned up thus far, and so I regret that I cannot include any such depictions in this chapter.

15 One likely candidate would be *Evangelicae Historiae Imagines ex Ordine Evangeliorum quae toto anno in Missae sacrificio recitantur, in ordinem temporis vitae Christi digestae* (Antwerp: Martinus Nutius, 1593), prepared under the direction of the Jesuit Jerome Nadal (1507–80). The book includes a set of 153 woodcuts prepared as an illustrated guide to the *Spiritual Exercises* (Rome: n.p., 1541) of Ignatius of Loyola (1491–1556).

16 John Amos Comenius, *The Great Didactic* (originally published in *Opera didactica omnia*, Amsterdam: Christophorus Cunradus and Gabriel à Roy, 1657), trans. Maurice Walter Keatinge (London: Adam and Charles Black, 1896), 336.

17 Ibid., 338.

18 Ibid., 335.

19 John Amos Comenius, *Joh. Amos Commenius's Visible world, or, A nomenclature, and pictures of all the chief things that are in the world, and of mens employments therein*, trans. Charles Hoole (London: John Sprint, 1705 [Nürnberg: Endterus, 1658]).

20 Jean Piaget, "The Significance of John Amos Comenius at the Present Time," introduction to *John Amos Comenius (1592–1670): Selections* (Paris: UNESCO, 1957), 14.

21 Comenius does discuss the pedagogical value of other senses, such as hearing and smell, but the heart of his curriculum, *Orbis Pictus*, is a book of images, not sounds or scratch-and-sniff stickers. (For his discussion of senses other than vision, see Comenius, *Great Didactic*, 336–7.)

22 Comenius, *Great Didactic*, 341.

23 Ibid., 339.

24 Manuel, *Utopian Thought in the Western World*, 315, quoting Comenius, *Pampaedia*, chap. 1, sec. 14, in Comenius, *De rerum humanarum emendatione consultatio catholica*, vol. 2 (Prague: Sumptibus Academiae Scientiarum Bohemoslovacae, 1966), 16.

25 Jacques Prévot, *L'utopie éducative: Coménius* (Paris: Belin Bibliothéque, 1981), 24–5. Author's translation.

26 John Amos Comenius, *The Labyrinth of the World and the Paradise of the Heart*, trans. Howard Louthan and Andrea Sterk, ed. Bernard McGinn (New York: Paulist Press, 1998 [Leszno, Poland: Bratrská tiskárna, 1631]), 69.

27 Ibid., 200.

28 In his essay "Utopia, the City and the Machine" (in Frank E. Manuel, ed., *Utopias and Utopian Thought* [Boston: Houghton Mifflin, 1966], 3–24), Lewis Mumford argues that the mechanical essence of utopia descends from the strict hierarchies and caste systems of the Neolithic monarchies of the eastern Mediterranean. The archeological evidence available may well suggest that Neolithic societies were highly regimented, but that does not entitle us to describe their social life as "mechanical." Also, the available evidence tells us almost nothing about life at the margins of these societies. So, on the one hand, Mumford unjustifiably deploys a modern notion to interpret Neolithic social life; and, on the other, he unfairly assumes that knowledge of a few facets of how the elite may have lived and thought entitles us to make sweeping generalizations about the entire society.

29 Eliav-Feldon, *Realistic Utopias*, 56.

Second Life: Identification, Parody, and Persona in William Burges's "Vellum Sketchbook"

Nicholas Roquet

Chora

THIS CHAPTER EXAMINES THE fascination exerted on nineteenth-century British architect William Burges by a rare surviving set of thirteenth-century drawings and inscriptions: the manuscript of Villard de Honnecourt. At the time of his death, William Burges (1827–81) was widely recognized by his peers as one the great medieval scholars of his generation. However, many also regretted that he had no greater opportunities to display his talent as a designer. Among the actors of the Gothic Revival in mid-century Britain, Burges was singular for the modest scope of his production and the fact that he directed much of his energy towards the production of drawings, decorative objects, and domestic interiors rather than towards major public undertakings.

Since J. Mordaunt Crook first published a monograph on Burges some thirty years ago, it has been known that he patterned his style of drawing on that of Villard.[1] However, no one has examined what purposes this emulation was meant to serve, whether Burges's outward imitation also expressed inward identification, or how this practice was related to ideas about the relation between medieval and modern art. This chapter addresses these questions by focusing in turn on three distinct bodies of material: the first critical readings of Villard's manuscript, made in France during the 1840s and 1850s; Burges's graphic re-enactment of Villard's portfolio during the 1860s; and, last, the artistic context in which Burges's engagement with Villard took place.

One thing I do not attempt here is to determine the veracity of early interpretations of Villard. All scholarship until at least 1901 was vitiated by two questionable assumptions: that the manuscript was the work of a single author and that this author was an architect. In the twentieth century, it was established that the manuscript was actually a palimpsest of three successive authors.[2] Moreover, though Villard de Honnecourt is sometimes still referred to as an architect, there is little evidence that he was a master mason or, indeed, a master of any craft connected with medieval buildings. Villard identified himself by name and commended his drawings to posterity, but nowhere did he state his trade, the reason for his travels, or the works with which he was connected.[3] In fact, the manuscript's enigmatic nature was key to its enthusiastic reception in the mid-nineteenth century because it allowed Villard to function as something of a blank screen. Successive interpretations of medieval practice were projected onto the manuscript's professed author, and, in turn, these imaginary Villards were projected back, as possible models, onto the practice of the nineteenth-century architect.

WRITING VILLARD

If there is a consistent image running through the writings on Villard in mid-century France, it is that of a new style coming into being. This image was crafted by Jules Quicherat, a historian and archaeologist at the École des Chartes in Paris, who, in 1849, contributed the first extended assessment of Villard's portfolio.[4] Quicherat dated the portfolio to between 1243 and 1251, placing its author at the genesis of the Gothic in northern France.[5] His reading of Villard was shaped by an evolutionary conception of architecture, according to which each historical style contained within it both the memory of its predecessors and the seeds of future change. Architectural styles, Quicherat argued, were similar to languages, and so they should be distinguished by their organizing principle, or "grammar," rather than by the "vocabulary" they inherited or imported from earlier idioms.[6] The emergence of a new style, however, was a chaotic process. Driven by a new cultural temper, artists were compelled for a while to operate outside established canons, and in this moment they were liable to false starts, to excesses, or to the awkward repetition of older formulae.[7]

Quicherat's work was pursued in the 1850s by architect Jean-Baptiste Lassus, whose project of a printed facsimile of Villard's portfolio was published posthumously in 1858. Lassus's facsimile drew heavily on Quicherat's ideas, but it was also filled with a new sense of grievance and anxiety. By the early 1850s, the project of a Gothic revival in France had come under threat from a younger generation of architects, who saw stylistic eclecticism as a means to express their sense of historical change, progress, and modernity.[8] In response, Lassus preceded his commentaries on Villard by a polemical essay that describes the state of architecture in modern France as one of anarchy.[9] Since the teaching of the École des Beaux-Arts had been shaken by the generation of 1830, no new foundation for architecture had emerged from the ensuing chaos. Instead, architecture in France had become a Tower of Babel, fought over by three distinct camps: "pagan" rationalism, eclecticism, and the Gothic school.[10] Moreover, this period of anarchy was more obscure and more dangerous than any previous artistic renewal because the chain of cultural transmission had been broken at the time of the Renaissance.

As Lassus understood it, "style" was a gift that one generation passed on to the next – a body of gestures and forms that might undergo gradual change but that, at a deeper level, retained its intrinsic identity. Thus, in Lassus's view, Villard had seen classical antiquity entirely through the lens of an inward, Gothic *sentiment*: "the architect of Cambrai ... belonged to a generation which drew its inspiration from the very air it breathed; which was so penetrated with Gothic feeling that it was quite unable to do anything other than what it did."[11] His drawing of a Roman tomb transformed the figure of an edile into a sceptred king, and classical urns into Christian cruets and ciboria (see fig. 12.1).[12] In contrast to modern eclecticism, such imitation was truthful because it was transformative. Just as the French language had assimilated earlier linguistic strata, the possession of a single, inherited language of forms enabled Villard to turn the remains of the classical past into something new.

Since a new style could not be invented, the only way out of the crisis of eclecticism was to retrieve earlier, national traditions.[13] It was in this sense that Lassus understood Villard's portfolio as a book of instruction: in studying it, a young architect might learn to build from first principles, in the same way as an apprentice in a medieval guild. He conceived of this process as akin to relearning a forgotten mother-tongue. The anxieties of the present and its conflicting languages would be resolved in a restored chain of generations.

Lassus's interpretation of Villard's portfolio was contested at the time of its publication, even by sympathetic observers. Prosper Mérimée dismissed the facsimile's polemical contents as belonging to an outworn debate. The production of architecture in France had ceased to be ruled by any "exclusive taste," and so there was no longer a need for impassioned defences of Gothic architecture.[14] Viollet-le-Duc submits Lassus's facsimile to a yet more radical criticism, arguing, in a review published in 1859, that the portfolio was a mere sketchbook, "of the kind we [architects] leave lying on our desks," and in which the trivial jostled with the sacred and the symbolic.[15] The understanding of Gothic architecture, he claims, would have been better served by an illustrated volume on the cathedrals of Paris or Reims.

Nonetheless, the figure of a forgotten, then rediscovered, medieval builder took hold of Viollet-le-Duc's imagination. The real interest of the

Fig. 12.1 Drawing of a Roman tomb, from the album of Villard de Honnecourt. Bibliothèque nationale de France.

portfolio, he writes, lay precisely in the fact that it was not a treatise: "the album of Villard de Honnecourt is a very interesting book, far more so than had it been an architectural treatise, for here one discovers the intimate life and daily labours of those lay architects who founded the great school of the thirteenth century. For if nowadays artists must work for the living, they must learn from the dead. Indeed, the latter are the only ones who can teach."[16] The fictionalized "apparitions" of an elderly Villard in Viollet-le-Duc's writings – materializing in his study late in the evening to discuss the current state of architecture – represent more than a rhetorical device; rather, Villard personifies a living tradition of building that still survives in the restorations of medieval monuments carried out by the Commission des monuments historiques. For all the deficiencies of Villard's drawings, Viollet-le-Duc claims, the curiosity and practical spirit they express are those of a layman, a realist, and a freethinker, a man independent of stylistic allegiances and aristocratic or ecclesiastical patrons.[17] What the past could teach the present was not a repertoire of forms but an intellectual attitude towards practice: one of patient experimentation, improvement, and innovation.

Significantly, Viollet-le-Duc always portrays Villard as one artist among many, the friend and equal of the cathedral builders "Pierre de Corbie, Robert de Luzarches, Pierre de Montereau, Renaud de Cormont, Jean de Chelles and so many others": a man practising a popular and collaborative art, and completely immersed in the concerns of his place, his time, and his race.[18] In order to regain control over his means of expression, the modern architect likewise had to free himself of the "caprice" of wealthy patrons and to meld into the society of equals – painters, sculptors, and craftspeople – that gathered on the building site.[19] Only under these conditions might architecture once again become a rational and progressive enterprise and a new form of art be born.

Compared to those of Lassus and Viollet-le-Duc, William Burges's essays on Villard are slight works, and I do not extensively discuss them here.[20] Their crucial feature is that Burges displaces the focus of interpretation from the archetype of "medieval man" to the singular fact of the drawings. Moreover, by insisting on the manuscript's material process and graphic manner, Burges strips Villard's "style" of its previous association with racial and historical necessity. In his view, the manuscript's sole unifying feature is the graphic shorthand that Villard had invented, condensing the world around him in quick, precise, abbreviated strokes.[21] Thus style, the essays imply, is above all a faculty of the individual imagination: it is what allows an artist to assimilate visible phenomena and bring them forth in new ways.

This was to read Villard through the lens of Ruskin's earliest architectural writings. In "The Lamp of Life," Ruskin defines the "force of assimilation" as an organic, productive, and self-conscious energy at work in every human being. This "true life" of the self is "the independent force by which [the individual] moulds and governs external things ... which converts everything around him into food, or into instruments; and which, however humbly or obediently it may listen to or follow the guidance of superior intelligence, never forfeits its own authority as a judging principle, as a will capable of either obeying or rebelling."[22] Like Ruskin at the turn of the 1850s, Burges's thoughts on practice were driven by the tension between ideals of labour and imagination. He believed an architect should be not only a thinker but also a producer of works, relying like the craftsperson on a practical knowledge of making; yet, in order to be in full possession of his means, an architect also had to stand apart from the collective of builders and to make his eye and hand the tools of a radically personal vision.

DRAWING VILLARD

Unlike Viollet-le-Duc, before whom the living Villard made a brief appearance, then vanished for good, Burges remained preoccupied by Villard's drawings for close to a decade. Whereas the French architect's engagement with Villard took place only in writing, Burges's essays played a relatively small part in his ongoing confrontation with the medieval artefact. Far more central was the so-called "Vellum Sketchbook," a slim volume containing eighteen sheets of thick vellum folded down the middle, sewn two by two into quires, and bound into a dark green leather portfolio. Few of the drawings in the Vellum Sketchbook are dated, but its material attributes correspond closely to the description Burges gave in 1858 of Villard's original manuscript, held in the Bibliothèque Impériale in Paris. Thus, it seems certain that production began only after Burges's first-hand encounter with the manuscript.[23]

For all its slightness as an object, the choice and arrangement of the Vellum Sketchbook's contents are decisive, as though for Burges it truly marked a new beginning. On opening its cover, one is confronted not with architectural drawings but with a scene from a London zoo. Eight small outline sketches of animals fill this first page (see fig. 12.2); seven similar drawings follow on the overleaf. Two hand-written annotations in fine lowercase script suggest to the reader that all of the drawings have been taken directly from Nature: "This is an insect called a caballa. I know that I found it in the garden of the Franciscans at Fiesole. The latin name is mantus religiosa & oratoria – because it says its prayers. / This is a little beast called a chameleon. I know that he changes his colour according to natural objects near which he is placed."[24] If one takes the descriptions at face value, then the author of these drawings has wiped clean the slate of his mind: if he was already an artist, then he has decided to start over again from first things, drawing only what he can see with his own eyes.

One way to read the Vellum Sketchbook is as a book of nature and life – as a series of faithful transcriptions of living things, real persons, and actual monuments that play out in real time according to Burges's peregrinations on the continent during the 1860s. Indeed, in terms of outward form, the Vellum Sketchbook is a straightforward re-enactment of Villard's graphic process. It is drawn with the same instruments on the same size and type of paper, on a comparable number of pages set inside an identical binding.[25] Moreover, Burges's self-imposed restriction of medium to quill and sepia ink led by necessity – as he believed had been the case with Villard – to the graphic simplification of the artist's living models.

The happenstance of travel pervades the sketchbook's contents. As one turns its pages, animal and human figures alternate pell-mell with plants and flowers, costumes and street scenes, buildings, furnishings, and statuary. Where these disparate subjects are woven together within a single leaf, the effect is that of a dense and intricate visual world. A striking instance of this occurs on the overleaf of folio 8. Here Burges gathers together fragments of plants and architecture. All are shown in perspective, their parts unfurling in the empty space of the page in a way that accentuates their physical reality (see fig. 12.3). But the status of these assembled fragments as real things in a real world is ambiguous, for Burges also inserts one of his flat decorative designs (a Crucifixion scene for the church at Fleet in Hampshire) among the blooms and carvings, and the page lies opposite his decorative scheme for Gayhurst Manor, conceived around the biblical theme of humanity's fall, expulsion from Eden, and cultivation of the wilderness. The juxtaposition of these contradictory fields of imagery – the timeless narrative of the Bible and the evidence of historical change embodied in architectural forms and natural life – raises the question of which one Burges held to be true.

To a certain extent, the Vellum Sketchbook is still a paean to a productive and sexually potent natural world. Burges's drawings of flowers emphasize their reproductive capacity, in one instance transforming a flower's petal into the faintest outline of a manikin, in another portraying

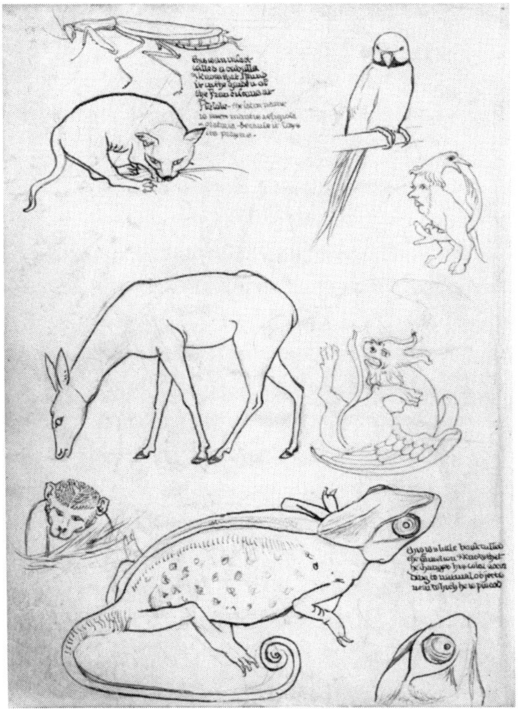

Fig. 12.2 William Burges, Vellum Sketchbook, folio 1 verso. RIBA Library Drawings Collection.

Fig. 12.3 Below: William Burges, Vellum Sketchbook, folio 8 verso and 9 recto. RIBA Library Drawings Collection.

blooms miraculously sprouting from a castellated vase in the shape of a medieval city. Conventionalized by means of plan or sectional views, plant life scrolls for page after page across painted diapers and carved friezes, spandrels and capitals, until, in Burges's drawing of a medieval house in Beauvais, it almost overgrows the building's façade (see fig. 12.4). Yet this "Nature" is no longer that – at once symbolic and familiarly English – of the Creation windows one finds in High Victorian churches. In the pages of the Vellum Sketchbook, common garden flowers lie next to exotic specimens from a Victorian hothouse. As for Burges's intensely observed

Fig. 12.4 William Burges, Vellum Sketchbook, folio 21 verso and 22 recto.
RIBA Library Drawings Collection.

drawing of animals, his uncanny graphic method of isolating them within pages of architectural specimens arguably transports all of them into the realm of the marvellous.

A key moment in the creation of the Vellum Sketchbook is Burges's undated addition, in the margin of the first page's overleaf, of two small grotesques, both of which are drawn in a lighter ink than are the neighbouring naturalistic studies (see fig. 12.2). The lower one represents a winged beast, a hybrid between a lion and a goat. Above, a woman's face rides two hoofed legs and is crowned by the head of a bird. Sprouting from the bird's beak, a winged tongue arches back and around between the beast's legs, emerging as a claw in front of its groin. Both are products of a post-Darwinian natural world that is equally fertile and monstrous. To borrow a term coined by Krzysztof Pomian to describe the world of the Baroque cabinet of curiosities, the Vellum Sketchbook is the product of an interim age, in which nature has lost its status as a revealed truth but has not yet been fully rationalized by science – an age, therefore, that is "exuberant, incoherent, disorderly, fraught with contradictions, and pulled in opposite directions."[26]

As Burges's grotesques make clear, the Vellum Sketchbook is not only a book of nature but also the locus of an elaborate fantasy. At the moment when Burges took in hand the archaic instruments of vellum and quill, he became an imagined other. The innocent gaze that the draftsman brought to bear on the world, the naïve voice in which he expressed his wonder at it, and the spontaneous vigour with which he rearranged what he found were not Burges's own; rather, they were those of a fictional "Villard" who had been made to materialize in mid-nineteenth-century Europe. Villard's pictorial universe provided Burges with an imaginary alternative to that in which he lived and practised. In his own words, modern England was a world in which religion had retreated into private worship and in which neither public buildings nor works of engineering were viewed as legitimate objects for ornament or expense.[27]

In his writings of the 1860s, Burges repeatedly invokes a future in which histories would no longer be written and pattern books no longer printed. Instead, the painted or carved image would give expression to shared beliefs; private wealth would sponsor public rituals; and architecture would serve once again as a living museum of the arts.[28] Yet it should be stressed that Burges always deferred this possible future to another century. He believed his age had lost the knack of forgetting and that it was impossible to cut oneself off from the nineteenth century's surfeit of historical knowledge. All historical styles now had been made available for use, and the question of which to employ could be answered only arbitrarily, as a matter of personal preference.[29] These convictions confronted Burges with a set of paradoxes. The first was that, though he doubted that an archaeological revival could bring forth live works, archaeology remained the only language at his disposal. The second was that, though he believed the purpose of architecture to be essentially representational, there was no longer an audience for public myths. Fundamentally, Burges's impulse as a creator was not to re-found art on a new basis, still less the society within which it was produced; rather, his resolution of these creative paradoxes took the form of a fictional second life, in which style still might be construed as "natural" and symbols as "true."

The product of this imaginative process is less a sketchbook than the simulacrum of one. Villard's drawings are incidental by-products of his travels. They are made on loose sheets of vellum, with no fixed orientation of top to bottom or right to left, and vacant spaces are filled in over time with little attention to narrative continuity. With Burges, these relationships are reversed, and the incidental construction of the medieval manuscript yields to the logic of a single, deliberately crafted representation. He carefully selects what to imitate in Villard's drawings and what to omit, leaving aside the diagrams of stone-cutting, machinery, and operative geometry that figure so prominently in the manuscript, and taking up only what might be construed as "studies from life." A similar shift between the two works took place in terms of architectural representation. In contrast to the schematic plans, sections, and elevations contained in the original manuscript, Burges's preferred mode in the Vellum Sketchbook is the sectional perspective. Such drawings abstract the building from any real physical context, instead giving access to a painted or inhabited life contained wholly within (see fig. 12.5).

Even though the Vellum Sketchbook contains several designs that would be materialized years later in Burges's house in Holland Park, the work's function as a whole is not primarily as a practical pattern book; rather, it acts as a threshold between two distinct worlds – external reality and fantasy. In this respect, a particularly revealing drawing in the Vellum Sketchbook is that of a medieval tomb Burges discovered at Beauvais (see fig. 12.6). Burges's caption for the image simultaneously insists on its

Fig. 12.5 William Burges, Vellum Sketchbook, folio 30 recto. RIBA Library Drawings Collection.

status as a first-hand observation and undermines the credibility of the world from which it issues: "This is the tomb of Saint Arnould near Beauvais & the holes are for the sick to pass thro' & when they have drunk from the fountain they are immediately cured & of this you may be certain."[30] Taken together, image and caption are an obvious parody of the fantastical elements in Villard's portfolio, such as his recipes for medicinal potions and his description of a device for perpetual motion. But they also function as a figuration of the Vellum Sketchbook and its maker.[31] The holes insistently drawn by Burges on the sides of the tomb mirror the mouths of the organically shaped vases drawn on the following page, out of which blooms spontaneously seem to grow. Like the mirror in *Alice in Wonderland*, these blackened orifices are metaphors of passage into a generative world, in which all formal combinations are possible. However, the resulting product has no clear claim to reality. As Burges's ironic annotations constantly remind us, the sketchbook's ostensible author is a naïf – a man prone to non sequiturs, to statements of the obvious, and to taking legends at face value. If the Vellum Sketchbook is a parody, then above all it highlights the artifice of Burges's assumed identity as a latter-day Villard. In a sense, it is no more authentic than his real identity as an architect in Victorian London.

The ambiguities of Burges's imaginative process are most apparent in the Jenner crosier, which Burges designed for the Anglican bishop of Dunedin in 1866–67, illustrated in the Vellum Sketchbook as a curiosity from the "isles where they eat one another" (a New Zealand unknown to the Middle Ages) (see fig. 12.7). At first hand, the figurines on the crosier's ivory handle seem to represent England's patron saint George slaying a dragon. Therefore, the crosier symbolizes the colony's inclusion in the British Empire and the Church of England's evangelical mission among its native population. But the figures of knight, dragon, and lady might also be a representation in Gothic dress of the Greek myth of Perseus and Andromeda. Viewed this way, the crosier embodies Burges's belief in the analogies between Gothic and classical Greek art. Furthermore, the imagery on the crosier relates to a constellation of private meanings that played out simultaneously in Burges's home in London. The dragon may be an iteration of the allegorical monsters – Contract, Arbitration, Law, etc. – painted on the cabinet in his study (ca. 1858); if so, then the bound female figure symbolizes art threatened by practice.[32] The contrasting poses of the armoured knight and the dragon's bound victim suggest yet another realm of imagery: the Sleeping Beauty panel Burges had painted over his bed (ca. 1865–67), in which a woman lying unconscious is silently approached by a man.[33] With this, the crosier enters a world of externalized sexual fantasies.

What makes Burges's work unusual is that the proliferating meanings embedded in the Jenner crosier also give rise to a proliferation of contradictory representations. In addition to the drawing in the Vellum Sketchbook, the crosier is portrayed in the decorative art magazine *L'art pour tous* as an original thirteenth-century artwork from France and in one of Burges's photographic albums as a modern manufactured object (see figs. 12.8 and 12.9).[34] The same is true of the tower for the Law Courts competition, designed to dominate the building's façade on the Strand. In a perspective drawn by Axel Haig for the competition boards, the

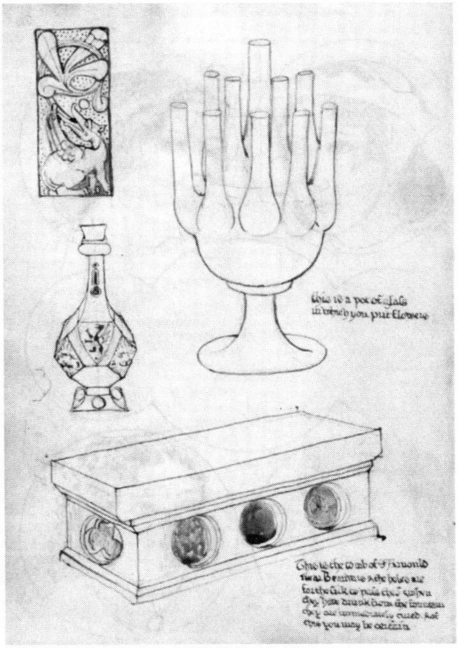

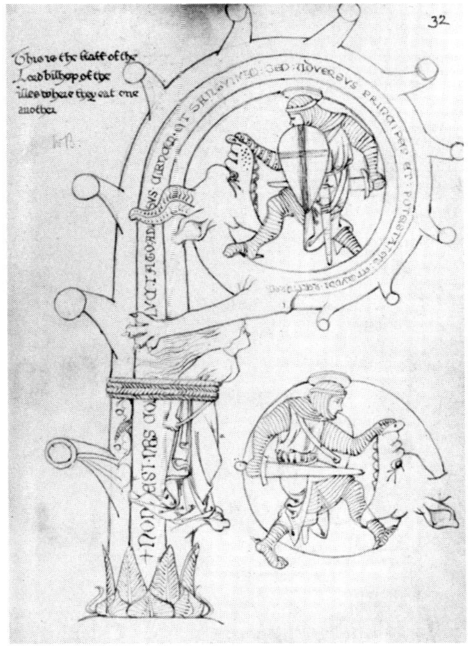

Fig. 12.6 Left: William Burges, Vellum Sketchbook, folio 20 verso. RIBA Library Drawings Collection.

Fig. 12.7 Right: William Burges, Vellum Sketchbook, folio 32 recto. RIBA Library Drawings Collection.

tower forms a picturesque backdrop to the traffic and trade of modern London.[35] In the Vellum Sketchbook, it is portrayed as a cosmology in stone, its symbolic meaning conveyed by sculpted personifications of the planets and the Zodiac.[36] Within the covers of the sketchbook, it proves possible to abstract the tower from its real setting in modern London and to relocate it to a world in which nature, myth, and art are still (or once again) wholly fused.

In this sense, the Vellum Sketchbook is not really a representation of history at all. Though clearly distinct from the London in which Burges actually lived and moved, the "age" figured within its pages is a flattened and fabricated time – neither past nor future – in which specimens from nature and medieval art co-exist alongside buildings and decorative objects Burges designed during the 1860s. More important, none of these disparate objects is unambiguously real. What Burges explores in the Vellum Sketchbook is the condition of architecture as pure ornament: could one still treat the building as a framework for symbolic imagery once the tie linking object and concept had dissolved?

Fig. 12.8 Left: The Jenner crosier as thirteenth-century original in *L'art pour tous* (1875). Bibliothèque nationale de France.

Fig. 12.9 Right: The Jenner crosier as modern manufacture in *The Designs of William Burges, A.R.A.* (1885). RIBA Library Photographs Collection.

If one judges by the cloud of representations with which Burges surrounded his works, then he found that such an architecture could generate multiple fictional truths about itself – existing, as it were, in several places and times at once.

BEING VILLARD

In November 1858, shortly after the publication of Burges's first essay on Villard in the pages of *The Builder*, his confrere Robert Kerr countered in the same periodical with a satire of anachronism as a heroic posture. Ostensibly, Kerr wished to commend to the readers' attention the manifesto of a young architect who, inspired by Villard's sketches, had cast off the classical pretensions of his father, adopted the biblical prosody of Thomas Carlyle, rechristened himself "John de Camden Town, master of the works," and dedicated himself to redesigning London shops in a style based on the Scandinavian sagas.[37] What Kerr suggests here is that the modern Gothic of the 1850s would prove to be yet another passing fashion and, more generally, that the promotion of one style over another said nothing essential about the condition or purposes of architecture in modern England.

Kerr's satire captures the potentially burlesque implications of patterning one's practice on that of a long-dead artist; but, in a deeper sense, it misread Burges's intentions, for the world in which Burges's fascination with Villard played out during the 1860s was not primarily one of professional architects or builders. Moreover, the question that preoccupied him during this time was not that of style but that of his social identity as a creator. Burges's imaginative portrait of the medieval architect as a "maker above other makers" reaffirms architecture's status as a fine art: independent of technology, of the systematic aims of industrial design, and of the repetitive standards of the modern builder. A less explicit aspect of this statement is that architecture, as an art, is also free of any moral and social purpose beyond its own formal integrity. The world in which this notion first emerged was a network of painters, poets, and art patrons loosely centred on the person of Dante Gabriel Rossetti.

Along with the painters John Everett Millais and William Holman Hunt, Rossetti was one of the central actors of the Pre-Raphaelite Brotherhood, a grouping of young artists founded in 1848.[38] By the time Burges came into contact with him in the late 1850s, Rossetti had already begun to "unpick" one of the central tenets of Pre-Raphaelite art: the nexus established by Ruskin between the character of the artist, the work of art, and the external world.[39] In Ruskin's view, a work of art is beautiful only if it reveals the moral dimension of visible reality. Moreover, revelation of this kind requires absolute truthfulness on the part of the artist, whose mind Ruskin likens to a "broad, white, lucid field."[40] But in a celebrated series of portraits of women begun in 1859, Rossetti resists both the evocation of any real time or place and the painting's ultimate resolution into moral or social narrative. Adorned and surrounded with an eclectic assortment of ancient and oriental jewels, textiles, and objets d'art, his female figures are contained in a shallow space with no obvious relation to external reality. For the first time in England, Rossetti's experiments in portraiture articulate the notion that sensual beauty constitutes a self-sufficient apprehension of reality, separate from moral truth and scientific fact.

Largely dedicated to the production of this autonomous beauty, the art of the 1860s played out in an increasingly exclusive and introspective milieu. In 1862, Rossetti set up an essentially masculine and self-consciously bohemian household at Tudor House in Chelsea that drew on the myths of the gypsy encampment and the "vie de Bohême" of Parisian artists.[41] An equally important aspect of Rossetti's self-transformation was his decision to withdraw his painterly production from the public realm. From the late 1850s on, his paintings were seldom exhibited, appearing instead within a narrow circle of "intimates and patrons."[42] As an architect in a community of painters, Burges's position within this rarefied world was necessarily insecure. Never one of Rossetti's intimates, his relationship with the painters' circle remained largely indirect, mediated in turn by institutions, patronage, and mutual acquaintances.[43] But far more important than these contacts was the way they nourished Burges's identity as an "art-architect," operating at the margins of conventional society.

An important document relating to Burges's self-image is the abstract of his diaries dictated shortly before his death. This exercise enabled him to cast his identity into a coherent and final shape, alternately omitting or emphasizing disparate events and people who had crossed his path. One of this document's more remarkable features is the place it reserved for London's Aesthetic circles. The following are among the things for which Burges wished to be remembered: he had attended the same school as Rossetti; he socialized with Edward Burne-Jones, William Morris, and the art critic W.M. Rossetti; he breakfasted with the poet Algernon Swinburne; he dined with the painter Frederic Leighton; he visited Morris's Red House in Bexleyheath and J.M. Whistler's Peacock Room in London; and, finally, he received deathbed visits from both Whistler and Oscar Wilde.[44] All of these men were relative outsiders in Victorian London, and the abstract of his diaries tells us that Burges believed himself to belong in their midst.

Like the abstract of his diaries, the Vellum Sketchbook also contains markers of Burges's identification with London's aesthetes and bohemians. Near the end of the sketchbook, he inserted a series of drawings depicting a woman or siren absorbed in her own reflection (see fig. 12.10).[45] Though the siren had a place in Villard's world as a Christian symbol of temptation, the addition of a mirror alluded to a whole gallery of Pre-Raphaelite and Aesthetic representations in which a female artist-figure either observes reality at a remove, mediated by a mirror, or focuses inward on a self-contained realm of fantasy or desire.[46] If one views these drawings as artistic self-portraits, then the early Pre-Raphaelites' ethos of masculine labour and engagement with society was superseded, in Burges's mind, by the feminine faculties of idea and imagination. Thus, what Burges seems to have appreciated in Rossetti's portraits of women is the power of painting to create a closed, decorative, and erotically charged world. By adopting Villard's portfolio as a model for his own practice of drawing, it is this world-creating power that he seeks to usurp.

In her recent work on beauty as a critical issue in the visual arts, Elizabeth Prettejohn stresses the empirical and speculative nature of Aestheticism in nineteenth-century Great Britain. In her view, Aestheticism should be understood less as a coherent set of practices or rules and more as the formulation of a question: what would a work of art be like if its sole aim were to bring forth beauty?[47] If one considers the Vellum Sketchbook as one possible answer to this question, then Burges's conclusion is that beauty – conceived as the realm of culture, myth, and the erotic – had become radically divorced from technology. The only form in which beauty could still be produced is that of a paradoxical counter-world to the objects it was meant to adorn. In a lecture delivered to the Society of Arts in 1864, Burges puts forward a quasi-surrealistic strategy for ornament, in which medieval imagery is made to collide with products of modern industry, imposing its own reality like an overlay on the world of machines:

> Formerly the two professions of engineer and architect were not divided, and if we look into the old books of the sixteenth and seventeenth centuries we shall find that even machinery was to a certain extent made ornamental … Hitherto we have done the reverse. The machines have been very strong and have done their work very well, but they have been dreadfully ugly, bearing about the same relation to what they ought to be as a skeleton does to the human body. One is very much tempted to imagine and try and think out

Fig. 12.10 William Burges, Vellum Sketchbook, folio 24 recto. RIBA Library Drawings Collection.

> how our ancestors of the twelfth and thirteenth centuries would have treated a royal locomotive with its tender and carriage ... : perhaps they would have converted the locomotive into the form of a dragon vomiting the smoke through its upraised head; his body and wings being rich with gold, colour, tin, and brass, and perhaps even great crystal balls would do duty for eyes.[48]

Was such an appropriation of medieval art inauthentic? If one addresses the question with Ruskin's expectation of an artist's uncompromising truthfulness, then the answer is yes. But Burges's sense of self is more complex than this: it, too, is informed by a conception of ornament and substrate as clashing and contradictory worlds. In Burges's eyes, Villard was nothing so intimate or determining as a master or ancestor. He would no doubt have agreed with Lassus that the Gothic of thirteenth-century northern France constituted a language, but it was a language with which he himself had no organic connection. On the contrary, his emulation of medieval practice plays on the obvious disjunctions between William Burges as actor, Villard as his chosen character, and the setting of 1860s London.

A more productive way to consider Burges's appropriation of Villard would be to view it as a persona. As C.G. Jung defined the concept in the early twentieth century, the persona is a psychological construct: not a sovereign, centred, and reified personality but a mask that mediates between the individual and the demands placed upon him or her by the community.[49] The persona is only one voice among many that issue from the self; it is not in itself a false or inauthentic expression, but it remains always incomplete and only partially true. Much as Rossetti found a vehicle for sensuality in the closed world of the decorative portrait, Burges's medieval persona provided him with a creative voice in a culture with little use for public symbols. By repeatedly inscribing himself into the fictional world of the Vellum Sketchbook, he creates the metaphorical equivalent of the six-mile-long wall that encircled William Beckford's home at Fonthill Abbey.[50] The underlying process is inherently theatrical – equivalent to donning a stage costume – but it makes room for a sexual and ornamental imagination that couples fish with fowl, heads with tails, and gnomes with mermaids.

NOTES

1 J. Mordaunt Crook, *William Burges and the High Victorian Dream* (Chicago: University of Chicago Press, 1981), 63–4.

2 François Bucher, *Architector: The Lodge Books and Sketchbooks of Medieval Architects* (New York: Abaris Books, 1979), 1:28–30.

3 Carl F. Barnes, Jr., "The 'Problem' of Villard de Honnecourt" (original English text of "Le 'problème' de Villard de Honnecourt," in *Les bâtisseurs des cathédrales gothiques*, ed. Roland Recht [Strasbourg: Les musées de la ville, 1989], 209–23), available at http://www.villardman.net/problem.html. Bucher nonetheless refers to Villard as a minor builder or subcontractor on cathedral work and to his manuscript as a lodge book.

4 Jules Quicherat, "Notice sur l'album de Villard de Honnecourt, architecte du XIIIe siècle," *Revue archéologique* ser. 1, vol. 6 (1849): 65–80, 164–88, 209–26, plates 116–18.

5 Ibid., 72.

6 Jules Quicherat, "De l'architecture romane," *Revue archéologique* ser. 1, vol. 8 (1851): 145–58; ser. 1, vol. 9 (1852): 525–40; ser. 1, vol. 10 (1853): 65–81; ser. 1, vol. 11 (1853): 668–90. See ser. 1, vol. 8 (1851): 148–9.

7 Ibid., ser. 1, vol. 10 (1853): 76.

8 Barry Bergdoll, "The Idea of a Cathedral in 1852," in *A.W.N. Pugin: Master of Gothic Revival*, ed. Paul Atterbury (New Haven: Bard Graduate Center for Studies in the Decorative Arts/Yale University Press, 1995), 104–20.

9 Jean Baptiste Antoine Lassus, *Album de Villard de Honnecourt, architecte du XIIIe siècle; manuscrit publié en fac-simile annoté, précédé de considérations sur la renaissance de l'art français au XIXe siècle et suivi d'un glossaire par J.B.A. Lassus; ouvrage mis au jour, après la mort de M. Lassus et conformément à ses manuscrits par Alfred Darcel* (Paris: L. Laget, 1968 [reprinted 1976], facsimile of the original edition of 1858), 1–41.

10 Ibid., 33–4.

11 "L'architecte de Cambrai … appartenait à une génération qui puisait dans l'air, pour ainsi dire, le souffle inspirateur; qui était tellement empreinte, enfin, du sentiment gothique, qu'il lui était impossible de ne pas faire ce qu'elle faisait." Ibid., 180.

12 Ibid., 69–70.

13 Ibid., 39.

14 Prosper Mérimée, "Album de Villard de Honnecourt," *Études sur les arts du Moyen Âge* (Paris: Éditions Flammarion, 1967 [1858]), 229–70.

15 Eugène Emmanuel Viollet-le-Duc, "Première apparition de Villard de Honnecourt, architecte du XIIIE siècle," *Gazette des Beaux-Arts* 1 (1859): 286–95; Viollet-le-Duc, "Album de Villard de Honnecourt, architecte du treizième siècle," *Revue archéologique* n.s. 7 (1863): 103–18, 184–93, 250–8, 361–70.

16 "L'album de Villard de Honnecourt est un livre plus intéressant, plus curieux que ne le serait un traité sur la matière, car il nous découvre la vie intime, les travaux journaliers de ces architectes laïques qui ont fondé la grande école du XIIIe siècle. Or aujourd'hui, si les artistes doivent travailler pour les vivants, il faut qu'ils vivent avec les morts. Car il n'est que ceux-là qui enseignent." Viollet-le-Duc, "Première apparition," 295.

17 Viollet-le-Duc, "Album de Villard," 362, 364–5.

18 Eugène Emmanuel Viollet-le-Duc, "Deuxième apparition de Villard de Honnecourt: à propos de la renaissance des arts en France," *Gazette des Beaux-Arts* 5 (1860): 24–31. See also Viollet-le-Duc, "Album de Villard," 109, 255. Pierre de Corbie is the only builder mentioned by name in the manuscript of Villard. Concerning the idea of the overdetermined medieval creator, see Jean Nayrolles, "Sciences naturelles et archéologie médiévale au XIXE siècle," in *L'architecture, les sciences et la culture de l'histoire au XIXe siècle*, introduction by François Loyer (Saint-Étienne: Publications de l'Université de Saint-Étienne, 2001), 25–49.

19 Viollet-le-Duc, "Deuxième apparition," 29–31; Viollet-le-Duc, "Album de Villard," 110.

20 Burges published three essays on Villard in the immediate aftermath of Lassus's facsimile. See William Burges, "An Architect's Sketchbook of the Thirteenth Century," *The Builder* 16 (1858): 758, 770–2; Burges, "Fac-simile of the Sketch Book of Wilars de Honecort," *The Building News* 5 (1859): 897–8; Burges, "Architectural Drawing," *Papers Read at the Royal Institute of British Architects* (1860–61): 14–23.

21 Burges, "Architect's Sketchbook," 770.

22 John Ruskin, *The Seven Lamps of Architecture* (New York: Farrar, Straus and Giroux, 1986), 143.

23 A little less than half of the drawings in the Vellum Sketchbook constitute visual records of buildings or monuments in places that Burges is known to have visited, or likely visited, during the first half of the 1860s: Florence (1860 and 1861); Prato, Milan, Monza, Bologna, Verona, Parma, Bern, Basel, and Langres (1861); Chartres (1862); Dublin (1862 and 1863); Bordeaux, Poitiers, and Carcassonne (1863); and Beauvais (1862, 1863, and

1864). The Vellum Sketchbook further includes six pages containing representations of Burges's own designs; for the most part, these, too, can be reliably dated to the period between 1860 and 1867.

24 Burges, Vellum Sketchbook, folio 1 verso.

25 The Vellum Sketchbook has seventy-two pages measuring around 235 by 170 millimetres; what survives of the original manuscript sixty-six was trimmed to 235 to 240 millimetres by 154 to 160 millimetres.

26 "Incarnée dans une *Kunst- und Wunderkammer*, dans la bibliothèque d'un érudit, dans le laboratoire d'un chimiste, praticien de la philosophie hermétique, ou d'un physicien pour qui l'optique reste une science des miracles, exubérante, incohérente, désordonnée, travaillée par des contradictions, tirée à hue et à dia, la curiosité a gouverné par intérim entre le règne de la théologie et celui de la science." See Krzysztof Pomian, *Collectionneurs, amateurs et curieux. Paris, Venise: XVIe–XVIIIe siècle* (Paris: Éditions Gallimard, 1987), 80.

27 William Burges, "Introductory," in *Art Applied to Industry: A Series of Lectures* (Oxford: John and Henry Parker, 1864), 1–12.

28 William Burges, "Art and Religion," in *The Church and the World; Essays on Questions of the Day in 1868*, ed. Rev. Orby Shipley (London: Longmans, Green, Reader and Dyer, 1868), 574–98.

29 William Burges, "History and Literature of Architecture, Early Middle Ages, 6th century to 12th century" (manuscript), *Voluntary Architectural Examination Lectures, 1865* (RIBA Archives, London), 19–39; Burges, *Art Applied to Industry*, 8.

30 Burges, Vellum Sketchbook, folio 20 verso.

31 On the notion of the "figuration" as a drawing that produces both the building and its architect, see Hélène Lipstadt, "Architectural Publications, Competitions, and Exhibitions," in *Architecture and Its Image: Four Centuries of Architectural Representation – Works from the Collection of the Canadian Centre for Architecture*, ed. Eve Blau and Edward Kaufman (Montreal: Canadian Centre for Architecture, 1989), 110.

32 Crook, *William Burges*, 320–1.

33 Ibid., 326.

34 "XIIIE siècle.—Orfèvrerie française. Crosse d'évêque en cuivre ciselé," *L'art pour tous; Encyclopédie de l'art industriel et décoratif* 14 (1875): 1457; William Burges, "Own Furniture," RIBA Photographs Collection, London. The same photograph appears in R.P. Pullan, *The Designs of William Burges, A.R.A.* (s.l.: s.n., ca. 1885), plate no. 14: "Pastoral Staff."

35 William Burges, *Report to the Courts of Justice Commission* (London: George Edward Eyre and William Spottiswoode, Printers to the Queen's Most Excellent Majesty, 1867).

36 Burges, Vellum Sketchbook, folio 3 verso.

37 R[obert] K[err], "Heroes and Hero-Worship: The Hero as Architect," *The Builder* 16 (1858): 794–5.

38 Tim Barringer, *The Pre-Raphaelites*, Everyman Art Library (London: Calmann and King, 1998), 32–3.

39 Elizabeth Prettejohn, *Beauty and Art: 1750–2000*, Oxford History of Art (Oxford and New York: Oxford University Press, 2005), 113–15.

40 John Ruskin, *The Stones of Venice*, 3 vols. (New York: John Wiley and Sons, 1880), 2:37–9.

41 Elizabeth Prettejohn, *Rossetti and His Circle* (New York: Stewart, Tabori and Chang, 1998), 17–19.

42 Barringer, *Pre-Raphaelites*, 136.

43 Burges was a member of the short-lived Hogarth Club in London in 1860–61, a meeting place for artists and their patrons founded in 1858 by Rossetti and Ford Madox Brown. He is also known to have commissioned Rossetti and other members of his circle to paint panels on his furniture in 1859. Finally, the watercolourist George Price Boyce, Burges's neighbour in Buckingham Street from 1856 to 1868, was also a close personal friend of Rossetti. See Deborah Cherry, "The Hogarth Club: 1858–1861," *Burlington Magazine* 122 (1980): 236–44; Crook, *William Burges*, 321; Barringer, *Pre-Raphaelites*, 87; Prettejohn, *Rossetti*, 15.

44 William Burges, *The Diary of William Burges* (original manuscript on deposit at the National Art Library, London).

45 Burges, Vellum Sketchbook, folios 23 verso, 24 recto, 25 verso.

46 The most famous of these works are William Holman Hunt's illustration of Tennyson's poem *The Lady of Shalott* (1857), D.G. Rossetti's *Fazio's Mistress* (1863), and J.M. Whistler's *The Little White Girl: Symphony in White No. 2* (1864). See Christine Poulson, "Death and the Maiden: The Lady of Shalott and the Pre-Raphaelites," in *Reframing the Pre-Raphaelites: Historical and Theoretical Essays*, ed. Ellen Harding, 173-3 (Aldershot: Scolar Press, 1995); Prettejohn, *Rossetti*, 26–31.

47 Prettejohn, *Beauty and Art*, 151–5; Prettejohn, "The Modernism of Frederic Leighton," in *English Art, 1860–1914: Modern Artists and Identity*, ed. David Peters Corbett and Lara Perry (New Brunswick, NJ: Rutgers University Press, 2001), 48.

48 Burges, *Art Applied to Industry*, 52.
49 C.G. Jung, excerpt from "The Relations between the Ego and the Unconscious," in *The Essential Jung*, ed. Anthony Storr (Princeton, NJ: Princeton University Press, 1983), 94–6.
50 Chris Brooks, *The Gothic Revival* (London: Phaidon Press, 1999), 155–7.

Perspective *Jing*: The Depth of Architectural Representation in a European-Chinese Garden Encounter*

Hui Zou

INTRODUCTION[1]

IN 1786 THE COURT PAINTER Yi Lantai created twenty copperplate drawings of the Western Multistoried-Buildings (Xiyang Lou),[2] a "Western-like" garden designed and co-built by European Jesuits for Emperor Qianlong of the Qing dynasty. The garden was located in a remote corner of the imperial Garden of Round Brightness (Yuanming Yuan). These copperplate drawings were composed in Western linear perspective, called "line-method" (*xianfa*) in eighteenth-century China. Commissioned by the emperor, Yi's copperplate set is the earliest application of Western linear perspective to the representation of a Chinese imperial garden.[3] The term "line-method" is also inscribed in the titles of these copperplate engravings. Yi used both line-method and Chinese traditional "frontal view" to construct drawings in which detailed buildings occupied a dominant position.

In Yi's set there are no shadows in any of the drawings.[4] Without shadows, the light in each picture is evenly distributed, with a diffused brightness. In my interpretation of these copperplates, three questions emerge: (1) How was perspective used to create depth in the Chinese gardens? (2) How was this received by the emperors? and (3) Was the diffused brightness in these representations related to the cosmic concept of Round Brightness in the imperial gardens? To explore these questions, the garden and drawings are placed in an interactive relationship in which the garden design and the garden representation can respond to one another. Because the emperor commissioned and was personally involved in both the design of this Western garden and its representations, their meanings may be revealed in its imperial context: Round Brightness.

The framed bright view in Chinese gardens and landscape paintings is traditionally called a *jing*. According to Chinese garden and landscape literature, the *jing* has been associated with brightness in landscape views since the Han dynasty. The idea of the *jing* as a view of a beautiful landscape was fully developed during the Tang dynasty.[5] In addition, according to Chinese painting theories, the *jing* as a framed view of a landscape or garden has been very popular in paintings since the Southern Song dynasty. It was not until the Ming dynasty that the *jing* began to be represented from a ground-level viewpoint (i.e., the viewpoint of someone standing within the garden) rather than from the traditional bird's-eye viewpoint. During the Qing dynasty it became a cliché that when people saw a beautiful landscape – a *jing* – they would say it was like a painting.[6]

My interpretation of the European-Chinese encounter in the Garden of Round Brightness focuses on the *jing* of this garden. The dual association between both the garden and its representation during the Qing dynasty makes the *jing* a useful historical concept for discovering perspective, depth, and diffused brightness. In order to analyze a *jing*, one must take note of three of its typical characteristics: depth, boundary, and brightness. My research focuses on how the emperors' cosmic vision of Round Brightness unified the multiple *jing* in the Garden of Round Brightness, and it investigates how the *jing* was created through line-method in the Western Multistoried-Buildings Garden. The comparison between the perspective *jing* and the *jing* of Round Brightness shows how the physical phenomena of depth, boundary, and brightness in a garden *jing* not only promoted cultural fusion but also maintained cultural difference.[7] The existence of a *jing* requires a careful study of the relationship between the *jing* and its immediate context. Unlike a landscape, a *jing* is a bright, deep, bounded view that is removed from its context. In this sense, the presence of the perspective *jing* depends on the *jing* of Round Brightness, which, in turn, depends on the cosmic vision of Round Brightness.

The Garden of Round Brightness was the most magnificent of the imperial gardens in the northwestern suburb of Beijing during the Qing dynasty (see fig. 13.1). This suburb was selected as an ideal garden site for many reasons, including cool weather conditions, rich spring waters, and proximity to the beautiful landscape of West Mountain and the wilderness. In 1710, Kangxi granted a piece of land north of his Garden of Uninhibited Spring (Changchun Yuan) to his fourth son, Prince Yinzheng. On this site, Yinzheng built the Garden of Round Brightness. After Yinzheng took the throne and became Emperor Yongzheng, he used the garden as his permanent residence and a place for receiving audiences. Emperor Qianlong, Yongzheng's fourth son, expanded the Garden of Round Brightness into a huge garden compound consisting of four gardens: three Chinese – Garden of Round Brightness, Garden of Eternal Spring (Changchun Yuan), and Garden of Gorgeous Spring (Qichun Yuan) – and the small European garden, Western Multistoried-Buildings Garden (see fig. 13.2).

By 1744, Qianlong made the first expansion of his father's Garden of Round Brightness by formally establishing the series of garden scenes, the so-called "Forty Jing." He named and poeticized the Forty Jing and commissioned the court painters to create a painting for each one.[8] Like his grandfather Kangxi, Qianlong visited the Jiangnan region six times and

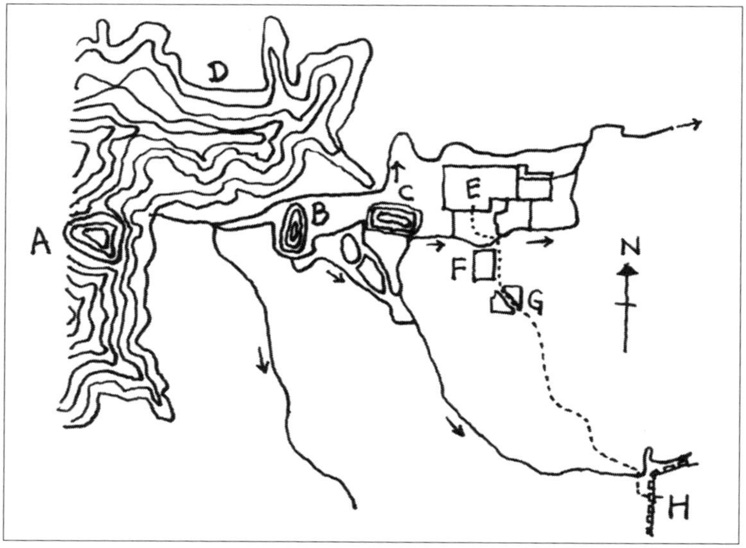

Fig. 13.1 Map of the northwestern suburb of Beijing, drawn by author.
A: Fragrant Hill; B: Jade-Spring Hill; C: Longevity Hill; D: West Mountain; E: Garden of Round Brightness; F: Garden of Uninhibited Spring; G: Town of Shallow Lakes; H: Old Beijing City.

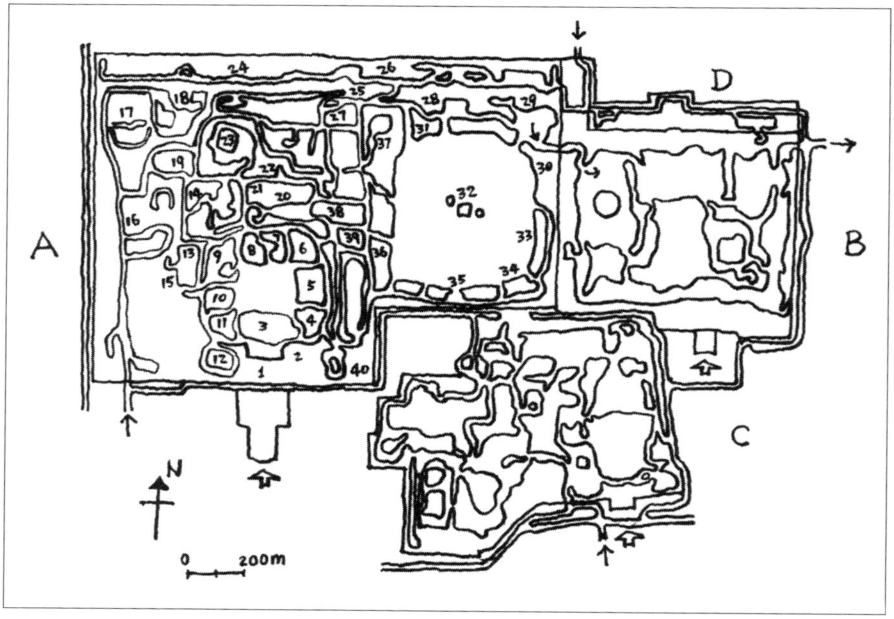

Fig. 13.2 General plan of watercourses in the Garden of Round Brightness compound, drawn by author. A: Garden of Round Brightness; B: Garden of Eternal Spring; C: Garden of Gorgeous Spring; D: Western Multistoried-Buildings Garden; Nos. 1–40: Forty Jing.

was impressed by the literati gardens he visited there.[9] For each garden he admired, he would ask a court painter to produce a painting and bring it back to Beijing as a reference for creating new gardens. In 1751, he built the Garden of Eternal Spring, east of the original Garden of Round Brightness, as the epitome of some famous Jiangnan gardens. Meanwhile, he was also building the Western Multistoried-Buildings Garden in the northeastern corner of the compound.

The Garden of Round Brightness had served continuously as the permanent residence for five Qing emperors before being destroyed by fires lit by foreign powers in 1860. The identity of the Garden of Round Brightness was somewhat ambiguous. Both the original garden and the entire garden compound were called Round Brightness. The garden was not purely Chinese: it was partly European, and the fire emphasized the distinction between its Chinese and European portions. Before the fire, the European portion was hidden within the Chinese portion; after the fire, the Chinese portion was burnt to cinders, while the European portion, built in stone, remained as ruins. The ruins of the Western Multistoried-Buildings Garden are now well known and are often identified as the Garden of Round Brightness.

VISION OF ROUND BRIGHTNESS

Unlike his father and son, Yongzheng was known for his philosophical thinking. While in the gardens, he would often think about the relation between human spirituality and the heavens. In his mind, the vision of Round Brightness was evident in both his heart and the full moon. In the poem "Hall of Wonderful Height," he states:

> The inherent character and heavens mix together without differentiation of the present and past [性天融会无今古],
> The heart and moon in *round brightness* brighten through the deep sky [心月圆明彻太虚].
> [I] get up and shout through the northern window [睡起北窗时一啸],
> One thousand mountains echo to me smoothly [千山答响自如如].[10]
> (My emphasis)

This is the only poem in which Yongzheng uses the phrase "round brightness" to associate the heart with the moon. In China, thought is usually believed to originate in the heart, which is considered to be the most remote and most opaque place in the human body. The depth of the heart is associated with the dark depth of the cosmos. If the heart can be brightened, the human being can become fully integrated with the surrounding world. The vision of Round Brightness unifies not only the heart and the moon but also the human being and the heavens, the present and the past, the individual and the landscape.

There are no known pictorial representations of the Garden of Round Brightness during the reign of Yongzheng. His vision of Round Brightness is best described by his prose, "Record of the Garden of Round Brightness" (1725). In it, he emphasizes that the garden name was granted by his father Kangxi, whose discovery of the sweet spring water in the northwestern suburb led to the construction of imperial gardens in that area. Regarding the construction of the garden, Yongzheng writes:

> I was granted an area here with clear, elegant, forested hills and still, deep and expansive waters. I built pavilions and houses following the lay of the land, rising with hills and diving with the waters. I chose to delight in nature and spare myself the vexations of construction. Flowers by the balustrades and trees on the dike flourished without watering. Flocks of birds enjoyed soaring; schools of fish dove freely. The place was bright, high and dry; fertile soil and abundant springs promised prosperity. How peaceful and auspicious it was to reside here![11]

The water for the garden came not only from springs on the site but also from the Hill of Jade-Spring in the west and the River of Ten Thousand Springs in the south. During the construction of the garden, earth that was removed for watercourses was used to create many hillocks. Yongzheng's phrase "I chose to delight in nature" alludes to the Daoist sage Zhuangzi's idea of *ziqu*, literally, "choose by oneself."[12] His descriptions of birds and fish enjoying their own nature allude to another of Zhuangzi's ideas, *zide*, literally, "obtain by itself."[13] Comparing himself to the birds and fish suggests Yongzheng's delightful strolls within the enclosure of Round Brightness.

Yongzheng hints that the enclosure of Round Brightness symbolizes the boundary of the nation. In the garden, plots were planted for vegetables and other crops: "With a casual glance into the distance, my reverie extends to the whole country, as well as wishes for a good harvest."[14] The bounded perfect brightness is extended further, to the cosmos:

When the forest light shines bright and clear, the pools are crystal clear and tranquil; the distant peaks break into this mirror. The morning sun and the evening moon; greenery is reflected and the sky is contained [by the water]. [Hence,] magic effects of Dao emerge unconsciously and the bosom of heaven suddenly becomes bright.[15]

The agricultural field in the garden alludes to Confucius's belief that a country must have sufficient provisions.[16] The emperor's description of the mirror-like surface of the water alludes to Zhuangzi's idea of *zhishui*, literally, "still water": the world is most clearly reflected and collected when water is still.[17]

Regarding his experience in the garden, Yongzheng states:

In the fine days of spring and autumn, when the scenery is fresh and fragrant, and birds sing a harmonious chord and limpid dew congeals on flower petals, I sometimes invite princes and ministers to appreciate the scenes at their own pace, ride in boats and enjoy fruits. We give free rein to our feelings, displaying accordingly our sense of well-being, looking up and gazing down and roaming at leisure. Nature discloses itself to the fullest; heart and mind exult with joy.[18]

The phrase "looking up and gazing down" alludes to the sentence "look up at the bigness of the cosmos, gaze down at the flourishing categories of things," which appears in the prose piece entitled "Recount of the Orchard Pavilion" by Wang Xizhi, a calligraphy artist of the Eastern Jin dynasty.[19] The phrase "roaming at leisure" originates in Zhuangzi's idea of *xiaoyaoyou*: when the heart is not burdened by things and expectations, it can move to infinity.[20] The sentence "nature discloses itself to the fullest; heart and mind exult with joy" expresses the vivid experience of Round Brightness.

As for the meanings of the phrase "Round Brightness," Yongzheng writes:

Round Brightness, the name granted by my father, has a deep and far-ranging

> meaning, not easily perceived. I have tried to research ancient books for the moral meaning of Round Brightness. "Round" means the perfection and concentration of the mind, implying the timeliness and moderation of the behaviour of a virtuous man. "Brightness" means to illuminate all things to reach human perspicacity and wisdom. Round Brightness is used to highlight the meaning of the residence, stimulate the body and mind, piously experience the idea of heaven, cherish forever [my father's] holy instruction, propagate all creatures and maintain harmony and peace.[21]

Yongzheng's method of interpretation was to "research ancient books." The chapter entitled "Xici shangzhuan" in the ancient cosmological book *Yizhuan* (ca. fourth century BCE) says: "Therefore, the virtue of *shi* becomes round and divine; the virtue of *gua* becomes square and intelligent ... Thus, the Dao of heaven is brightened."[22] This quotation is probably the oldest available source on the meaning of "round brightness." Yongzheng's phrase "concentration of the mind" alludes to Zhuangzi's concept of "condensation of the mind," *ningshen*.[23] According to Qing scholar Wang Fuzhi, this condensation of the mind enables the world to be fully occupied by an individual's spirit.[24] The phrase "timeliness and moderation," *shizhong*, literally "timely middle," comes from a central idea of Confucius, who said in the book *Zhongyong*: "A virtuous man acts timely and moderately."[25] The notion of "middle" also may suggest roundness.

At the end of the record, Yongzheng reinforces his primary intention that his garden be a symbol of the whole country: "I do not ask for peace for myself but rather wish it for the whole country. I do not seek leisure for myself but rather long for happiness for all the people, so that generation after generation can step on the 'spring terrace' and wander in the 'happy kingdom.'"[26] Here he uses two Daoist metaphors to describe his garden as a model of the ideal nation, where "happiness" is shared by "all people." The first phrase, "spring terrace," is from the Daoist sage Laozi ("Lustily, the people seem to be enjoying a feast or ascending a terrace in springtime")[27] and refers generally to a beautiful place for wandering. The second phrase, "happy kingdom," is from Zhuangzi's description of the freedom of fish: "To wander leisurely is fish's happiness."[28]

Compared to his father's philosophical vision of Round Brightness, which emphasizes the symbolic relationship between the garden and the country, Qianlong's more worldly vision identifies the garden with the cosmos. This led him to increase the size and inclusiveness of the garden. In 1737 he ordered the court painters to paint a huge panorama of the Garden of Round Brightness. Qianlong called the painting "Grand View," which was later poeticized by a Qing scholar: "move the sky and reduce the earth into the imperial bosom [移天缩地在君怀]."[29] The Chinese term "sky-earth" signifies the cosmos. Within the enclosure of Round Brightness, the distance between the cosmos and the individual's bosom is reduced.

Qianlong's vision of Round Brightness is well represented by the forty paintings of the Forty Jing (1744), created by the court painters Tang Dai and Shen Yuan. The emperor named each *jing* through the use of a four-character poetic phrase. In Chinese gardens this act of naming is called "thematicizing a *jing*" (*tijing*). Qianlong intended to "brighten up the *jing*"[30] by pairing each painting with a poem he had written. Like traditional landscape paintings, the forty paintings of the Forty Jing were represented by a bird's-eye view and presented a diffused brightness with no shadows. The *jing* depicted in each painting shows a place where the emperor stood, while the poem describes what he saw while he stood there. This unifies the two *jing* under the same title and fuses them into one.

The fact that the titled *jing* includes both the view of a place and the view seen from that place reminds us that a painting of a *jing* should consider how that particular *jing* was used in the garden. A poem about a *jing* provides an additional way of understanding it. Together, the painting and the poem interpret the diffused brightness and the emperor's perceptions. On the first *jing*, "Uprightness and Brightness," Qianlong writes:

> Poetical books are as many as the trailing plants in the courtyard
> [义府庭萝壁];
> Grace is as extensive as silvery water waves [恩波水泻银].
> A green grass reminds me of being thrifty [草青思示俭];
> Still mountains recall benevolence [山静体依仁].[31]

His thoughts shift among different components of the garden – to and fro, near and far. These ramblings through the bird's-eye view of the *jing* brighten his mind (see fig. 13.3). The buildings in this painting are constructed from an oblique, one-point perspective, but their focal point falls far beyond the upper right corner of the painting. As in traditional landscape paintings, the remoteness of this focal point enhances the back-and-forth motion of the viewer. This subtle perspective convergence departs from the parallel projection used in traditional landscape paintings and was probably influenced by the Jesuit painters in the court.

Qianlong's desire for perfect brightness in his vision of Round Brightness is also represented in his portraits. Every imperial portrait had to be painted frontally, with the eyes looking straight ahead, because the full face is supposed to be brightest. When Jesuit painters presented an oblique portrait with shadows, similar to the Renaissance three-quarter view, the emperor rejected it and insisted on the frontal view to show the

Fig. 13.3 Painting of the first *jing*, Uprightness and Brightness, drawn by Tang Dai and Shen Yuan (1744).

face with perfect brightness.[32] Two different frontal representations, the imperial face and the Jesuit central perspective, are integrated in a portrait of Prince Hongyan, Qianlong's younger brother (see fig. 13.4). The prince sits in an armchair in front of a painted screen that depicts a Western portal. The central perspective of the screen echoes his frontal posture, and his head is aligned exactly with the focal point. The perspective view depicted beyond the portal is a *jing* of a distant landscape. It is interesting that the outer edge of the screen was cut from the original paper and remounted on another piece of paper.[33] The thickness of the cut edge of the portal not only reinforces the perspective effect but also suggests the artificiality of line-method.

To construct the Garden of Eternal Spring as part of his expansion of the Garden of Round Brightness, Qianlong imitates the famous gardens in Jiangnan, including the Lion Grove in Suzhou, which was well known for its rocks and for being depicted in the paintings of Ni Zan of the Yuan dynasty. Replicating a famous existing garden in the design of a new imperial garden unavoidably raised the question of truth. In a poem about the new Lion Grove, Qianlong writes:

> I want to ask about the *bounded environment* [emphasis mine] of the Lion Grove [试问狮林境],
> Which one is fictional and which one is truthful [孰为幻孰真]?
> The She Garden [of today's Huang family, the current garden of the old Lion Grove] is in fact an imitation [of Ni's painting] [涉园犹假借],
> The original image [of the Lion Grove] is actually in the Treasure Box of the Stone Ditch [宝笈实源津].[34]

The Treasure Box of the Stone Ditch was the imperial place where masterpiece paintings were stored. Of the three sites – the garden site of the old Lion Grove in Suzhou, the new Lion Grove on the outskirts of Beijing, and Ni's painting of the original Lion Grove – which one was most truthful to the original garden? For Qianlong, it is the last one. This does not mean that the painting is more valuable than the actual gardens; rather, it demonstrates that the intention expressed by the pictorial representation of the garden is at least as important as the garden itself. As long as the pictorial intention was preserved, the fact that the garden was a replica was a secondary consideration.

Fig. 13.4 Portrait of Prince Hongyan, painter unknown (mid- to late eighteenth century). Freer Gallery, Washington, DC.

LABYRINTHS

The Forty Jing are organized into a numeric series throughout the garden. The multiple *jing* define a virtual path that appears mystical and confusing – "a beautiful disorder," according to the Jesuit painter Jean-Denis Attiret.[35] Connecting the sites of the Forty Jing with straight lines produces a zigzag diagram, like a constellation in the sky (see fig. 13.5). Surprisingly, these lines do not overlap. The hidden order of this meandering path describes the emperor's poetic journey towards infinity.

After the completion of the Forty Jing, Qianlong began to construct the Western Multistoried-Buildings Garden. This garden was built in two phases: the first was arranged on a short south-to-north axis, the second on a long west-to-east axis (see fig. 13.6). This European garden is also composed of many exotic *jing*, which includes the Western multistoried buildings, mechanical fountains, geometric pools, and a geometric hill.

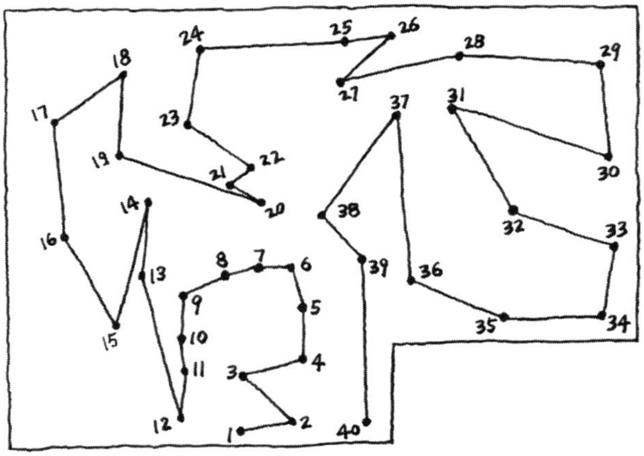

Fig. 13.5 Diagram of the path of Forty Jing, drawn by author.

At the northern end of the first axis is a Western labyrinth with an imperial throne at the centre. At the eastern end of the second axis stands an illusionary stage set. In Yi Lantai's copperplate drawings, all of these *jing* are depicted using line-method, the Chinese translation of the Western technique of linear perspective.[36]

According to an imperial archive, on the eleventh day of the fourth moon of the twenty-first year of the Qianlong reign (1756), the emperor decreed:

> Ask Lang Shining [Giuseppe Castiglione] to sketch a plan of a *Western garden* [*xiyang huayuan*] east of the Harmony, Wonder and Delight [Pavilion] of the Garden of Eternal Spring [n.b., the Western Multistoried-Buildings Garden was usually considered part of the Garden of Eternal Spring]. The design should be presented for review and only after it is permitted can it be sent to the Construction Department of the Garden of Round Brightness for building.[37] (My emphasis)

Castiglione's plan is actually the second phase of the European garden; the Harmony, Wonder, and Delight Pavilion belongs to the first phase. It is significant that Qianlong calls the plan "a Western garden" as this is the clearest proof that the site of the Western Multistoried-Buildings was intended as a garden. It is recorded that "Lang Shining finished the sketch of a *Western-like and garden-like plan* and presented it [my emphasis]." Qianlong approved the construction of the garden on the same day that

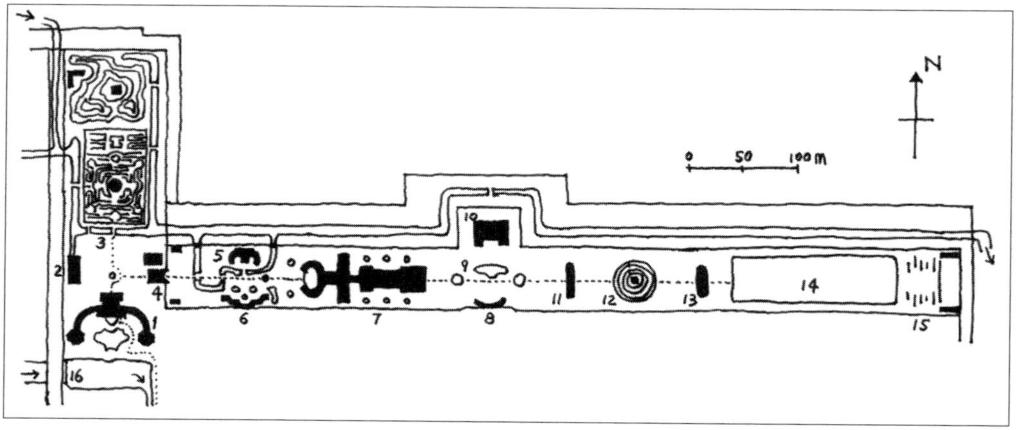

Fig. 13.6 Plan of the Western Multistoried-Buildings Garden, drawn by author. (1) Harmony, Wonder, and Delight Pavilion; (2) Water-Storage Building; (3) Flower Garden; (4) Cages for Raising Birds; (5) View beyond the World; (6) Bamboo Pavilions; (7) Hall of the Peaceful Sea Pavilion; (8) Viewing the Water-Method Throne; (9) Big Water-Method; (10) View of the Distant Sea Pavilion; (11) Gateway of the Hill of Line-Method; (12) Hill of Line-Method; (13) Eastern Gateway of the Hill of Line-Method; (14) Square River; (15) Paintings of Line-Method; (16) Bridge of Line-Method.

he was presented with the plan. He then decreed: "It is permitted to construct according to the design. Wherever Western paintings are needed [in the garden], ask the Lodge of As-One-Wishes [studio] to make moving-through-*jing* paintings."[38] "Moving-through-*jing* painting" (*tongjing hua*) was a court term for a painting with a Western-like perspective.[39] It suggests that perspective depth was attractive to Chinese eyes. Although construction had not yet begun, the emperor already visualized a garden that would be created with the line-method used in Western paintings.

The path through the European garden starts at the western end and moves directly eastward. The main entrance is located over a "water-mouth" (*shuikou*), where the water from the Garden of Round Brightness flows into the Garden of Eternal Spring (see fig. 13.7).[40] This water-mouth symbolizes the father-son relationship between the two gardens. It is interesting that this crucial water-mouth is spanned by a Western bridge with a trompe l'oeil portal that was composed through the use of line-method. This portal not only extends the depth of view but also energizes the bridge and the watercourse underneath. The appearance of the portal creates the illusion that people could step from the bridge into another world.

The Western labyrinth located at the northern end of the first axis is called Formation of Yellow Flowers (see fig. 13.8). Given the square layout of the labyrinth, the word "formation" hints at the formation of troops. Compared to the winding path in the Garden of Round Brightness, the zigzag path of the labyrinth follows a strict geometric pattern. It is interesting that the emperor apparently accepted the straight but winding path and called the labyrinth a "garden" (*huayuan*). Although labyrinths and mazes were common in European Baroque gardens, the emperor and the Chinese people probably referred to the exotic labyrinth as a "garden" because of its zigzag movement (even though the path was laid out according to line-method). In Chinese gardens, a winding path is believed to lead to a "deep and remote" area within the mind. According to the theory known as "abstruse as such" (*aoru*) advanced by the Tang landscape essayist Liu Zongyuan, meandering through nature procures the "delight of the abstruse."[41] Perhaps the zigzag path of the labyrinth reminded the emperor of the meandering journey of the Forty Jing.

The labyrinth was also called Lanterns of Yellow Flowers, after a Chinese folk tale. It is said that, on the night of the Mid-Autumn Festival, when the moon was most round and its light most clear, the emperor would peer down from the pavilion at the centre of the labyrinth, watching the court ladies meandering about carrying lamps of yellow flowers. As the traditional celebratory fireworks brightened the Chinese portion of

Fig. 13.7 Southern face of Harmony, Wonder, and Delight Pavilion, the first copperplate, drawn by Yi Lantai (1786).

Fig. 13.8 Frontal face of the Flower Garden, the fifth copperplate, drawn by Yi Lantai (1786).

the Garden of Round Brightness at night, the yellow-flower lanterns brightened the labyrinth.

North of the labyrinth was a hillock covered with dense trees that hid a Chinese square pavilion. This hillock behind the flat labyrinth may have prevented the emperor's back from being exposed to the outside of the garden as he sat in the central pavilion, facing south. This can be seen in the fifth copperplate, where the densely treed hillocks block the distant view and hide the water-mouth of a canal flowing in from outside.

THE MOUNTAIN AND WATERS OF LINE-METHOD

Among the emperors who lived in the Garden of Round Brightness, Jiaqing, son of Qianlong, wrote the most poems on the European portion, especially on the View of the Distant Sea Pavilion as this *jing* may have been his favourite (see fig. 13.9). His poetry shows how the Western multistoried-buildings were used and how he was impressed by these "Western style" buildings. In his poem "Chanting at the View of the Distant Sea," Jiaqing states:

> Stone steps go up and down between pearl trees [石级参差列珠树],
> Glass windows compose beautiful views [玻璃为牖佳境布].
> Wide-open windows on all sides lead to cool breezes [八窗洞开引清风],

Fig. 13.9 Frontal face of the View of the Distant Sea Pavilion, the fourteenth copperplate, drawn by Yi Lantai (1786).

On the emerald-green screen the purple phoenix lingers in fragrant mists [翠屏紫凤萦香雾].
A room with clear views is prepared for the distant sea [一室澄观备远瀛],
The imperial mind embraces the great world [圣念包罗九有宏].
Look with reverence at the grand building and caress in deep concern its structure [瞻临堂构切抚宇],
Its majesty resists decay and remains full [凛乎驭朽弥持盈].[42]

The *jing* of the distant lake framed by the bright room extends the emperor's mind into the cosmos, and the "grand" view expresses the "fullness" of his majesty. According to an imperial archive, the windows of the building were fitted with more than twelve hundred glass plates in 1782,[43] bringing light into the room and creating a "room with clear views." The phrase "prepared for the distant sea" implies that the emperor was facing the Garden of Eternal Spring to the south.

In other poems on the same *jing*, Jiaqing presents more descriptions of the building:

The stone door is connected with lip windows [石牖层窗接],
The form imitates the Western [规制仿西洋].[44]

Clearly, the "Western" style impressed him. The "lip windows" refer to the decorations on the window frames. Jiaqing continues:

> The structure imitates the Western [结构仿洋式],
> For entertainment and leisure, I occasionally come [here] to stroll about [娱情偶来游].
> The view is like a *jing* of a painting [如披画图景],
> My eyes are pleased and my intention remains free [悦目意漫留].[45]

The poem clearly states that the scene around the View of the Distant Sea Pavilion was "a *jing* of a painting," where Jiaqing's eyes and heart met. Penned by Qianlong, the name board "View of the Distant Sea" was made of glass and decorated with Western lace borders, and it officially hung on the inner eave of the pavilion in 1781.[46] A name board indicates the official name of a *jing*, typically inscribed on a wooden board and hung on the inner or outer eave of the main building of that *jing*. When the emperor sat on his throne and looked outside, the *jing* he saw was the reverse of the *jing* shown in the copperplate, which focused on the building. The *jing* described on the name board on the eave and the *jing* depicted in the corresponding copperplate had the same title but were complementary opposites.

In the perspective *jing* of the European portion of the Garden of Round Brightness, the Western multistoried-buildings were closely tied to the mechanical fountains known as "water-methods" (*shuifa*). Early descriptions of water-methods appear in the Chinese books written by the Jesuits during the Ming dynasty. The biggest water display in the garden, the so-called Big Water-Method, stood just south of the View of the Distant Sea Pavilion (see fig. 13.10). In a poem titled for the pavilion but describing the fountain, Jiaqing writes:

> Continuous lofty towers imitate the Western style [连延崇阁仿重洋],
> Dig a pool and draw the water with detailed mechanical running [鑿沼引水机运详].
> Water meanders and pours into [the movement of] surging and stirring [曲折灌注互荡激],
> Three times disappearing and three times appearing, the vein is hidden [三伏三见脉络藏].[47]

The poem demonstrates the interactive relation between the water-method and the building depicted in line-method. Several features of the fountain setting impressed the emperor: the lofty building in the "Western style," the complex mechanism of the fountains, the waterspouts, and the hidden watercourse. His description of the covered water channel leading to the fountains as a "vein" suggests that he was interpreting the water-method according to the concepts associated with a watercourse in Chinese gardens.

South of the Big Water-Method was a throne called Viewing the Water-Method, primarily for appreciating the theatrical water play of the fountains (see fig. 13.11). Behind the throne was a curved stone screen with five relief panels of panoplies, arms, helmets, and breastplates. Because the View of the Distant Sea Pavilion sat high on a terrace, just behind the Big Water-Method, the emperor's view from the Viewing the Water-Method Throne concentrated on the fountains and did not extend further north. In the opposite direction, the emperor could sit in the View of the Distant Sea Pavilion and look far to the south, towards the Garden of Eternal Spring.

The title of this *jing*, Viewing the Water-Method, indicates the shift between view and viewing. A view of a fountain in the garden was not an isolated image in itself; rather, it became an appreciable "view" because

Fig. 13.10 Frontal face of the Big Water-Method, the fifteenth copperplate, drawn by Yi Lantai (1786).

Fig. 13.11 Frontal face of the Viewing the Water-Method, the sixteenth copperplate, drawn by Yi Lantai (1786).

the fountain was integrated into a line-method picture. As shown in the twenty copperplates, the line-method lowered the horizon to eye level and established a central focal point within the picture. It drew the beholder's eye to this focal point, which then became a counter-eye with a reciprocal role. The throne was both the focal point and the viewpoint, the view and the act of viewing. In the garden, the emperor watched the play of water from the throne; in the copperplate, the empty throne indicates his absence and becomes the new frontal focal point.

Line-method was used to create not only water-methods but also the hill in the garden, known as Hill of Line-Method, located east of the Big Water-Method (see fig. 13.12). The path from the bottom to the top of the hill is arranged in concentric circles, similar to a labyrinth. Although the path looks simple in plan, it is disorienting because the hill is covered with pine trees. The labyrinthine path, used for equestrian activities, provides the emperor with much more entertainment and opportunities to appreciate the surrounding views than would a single spiral path or a straight stairway. In the eighteenth copperplate, the hilltop pavilion appears without any obstruction by the pine trees, suggesting that the emperor wanted a clear panoramic view from the hilltop. Unlike the spiral hills in European gardens, the Hill of Line-Method did not stand by itself but was carefully composed, as the title of the copperplate indicates, to present a "frontal face" (*zhengmian*) according to line-method.

Fig. 13.12 Frontal face of the Hill of Line-Method, the eighteenth copperplate, drawn by Yi Lantai (1786).

THEATRE

Climbing over the Hill of Line-Method and facing east, one encounters the so-called Eastern Gateway of the Hill of Line-Method, with a view of distant mountains and water beyond (see fig. 13.13). Unlike the western gateway of the hill, which enhances the centrality of line-method, the eastern gateway acts as a frame to draw the mind to a distant *jing* that looks like a typical "head-on *jing*" (*duijing*) in Chinese gardens. The dynamic and exotic decorations on the gateway enhance the theatricality of the framed view, recalling the mythical islands in the East Sea where immortals were said to dwell.[48]

After passing through the Eastern Gateway, one would realize that the previous framed view is part of an open-air theatre that includes a rectangular lake called Square River. East of the lake is a stage set with line-method murals, based on stage designs attributed to the Jesuit painter Andrea Pozzo.[49] The stage is called the Paintings of Line-Method or the Walls of Line-Method. According to a construction plan drawn up by the Lei family (see fig. 13.14), the court contractors who built the Garden of Round Brightness as well as its European portion,[50] a small body of water from the external canal branches into two smaller canals: one flows west and passes alongside the eastern gateway of the hill, while the other flows east along the northern bank of the Square River and passes in front of the stage set. Both canals function as a symbolic boundary to mark specific territories and to increase the apparent depth of the view through the gateway near the stage. The multiple layers of watercourses across the front and the illusory mountain ranges in the background compose a picture of "ten-thousand waters and one-thousand mountains," symbolizing the extensive landscapes of nature. As usual in Chinese gardens, the earth that was removed to make the Square River was used to create the Hill of Line-Method. The Square River is mainly intended to enhance the perspective illusion of the Paintings of Line-Method.[51] The complementary relation between the "square" lake and the "round" hill also symbolizes a cosmological idea: "heaven [is] round and earth [is] square."

Unlike open-air theatres in Italian gardens, the stage at the eastern end of the Square River could be appreciated only by standing on the western bank of the lake or from a boat moving straight towards the eastern bank (see fig. 13.15). The line-method of stage-set perspective is explicated in Nian Xiyao's *Shixue* (1729), which imitates the Jesuit Jean Dubreuil's illusory perspective by emphasizing the eye-level position of "frontal viewing" (*zhengshi*). In the prefaces of the treatise (both the 1729 and the 1735 editions), Nian acknowledges the assistance of Giuseppe Castiglione, the designer of the Western Multistoried-Buildings Garden.[52] In Pozzo's stage designs, the frontal view is only one of many possible views for the audience in an amphitheatre, but the frontal view of the Paintings of Line-Method was the only one that appealed to the emperor. Unlike the oblique arrangements in Pozzo's stage designs, the site plan drawn up by the Lei family shows each painted wall oriented as a "frontal face," arranged orthogonally along the west-to-east axis of the lake so that the overall frontal view, the *jing*, consists of many small frontal views.

In the framed *jing* of line-method, the point of view is no longer random and free to move, as it is in traditional Chinese paintings; instead, the view is fixed to promote an illusion of depth. This static frontal view recalls Zhuangzi's idea of "condensation of the mind" (*ningshen*), which he explicates as "[to] gaze fixedly and stop [on something]."[53] In a focused gaze, the smallest thing, including the focal point of line-method, could coincide with the cosmos. As in the final scene of the Forty Jing, "In Depth of Remote Dwelling," this illusory *jing* of mountains and waters in line-method presents a remote dwelling for the emperor's mind.

The theatre was located at the eastern end of the Western Multistoried-Buildings Garden, which was also the most northeasterly part of the

Fig. 13.13 Eastern Gateway of the Hill of Line-Method, the nineteenth copperplate, drawn by Yi Lantai (1786).

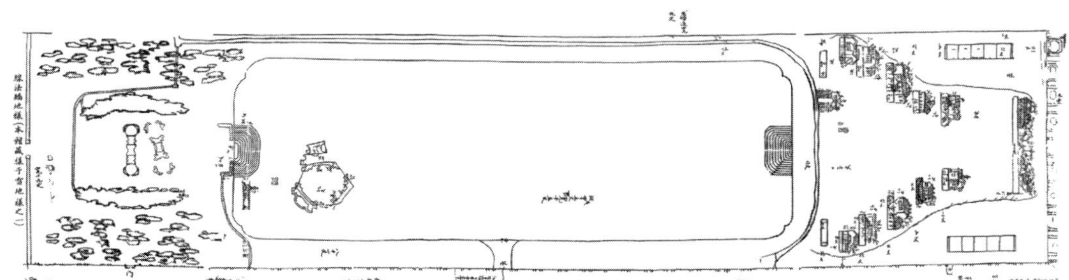

Fig. 13.14 Plan of the Walls of Line-Method, drawn by the Lei family (1750s).

Fig. 13.15 Paintings of Line-Method East of the Lake, the twentieth copperplate, drawn by Yi Lantai (1786).

Garden of Round Brightness compound. In the ancient cosmological diagram *bagua* (see fig. 13.16),[54] the northeast direction is called *gen*. Beijing, the capital, is located in northeast China. According to an explanation from the Qing dynasty:

> The [ancient book] *Yi*[*jing*] says: The *gen* is the cosmological mark of the northeast direction where all things end and begin ... The capital Beijing is located on the *gen* spot, which is a place of both the beginning and end of change ... and can receive the return of all things. It can hold the esteem of the north and face the brightness from the south.[55]

Following the same cosmological consideration, the location of the theatre in the Western Multistoried-Buildings Garden can be understood as a place where the journey for physical brightness ends and the journey for metaphysical brightness begins. The search for worldly truth arrives at this most remote location in the garden. In the pursuit of metaphysical brightness, the theatre at the eastern end of the European portion resembles the altar of a Roman Catholic church. It is at this *gen* spot, the most northeasterly site in the Garden of Round Brightness compound, that the Chinese cosmological brightness of the north and the Christian metaphysical brightness of the east are integrated into a unity.

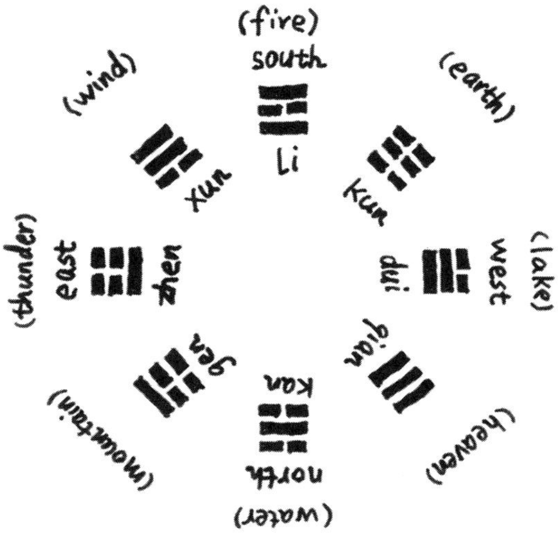

Fig. 13.16 *Bagua* diagram of King Wen of the Zhou dynasty, drawn by author.

NOTES

* This chapter is adapted from Hui Zou, "The *Jing* of Line-Method: A Perspective Garden in the Garden of Round Brightness" (PhD diss., McGill University, 2005).

1 Unless otherwise stated, all the translations from classic Chinese into English are my own. The Chinese dynasties relevant to this research are: Western Zhou (eleventh century BCE–771 BCE); Spring and Autumn (770–476 BCE); Warring States period (475–221 BCE); Western Han (206 BCE–CE 8); Eastern Han (CE 25–220); Southern-Northern Dynasties (317–589); Tang (618–906); Five Dynasties (907–960); Northern Song (960–1127); Southern Song (1127–1279); Yuan (1279–1368); Ming (1368–1644); and Qing (1644–1911). The Qing dynasty includes emperors Kangxi (r. 1662–1722), Yongzheng (r. 1723–35), Qianlong (r. 1736–96), Jiaqing (r. 1796–1820), Daoguang (r. 1821–50), Xianfeng (r. 1851–61).

2 The twenty copperplate engravings are reprinted at their original size in *Palais, pavillons et jardins construits par Giuseppe Castiglione: Dans le domaine impérial du Yuan Ming Yuan au Palais d'Été de Pékin: 20 planches gravées, de 1783 à 1786* (Paris: Jardin de Flore, 1977). A copy is in the Dumbarton Oaks collections in Washington, DC.

3 The first copperplate set of a Chinese imperial garden was drawn and en-

graved by Italian missionary Matteo Ripa for Emperor Kangxi's retreat garden, Mountain Hamlet for Summer Coolness (Bishu Shanzhuang), in Chengde, north of Beijing. In Ripa's set (1713), the perspective effect of line-method was not obvious because, as in Chinese landscape paintings, a universal bird's-eye view was applied and buildings looked small in extensive landscapes. Compared with traditional Chinese woodcut prints, the "precise" representation of the copperplate engravings impressed Kangxi's mind.

4 In the drawings the author applied shading to certain surfaces to emphasize volume and depth. The shading did not follow the Western principle of shades and shadows with a single light source; rather, it was probably related to the traditional watercolour and ink rendering, called *xuanran*, of Chinese paintings. The *xuanran* depicts the depth of a view by applying multiple layers of light shades. The perspective effect resulting from *xuanran* is close to atmospheric perspective in the modern sense.

5 Refer to sec. 2.1 in Zou, "*Jing* of Line-Method."

6 Ibid., sec. 2.2.

7 It is in consideration of the intrinsic relationship between the Round Brightness and the *jing* that I translate the garden name, Yuan-Ming, literally as "Round Brightness" rather than borrow the popular metaphoric understanding, "Perfect Brightness," which is based on the Jesuit translation "jardin de la clarté parfaite."

8 The original set of forty paintings and forty poems in calligraphy of the Garden of Round Brightness is now stored in the Bibliothèque Nationale in Paris. These paintings and poems are reprinted in colour in Chebing Chiu, *Yuanming yuan: Le jardin de la clarté parfaite* (Paris: Les Editions de l'Imprimerie, 2000).

9 The Jiangnan region includes the cities of Suzhou, Wuxi, Hangzhou, and Yangzhou, which are well known for their history of literati gardens.

10 Yongzheng [Qing emperor], "Miaogao Tang," in *Yongzheng shiwen zhujie*, anno. Wei Jianxun (Shenyang: Liaoning guji chubanshe, 1996), 57.

11 My translation is based on the punctuated and annotated version of the record by Yongzheng, "Shizong xianhuangdi yuzhi Yuanmingyuan ji," in *Zhongguo lidai zaoyuan wenxuan*, ed. and anno. Chen Zhi (Hefei: Huangshan shushe, 1992), 194–5. It also refers to another punctuated version edited by Zhongguo Yuanmingyuan xuehui, in *Yuanmingyuan: Xueshu lunwen ji* 4 (1986): 102; and the unpunctuated version in Qianlong [Qing emperor], *Yuzhi Yuanmingyuan tushi* (Tianjing: Shiyin shuwu, 1887), 1–19.

12 See chapter entitled "Qi wu lun," in Guo Qingfan [Qing dyn.] anno., *Zhuangzi ji shi*, 4 vols., (Beijing: Zhonghua shuju, 1982), 1:50.
13 See chapter entitled "Xiaoyao you," in Guo Qingfan [Qing dyn.] anno., *Zhuangzi ji shi*, 4 vols., (Beijing: Zhonghua shuju, 1982), 1:24-6.
14 Yongzheng, "Shizong xianhuangdi yuzhi Yuanmingyuan ji."
15 Ibid.
16 Zhang Dainian, ed., *Kongzi da cidian* (Shanghai: Shanghai cishu chubanshe, 1993), 280.
17 See chapter entitled "De chong fu," *Zhuangzi*, 193–4.
18 Yongzheng, "Shizong xianhuangdi yuzhi Yuanmingyuan ji."
19 Wang Xizhi [Eastern Jin], *Lanting ji* (Shanghai: Guangyi shuju, 1915).
20 See chapter entitled "Xiaoyao you," *Zhuangzi*, 1.
21 Yongzheng, "Shizong xianhuangdi yuzhi Yuanmingyuan ji."
22 See chapter entitled "Xici shangzhuan," *Yizhuan*, in Tang Mingbang, ed. and anno., *Zhouyi pingzhu* (Beijing: Zhonghua shuju, 1997), 216. The *shi* and *gua* are cosmological characters.
23 See chapter entitled "Xiaoyao you," *Zhuangzi*, 28. According to the Qing editor Guo Qingfan's annotation, when the mind is condensed, one can accomplish anything without being conscious of it; once the mind is condensed, all things will be obtained without effort. Zhuangzi's "condensation of the mind" does not simply mean to focus attention; on the contrary, at the precise moment when the mind is condensed, there is nothing in the mind on which to focus, and true freedom is thus released.
24 See Wang Fuzhi [Qing dyn.] anno., *Zhuangzi jie* (Hong Kong: Zhonghua shuju, 1989), 7.
25 See *Zhongyong*, in Zhen Xuan [Han dyn.], *Daxue, Zhongyong* (Shanghai: Shanghai guji chubanshe, 2003), 1.
26 Yongzheng, "Shizong xianhuangdi yuzhi Yuanmingyuan ji."
27 See chapter entitled "Laozi," in *Laozi, Zhuangzi*, anno. Fu Yunlong and Lu Qin (Beijing: Huaxia chubanshe, 2000), 27.
28 Chapter entitled "Qiu shui," in Wang Fuzhi, *Zhuangzi jie*, 148.
29 Wang Kaiyun [Qing dyn.], "Yuanmingyuan ci," in *Qingren shuohui* (Shanghai: Saoye Shanfang, 1928), 260.
30 Chen Congzhou, *Shuo yuan* (Shanghai: Tongji daxue chubanshe, 1984), 46.
31 Qianlong [Qing emperor], "Zhengda Guangming," in *Yuanmingyuan sishijing tuyong*, ed. Zhongguo yuanmingyuan xuehui (Beijing: Zhongguo jianzhu gongye chubanshe, 1985), 7.

32 Jean Denis Attiret, "Lettre du frère Attiret à M. Papillon d'Assaut, Pekin, 1 Nov. 1743," in *Lettres édifiantes et curieuses, écrites des missions étrangères*, nouvelle édition, tome 12 (Lyon: J. Vernarel Libraire, 1819), 400.

33 I thank Dr Stephen Allee of Freer Gallery (Washington, DC) for pointing out this detail to me.

34 Qianlong, "Tianzhen Shuwu," in *Yuanmingyuan sishijing tuyong*, 68.

35 Jean-Denis Attiret, "A Letter from a French Missionary in China, Peking, Nov. 1, 1743," in *The Genius of the Place: The English Landscape Garden*, ed. John Dixon Hunt and Peter Willis (New York: Garland, 1982), 38.

36 The term "line-method" (*xianfa*) first appeared in Nian Xiyao [Qing dyn.], *Shixue* (1729), the first Chinese treatise on Western linear perspective. An unpunctuated reprint is in Ren Jiyu, ed., *Zhongguo kexue jishu dianji tonglu*, shuxue juan: juan 4 (Zhengzhou: He'nan jiaoyu chubanshe, 1993).

37 "Neiwufu Zaobanchu ge zuochengzuo huoji qingdang" (hereafter "Neiwufu"), in *Yuanmingyuan: Qingdai dang'an shiliao*, ed. Zhongguo diyi lishi dang'an'guan, 2 vols. (Shanghai: Shanghai guji chubanshe, 1991), 2: archive 419.

38 Ibid. Located at the final *jing*, In Depth of Remote Dwelling, of the Forty Jing, the Lodge of As-One-Wishes studio was the painting studio occupied by the Jesuit painters.

39 The concept of "moving-through the *jing*" (*tongjing*) emerged in the Yuan dynasty to describe a type of landscape painting that maintains a high viewpoint so that the observer can look through the whole pictorial *jing*. In Qing imperial gardens, this concept was also used to describe the paintings that were composed in linear perspective. The commonality of Chinese and Western paintings in this respect probably lies in the intention of "seeing though into the distance," which is close to Albrecht Dürer's concept of *Durchsehung*. Dürer emphasized the fact that the semantic root of the Latin word *perspectiva* means "seeing through." Dürer's *Durchsehung* is discussed in Erwin Panofsky, *Perspective as Symbolic Form*, trans. Christopher S. Wood (New York: Zone Books, 1991), 27. Tang Dai, one of the two painters of the Forty Jing, emphasized in his painting theories that the depiction of each turn and undulation of the frontal view of a mountain should match the posture of the mountain in a "moving-though *jing*." See Tang Dai [Qing dyn.], "Huishi fawei," in Yu Jianhua, ed., *Zhongguo gudai hualun leibian*, 2 vols. (Beijing: Renmin meishu chubanshe, 2000), 1:863.

40 The "water-mouth" indicates the entrance or exit of a watercourse in a garden or landscape. It holds the symbolic meaning of the gateway into a mys-

tic world in both Chinese gardens and landscape paintings. According to a landscape-painting theory of the Yuan dynasty, the "water-mouth" is the most difficult to paint. See Huang Gongwang [Yuan dyn.], "Lun shanshui shushi," in Shen Zicheng, ed., *Lidai lunhua minzhu lubian* (Beijing: Wenwu chubanshe, 1982), 165.

41 Liu Zongyuan [Tang dyn.], "Yongzhou Longxingsi dongqiu ji," in Sun Xiaoli, *Zhichi shanlin: Yuanlin yishu wencui* (Shanghai: Dongfang chubanshe, 1999), 26.

42 Jiaqing [Qing emperor], "Yuanyingguan ge," in Zhang Enyin, *Yuanmingyuan bianqian shi tanwei* (Beijing: Beijing tiyu chubanshe, 1993), 228.

43 "Neiwufu," archive 830.

44 Jiaqing, "Yuanyinguan yougan," in *Renzong yuzhi shi sanji*, juan 23, in *Qing liuchao yuzhi shiwen ji*, ed. Yi Xin [Qing dyn.] 542 vols. (Beijing: Qing imperial court, 1876).

45 Jiaqing, "Yuanyinguan," in *Renzong yuzhi shi sanji*, juan 34, in *Qing liuchao yuzhi shiwen ji.*

46 "Neiwufu," archive 822.

47 Jiaqing, "Yuanyinguan ge," in *Renzong yuzhi shi chuji*, juan 12, in *Qing liuchao yuzhi shiwen ji.*

48 According to the ancient history book *Shiji*, the Chinese emperor's fantasy with the three divine island hills in the East Sea can be traced back to Shi Huangdi of the Qin dynasty. See Sima Qian [Western Han dyn.], *Shiji* (Beijing: Jinghua chubanshe, 2002), juan 28: 13c. Refer to a published translation of this record in Burton Watson, "The Treatise on the Feng and Shan Sacrifices," *Records of the Grand Historian of China: The Shi chi of Ssu-Ma Ch'ien*, 2 vols. (New York: Columbia University Press, 1961), 2:26. This imperial fantasy of the three divine island hills in the sea was later transformed into the typical layout, "one pool, three [island] hills," in Chinese imperial gardens. One example is the Fortunate Lake with three islands at the thirty-second *jing*, entitled Immortal Abode on a Fairy Island, in the Garden of Round Brightness.

49 For further research on the Jesuit perspective in China, see Hui Zou, "Jesuit Perspective in China," *Architectura: Zeitschrift für Geschichte der Baukunst* 31, 2 (2001): 145–68.

50 The Lei family was also called Model Lei (Yangshi Lei or Yangzi Lei), which was the popular name for the official title of "Head of the Division of Model Construction – Lei family." Six generations of this family held this position in the Qing court. After the Qing dynasty ended, the descendants

of the family sold the drawings and models of the imperial projects for economic reasons. The largest part of the collection was purchased by Beiping Library (now the National Library in Beijing) in the summer of 1930. Ten construction drawings of the Western Multistoried-Buildings Garden from the Lei collection were published in *Guoli Beiping tushuguan guankan* 7, 3–4 (1932).

51 Alexander Schulz, *His Yang Lou: Untersuchunger zu den "Europaische Bauten" des Kaiser Chien-lung* (Isny: Schmidt Schulz oHG, 1966), 70.

52 For the annotated full translations of Nian's two prefaces, see Zou, "Jesuit Perspective in China."

53 See chapter entitled "Xiaoyao you," in Wang Fuzhi, *Zhuangzi jie*, 7.

54 The first *bagua* diagram was created by King Wen of the Western Zhou dynasty. According to the diagram, the world is evenly divided into eight directions, each marked by a geomantic character and graph that is related to a particular natural phenomenon: water, fire, earth, mountain, lake, thunder, wind, or heaven. In King Wen's diagram, contrary to the modern convention, south is located at the top rather than the bottom. In the Chinese tradition, a king or emperor always placed his throne at the north in order to face south. This diagram places a beholder in the same position.

55 Yu Minzhong [Qing dyn.] ed., *Rixia jiuwen kao*, 4 vols. (Beijing: Beijing guji chubanshe, 2001), 1:82.

About the Authors

Lawrence Bird
Lawrence Bird is an architectural and urban designer whose work tends to veer off into film and other media. He completed his PhD in history and theory of architecture at McGill University in 2009, after earlier studies in urbanism at Kanazawa Institute of Technology, Japan, and the London School of Economics. His dissertation focuses on three versions of *Metropolis*: Fritz Lang's film of 1926, Osamu Tezuka's *manga* of 1949, and the 2001 work of *anime* by Rintaro, which folds these two stories together. He is currently SSHRC postdoctoral fellow at the University of Manitoba's Faculty of Architecture, where he is carrying out a research-creation project on the representation of the city in video and ubiquitous media, involving architectural students and members of the community in a remapping of Winnipeg.

Lian Chang
Lian Chang received her PhD from McGill University in 2010, with a dissertation entitled "Articulation and the Origins of Proportion in Archaic and Classical Greece." In between tending her garden and miniature zoo, she has taught studios and has served as a guest lecturer and critic in the professional and post-professional programs in architecture at McGill. She is currently an MArchI student at Harvard University's Graduate School of Design, with plans to become an architect one day.

Jason Crow
Jason Crow is a PhD candidate in the School of Architecture at McGill University. He is currently working on a dissertation concerning the interrelationship of the histories of vision and stone, under the working title "Animate Matters: Stone 1100–1600." His research explores changes in the understanding of the artisan's ability to transform matter, which he sees as comparable to the inherent power of stone to change itself. He presented a paper, "Light, Stone, and Tears: Bernard of Clairvaux and Stone as Flesh in the Cistercian Church," on the understanding of stone and light in Bernard's sermons, at the second Architecture and Phenomenology Conference in the summer of 2009. As a registered architect, he has worked at the forefront of sustainable design for the United States National Park Service and the Episcopal Diocese of Massachusetts.

Donald Kunze

Donald Kunze has taught architecture theory and general arts criticism at Penn State University since 1984. He studied architecture at North Carolina State University (BArch) and received his PhD in cultural geography in 1983. His articles and lectures engage a range of topics dealing with the poetic dimensions of experience. His book on the philosophy of place of Giambattista Vico studies the operation of metaphoric imagination and memory. As the 2008 Nadine Carter Russell Visiting Chair at Robert Reich School of Landscape Architecture at Louisiana State University, he applied boundary language theory – an interdisciplinary notation system he developed to describe conditions of reception in architecture, landscape, literature, film, and art – to the problem of the surrealist garden.

Mari Lending

Mari Lending is a professor of architectural history and theory at the Oslo School of Architecture and Design, and since 2009 has been head of its Institute of Form, Theory, and History. She holds an MLitt in comparative literature, focusing on Marcel Proust (1997), and a PhD in architectural historiography (2005). She has been a visiting scholar at Harvard University's Graduate School of Design and at Columbia University's Department of Art History. Her latest book, *Omkring 1900: Kontinuiteter i norsk arkitekturtenkning* (2007), is a critical rethinking of the concepts of historicism and modernism in nineteenth- and twentieth-century Norwegian architectural discourse. Recent articles include "Negotiating Absence: Bernard Tschumi's Design for the New Acropolis Museum in Athens," *Journal of Architecture* (2009); and "Landscape vs. Museum: J.C. Dahl and the Preservation of Norwegian Burial Mounds," *Future Anterior: Journal of Historic Preservation, History, Theory, and Criticism* (2009). She is currently working on "Place and Displacement: Exhibiting Architecture," a research project on architectural representation, decontextualization, and architectural models.

Rachel McCann

Rachel McCann is a professor of architecture at Mississippi State University, where she teaches architectural history, theory, and design. She received a PhD in architectural histories and theories from the Architectural Association School of Architecture in London. Her essays on architecture have appeared in *Intertwinings: Interdisciplinary Encounters with Merleau-Ponty*; *Writings in Architectural Education:* EAAE *Prize 2003–2005*; *Dictionary of Jewish-Christian Relations*; and *Architecture and Civilization.* Her research weaves Merleau-Pontian thought and architectural theory to investigate the intercorporeal experience and design of architecture.

Maria Elisa Navarro Morales
Originally from Colombia, Maria Elisa Navarro Morales first studied architecture at the Universidad de los Andes in Bogota. After practising in Colombia and the United States, she moved to Montreal in 2005 to pursue a master's degree in history and theory of architecture at McGill University. She is currently a PhD candidate at McGill, studying the work of the Spanish polymath Juan Caramuel de Lobkowitz. Her research revolves around connections between mathematics, theology, and architecture in early modern Europe.

Marc J. Neveu
Following a professional education and a few years of work in Boston, Marc J. Neveu travelled to Montreal to pursue studies towards a PhD. His dissertation, "Architectural Lessons of Carlo Lodoli (1690–1764)," examines the origins of architectural education in the Veneto during the eighteenth century. Its main focus is Carlo Lodoli's bifold understanding of *indole* (inherent nature) – with respect to the meaning of materials and architectural education – and includes the first ever translation of Lodoli's architectural fables, *Apologhi Immaginati* (1787), into English. Neveu has taught at the Wentworth Institute of Technology in Boston, the University of Manitoba in Winnipeg, and SCI-Arc in Los Angeles. In 2007 he began work at Cal Poly in San Luis Obispo, California, where he teaches history courses and studio. He has lectured and published on issues of architectural pedagogy in both historical and contemporary contexts. Like another, more famous, Marc, Neveu longs to return to Venice one day.

Peter Olshavsky
Peter Olshavsky is a devout 'Pataphysician and a lover of exceptional machines. After spending much of his youth tending to his own machines, he went on to study architecture at the Pennsylvania State University

and the history and theory of architecture at McGill University as a Canada-US Fulbright Fellow. He has taught at McGill, Philadelphia University, and Temple University. He is now a PhD candidate in the history and theory of architecture at McGill, investigating the architectural implications of 'Pataphysics via the machine.

Santiago de Orduña
Santiago de Orduña hails from Mexico City. At Universidad Iberoamericana in Mexico City he completed an undergraduate degree in architecture and a graduate degree in philosophy, then taught there for ten years. In 2000 he moved to Montreal and completed a post-professional MArch and a PhD in the history and theory of architecture at McGill University. His doctoral dissertation is entitled "Coatepec, the Great Temple of the Aztecs: Recreating a Metaphorical State of Dwelling," and it addresses the origins of the ambiguous but highly poetic character of contemporary Mexican cultural manifestations. He lives with his wife and two children in Coatepec, Veracruz, Mexico.

Jonathan Powers
Jonathan Powers is currently pursuing his doctorate in the history and theory of architecture at McGill University in Montreal. His dissertation concerns the relationship between architecture, rhetoric, and utopia. Jonathan holds an MA in philosophy from Boston College, where he focused his studies on ethics, and a BA in philosophy from Amherst College, where his senior thesis compared the thought of Friedrich Nietzsche with that of Nishitani Keiji. Between degrees, Jonathan has worked for the École de Management Strasbourg, the United States Department of Housing and Urban Development, and the Affordable Housing Institute.

Nicholas Roquet
Nicholas Roquet is an architect and associate professor in the School of Architecture at Université de Montréal. Since graduating from Université de Montréal in 1991, he has combined teaching, research, and participation in design competitions with work in private practice and public service (urban design, historic preservation, and museum design). He is currently completing a doctoral dissertation at McGill University entitled "Life in Costume: The Architectural Fictions and Anachro-

nisms of William Burges." This project examines different facets of the concept of authenticity – in particular, the nineteenth-century intersection of historical imagination and personal identity.

Hui Zou
Hui Zou was born in southwestern China and completed graduate studies in architecture in China, the United States, and Canada. He obtained his PhD from McGill University at the end of 2005. He taught at Tongji University in Shanghai and has been teaching at the University of Florida in Gainesville since 2003. He was a former Fellow of the Garden and Landscape Studies at Dumbarton Oaks (Harvard University) in Washington, DC.